Tear Down These Walls

ETHICS AND INTERSECTIONALITY
An Orbis Series in Theological Ethics

SERIES EDITORS

Miguel A. De La Torre
Stacey M. Floyd-Thomas
David P. Gushee

Titles include:

Juan M. Floyd-Thomas, *Critical Race Theology: White Supremacy, American Christianity, and the Ongoing Culture Wars*

Melanie Jones Quarles, *Up Against a Crooked Gospel: Black Women's Bodies and the Politics of Redemption*

Miguel A. De La Torre and Mitri Raheb, *Tear Down These Walls: Decolonial Approaches to Barriers and Liberation*

ETHICS AND INTERSECTIONALITY SERIES

Tear Down These Walls

*Decolonial Approaches to
Barriers and Liberation*

MIGUEL A. DE LA TORRE
MITRI RAHEB

Editors

Maryknoll, New York 10545

Founded in 1970, Orbis Books endeavors to publish works that enlighten the mind, nourish the spirit, and challenge the conscience. The publishing arm of the Maryknoll Fathers and Brothers, Orbis seeks to explore the global dimensions of the Christian faith and mission, to invite dialogue with diverse cultures and religious traditions, and to serve the cause of reconciliation and peace. The books published reflect the views of their authors and do not represent the official position of the Maryknoll Society. To learn more about Maryknoll and Orbis Books, please visit our website at www.orbisbooks.com.

Copyright © 2025 by Miguel A. De La Torre and Mitri Raheb

Published by Orbis Books, Box 302, Maryknoll, NY 10545-0302.

All rights reserved.

Scripture quotations, unless otherwise noted, are from New Revised Standard Version Bible: Catholic Edition, copyright © 1989, 1993 National Council of the Churches of Christ in the United States of America. Used by permission. All rights reserved worldwide.

No part of this publication may be reproduced or transmitted in any form or by any means, electronic or mechanical, including photocopying, recording, or any information storage or retrieval system, without prior permission in writing from the publisher.

Queries regarding rights and permissions should be addressed to: Orbis Books, P.O. Box 302, Maryknoll, NY 10545-0302.

Manufactured in the United States of America

Library of Congress Cataloging-in-Publication Data

Names: De La Torre, Miguel A., editor. | Raheb, Mitri, editor.
Title: Tear down these walls : decolonial approaches to barriers and liberation / Miguel A. De La Torre, Mitri Raheb, editors.
Description: Maryknoll, NY : Orbis Books, [2025] | Series: Ethics and intersectionality | Includes bibliographical references and index. | Summary: "A study on the impact of walls on colonized people living in occupied lands"— Provided by publisher.
Identifiers: LCCN 2025016050 (print) | LCCN 2025016051 (ebook) | ISBN 9781626986244 (paperback) | ISBN 9798888660799 (epub)
Subjects: LCSH: Boundaries--Religious aspects—Christianity. | Christianity and geography. | Boundaries—Political aspects. | Christianity and politics. | Decolonization. | Imperialism.
Classification: LCC BR115.G45 T43 2025 (print) | LCC BR115.G45 (ebook) | DDC 230.09—dc23/eng/20250602
LC record available at https://lccn.loc.gov/2025016050
LC ebook record available at https://lccn.loc.gov/2025016051

Dedicated to

those trapped by a wall

yet determined to tear it down

Contents

Preface ix
    Mitri Raheb

1. Walls: A Philosophical Perspective 1
    Miguel A. De La Torre

2. The Wall of Impunity 21
    Mitri Raheb

3. About the Berlin Wall and the Iron Curtain:
Building and Deconstructing Walls 39
    Johanna Erzberger

4. The Great Wall and Eggs:
A Hong Kongers' Social-Spiritual Movement in the
Post–National Security Law Era 56
    Lap Yan Kung

5. Peace at the Korean Demilitarized Zone:
A Feminist Praxis of De-Imperialization, Decolonization,
and Demilitarization 76
    Boyung Lee

6. Israel's Apartheid Wall 100
    Mitri Raheb

7. South Africa and Apartheid 116
    Brian Joseph Brown

8. A Denationalized, Decolonizing, and Transborder
Hermeneutic in an Age of Border-Wall Politics 136
    Gregory L. Cuéllar

9. Extraction, Militarization, and Trump's Border Wall: The Circumstances That Led Up to the O'odham Revolt of 2020 153
   Nellie Jo David

10. *El Bloqueo*: Walling In a Nation. 163
    Miguel A. De La Torre

11. This Is US: Borderline Citizens, Borderscape Colonialism, and the Borderlands of Black Folk in America 183
    Stacey Floyd-Thomas

Conclusion 203
   Miguel A. De La Torre

Contributors 213

Bibliography 219

Index 231

Preface

Mitri Raheb

The idea for a book on walls was conceived during an American Academy of Religion meeting in San Antonio in November 2021. During COVID time, with people wearing masks, Miguel and I were having a drink at a hotel bar when we decided to embark on writing this book. Being in San Antonio, Texas, in proximity to the Trump wall might have played a role in our brainstorming, but certainly the apartheid wall, in whose shadow I live daily in Bethlehem, influenced our decision. In that meeting, we agreed that the book should focus on how physical or virtual walls—or both—have fortified and continue to fortify oppressive structures that separate privilege from disenfranchisement. Furthermore, we agreed that we must engage these walls through multivocal decolonial perspectives. Writing and editing this book on walls was not only an academic enterprise. It was a lived reality for both of us in different forms. Before departing, we agreed that it is essential for me to plan a visit to the US/Mexico border and for Miguel to visit Palestine.

After securing a small grant from the Latinx Center at the University of Denver, Miguel and I traveled in March 2022 to Tucson, Arizona. By a mere coincidence or divine planning, a conference organized by a group of Americans, Mexicans, and Palestinians was being held that weekend at St. Mark's Presbyterian Church under the title "All the Walls Must Fall." The conference explored "the realities, the struggles, and the vision we must mobilize around, so that walls indeed fall, connecting our lives and similarities despite the thousands of miles distance." On their website, we read,

> From the US/Mexico border to the borders around Palestine—walls and militarization, dispossession of lands and cultural genocide, brutality and murder, mass detentions and lack of rights, forced migration and criminalization, environmental damage—these and other shared abuses have all defined these experiences. Walls expel, exclude, oppress, discriminate and exploit. Walls cause thousands of deaths every year and destroy lives on a daily basis. For many, the logic of security seeks to justify the construction of walls separating territories and states. The creation of borders often conceals racist logics and is based on the idea of the external enemy in order to place a stigma of otherness on people and not recognize them as people with rights.[1]

Presenting and participating at this conference showed us the importance of such a book, especially since nothing of this perspective is available on the market.

The next day, Miguel arranged a Samaritan trip along the border wall with BorderLinks, a community-based organization that facilitates educational immersion trips in the Arizona-Sonora region.[2] We met at their center early in the morning; took water, food, blankets, and other supplies; and drove to Sasabe crossing. We were supposed to cross over to Mexico to experience "being on the other side of the wall," but I was concerned that, with my

---

[1] "All the Walls Must Fall," All the Walls Must Fall Conference, Tucson, AZ, 2022.

[2] "BorderLinks: Who We Are," 2025, borderlinks.org.

Palestinian passport, I might encounter delays at border control while reentering the United States. We continued our trip, driving for twenty miles along a twenty-seven-foot-high steel wall that dominated the landscape. It was painful to see the erosion along the wall, the rockslides, and the damage done to the environment. Coming from Palestine, seeing twenty or more gaps in the wall blew my mind. So, I had to step a foot in Mexico, just to say I was there.

The most heartening experience was when we encountered two Mexican emigrants. They were two women; the older woman was in her mid-forties and her niece was nineteen years old. They saw us from afar, got scared, and tried to hide, with the older woman holding her niece's hand. We stopped the car near them, and they were shivering. Their water bottle had run dry, and their feet were blistered. We gave them some food and water. I was eager to hear their story.

Each one of them had to pay around ten thousand dollars to Mexican cartels to get them near the border. They started as a group, but then they had to separate. Walking through the desert landscape for days without their companions must have been very frightening, especially for the younger woman. Knowing that, though they were able to cross the border, several miles in the desert were still awaiting them, with wild animals, coyotes, javelinas, bobcats, was not reassuring. If they survived the animals, they might fall into the hands of other gangs, and the possibility of being raped was ever-present.

We asked them what they wanted to do and how we could help. Talking among themselves in Spanish, it was obvious that the older woman wanted to take the risk and continue the trip. Half of the journey was behind them, and they had paid a fortune to get to that place. They were now on US soil, close enough to reach the elusive American dream. The younger woman was hesitant, tired, and afraid. I could tell that such a discussion must have accompanied them all along the road. Such thoughts and reasoning must be on the mind of migrants trying to cross walls everywhere. We left them alone for a few minutes so that they could come to a decision. The older woman came back, saying that they decided to go back to Mexico. Such a decision must have been very painful for the older woman, but she was concerned with the safety of her niece. She was ready to give up the American dream and return to their home in Mexico. In the meantime, an American rancher drove by, stopped, and asked if he could help. At the woman's request, he called the border patrol police to come and pick them up. They came, took the two women, and slowly disappeared behind the hills. We, in return, drove back west to our hotel, through the old mining town of Ruby. The encounter with the two Mexican women haunted me, experiencing firsthand when warm brown bodies encounter a cold steel wall with all the emotions and fears connected to crossing borders.

Two months later, Miguel was able to come visit Palestine. He stayed in Bethlehem, a city surrounded from three sides by a twenty-five-foot-high concrete wall. He witnessed how Palestinian workers are treated and humiliated on a daily basis when crossing the Israeli checkpoint to work in Jerusalem or inside Israel. He spoke with young people who never got a permit to visit the holy shrines in Jerusalem or to swim in the sea.

From Bethlehem, Miguel took the No. 231 bus to Damascus Gate in Jerusalem. About his experience there, he wrote,

> At the checkpoint, all Palestinians were forced to disembark and have their papers examined. They stood in long lines under a hot beating sun—no shade—as pimple-faced teenagers with assault rifles draped over their shoulders checked their papers with disgust and contempt. I was forbidden to join them. I just had to wave my golden ticket—a U.S. passport—to stay in my comfortable seat on the bus. On this particular day, an elderly Palestinian woman refused to get off the bus. Maybe she was tired.

> Maybe she had had enough of the daily indignations. Maybe she was standing—or should I say sitting—for her rights to be treated as a human, to be treated with dignity. I noticed the two teenage soldiers approach her. Their voices rose. I did not understand what they were saying but it was obvious they were demanding she gets off the bus. One held her IMI Galil assault rifle in a menacing manner. She defiantly yelled back. The atmosphere was tense. I was witnessing a Rosa Parks moment.[3]

In summarizing his experience over six weeks in Palestine, Miguel concluded, "I witnessed apartheid. I witnessed settler colonialism. I witnessed oppression. I witnessed the attempt to systematically humiliate people."[4]

Tear Down These Walls is sociopolitical, theological, and philosophical book written by a diverse group of scholars from seven regions of the world. This book helps us connect the dots between all these walls of imperial domination while understanding their local context and reasoning. The book starts with a philosophical perspective on walls followed by denationalized, decolonized, and transborder hermeneutics. The book invites readers on a journey from the wall of Berlin to the Israeli apartheid wall. Different chapters introduce several concepts to deal with walls: from a social-spiritual approach to a post–National Security Law era in Hong Kong, to a feminist praxis of deimperialization, decolonization, and demilitarization in face of Korea's (most heavily militarized) Demilitarized Zone (DMZ). While some authors look at a very specific case, like the revolt of the O'odham people along the Trump border wall, others look at walls that separate people along racial lines, as the case in the United States and South Africa.

---

[3] Miguel A. De La Torre, "When the Oppressed Become Oppressors," *Good Faith Media*, November 17, 2022.

[4] De La Torre, "When the Oppressed Become Oppressors."

The two editors look at invisible walls, like the blockage (*el Bloqueo*) in Cuba and the wall of impunity that Israel enjoys, which became obvious in the Gazan genocide.

We would like to extend our gratitude to the scholars who have shared their stories, insights, and wisdom as well as their commitment to tear down all walls.

1

Walls

A Philosophical Perspective

Miguel A. De La Torre

Walls are an abomination. Today, they are the consequence of the eurocentric commodification of land, transforming that which has existed naturally for all creatures, including humans, to use and enjoy into an artificial concept that has come to be called "private property." Digging a ditch, erecting a fence, building a wall are acts of violence committed against land that is perpetrated by the erector of the barrier who can proclaim, "This is mine. Keep out." Any philosophical discourse that is focused on walls must begin with seeking to comprehend what the wall is attempting to protect—either by keeping resources, including humans, within the enclosure or preventing those beyond the partition from trespassing to threaten those resources. Regardless of the reason for erecting the barrier, an attempt is made to safeguard and secure what has been commodified, whether it be tangible land or the profit, privilege, or power derived from said land. To better comprehend the philosophical mooring of land, this opening chapter seeks to first identify why private property developed as a eurocentric construct, including the role it played and still plays in justifying the colonial venture. This Western understanding of land is then contrasted with more indigenous perspectives. Finally, the discussion considers walls that are built upon land today, including what they signify and their ethical ramifications.

Life, Liberty, and the Pursuit of Happiness

Under all, there is land. This land is neither produced nor created by humans, for it predates them. Humans—along with all land-based creatures—literally live off the land, dependent upon it for their sustenance and existence. This kind of use is limited, not absolute, for the land is its own entity that is due respect, rather than the modernist concept that humans possess certain rights to land. The rise of the so-called Enlightenment reduced land to just another possession humans can own, becoming the blueprint for the horrors triggered by the colonial enterprise. Social philosopher Jean-Jacques Rousseau (1712–1778) was among the first eurocentric thinkers to sound the warning:

> The first man who, having enclosed a piece of ground, to whom it occurred to say "this is mine," and found people sufficiently simple to believe him, was the true founder of civil society. How many crimes, wars, murder, how many miseries and horrors Mankind [*sic*] would have been spared by him who, pulling up the stakes or filling in the ditch, had cried out to his kind: Beware of listening to this impostor; You are lost if you forget that the fruits are everyone's and the Earth no one's.[1]

Those colonized by the fences and walls erected around land to defend their so-called property rights, as opposed to centering

---

[1] Jean-Jacques Rousseau, "A Discourse upon the Origin and the Foundation of the Inequality Among Mankind," II;1, in *The Discourses and Other Early Political Writings,* ed. and trans. Victor Gourevitch (Cambridge University Press, 1997 [1755]), 164.

a respect for property, makes them complicit with their own colonization.

The father of classical political liberalism, English philosopher John Locke (1632–1704), was among the first to advance the exclusive use of real property as one of the "self-evident natural rights," becoming the third of inalienable rights, succeeding "life and liberty." Based on personal interest and self-preservation, he argued that individuals had an inalienable right to hold whatever property they possessed regardless as to how the property was originally acquired or any ability to use all its resources. Accumulation of land, as well as wealth in the form of gold or silver, becomes unlimited. To safeguard these inalienable rights, the state's purpose and duty is to defend and protect them.[2] Said protection of property, regardless of how it was acquired, often requires the state to erect walls. The inconvenience of considering how land acquisition occurred masks how Locke was an international enslaver trading in human flesh who was part owner in a slave-run plantation (Bahamian Adventurers) and a slave acquisition and selling firm (Royal Africa Company). Additionally, he worked as a business manager for a colonial land holding corporation with interests in North America along with a seat in the colonial legislature of the Carolina territory. Locke's philosophical musings were more influenced by his own pursuit of wealth than the pursuit of knowledge. Colonial theft of the land of others—North American Indigenous Peoples—was facilitated through the facade of the legal and moral reasoning he created.

Locke's pursuit of self-interest, defined as private property, becomes the basis for the eurocentric economic concept of nonstate interference advocated by Adam Smith (1723–1790): *laissez-faire*, French for, "let it happen." The pursuit of economic self-interests within the context of a competitive society, according

---

[2] John Locke, *The Second Treatise of Government*, ed. Thomas P. Peardon (Bobbs-Merrill Educational, 1952 [1689]), 5–6, 17, 23, 29.

to Smith, would benefit everyone.[3] To that end, no restraints should be placed on the accumulation of wealth, including land. For Smith, the myth of land accumulation prior to capitalism was due to the natural abilities of the accumulator. Those lacking wealth either lacked intelligence or were lazy.

Coining the term "the survival of the fittest," British philosopher Herbert Spencer (1820–1903) appropriated Charles Darwin's insights concerning biological evolution theory and natural selection, extending these concepts to the realm of sociology and ethics. Colonialist and colonial settlers' financial successes due to the conquest of land was due to them being fitter—mentally, genetically, physically, morally—than those conquered and relegated to live in squalor. Their wealth becomes scientifically justified while providing an ethical excuse to do nothing for the victim of land conquest. Eurocentric economic ruthlessness became the new morality.

With time, land was re-signified from being part of the natural environment to becoming an economic unit, one more commodity that could be subject to domination. Walls and fences enclosing private property secured the liberty of landlords or the state by means of the government and at the expense of those allowed to live on land as tenants whose interests become subordinated to the interests of this ruling class. Private property became a sacred building block of Western civilization. To question this economic arrangement became, at best, heterodoxy, for it questioned the legitimized and normalized eurocentric concept of inalienable rights. Such questionings would be seditious or treasonous. At worst, questioning the concept of private property, suggesting the resumption of land as common property, becomes paramount to advocating a cultural and societal regression toward

---

[3] Adam Smith, *An Inquiry into the Nature and Causes of the Wealth of Nations*, vol. 1, ed. R. H. Campbell, A. S. Skinner, and W. B. Todd (Clarendon, 1976 [1776]), 13.

some premodern, primitive, uncivilized existence. In the mind of colonizers, consideration of more indigenous understandings of land is akin to returning to a more barbaric human existence, where land is worthless for not being commodified.

There's Gold in Them Thar Hills

Land has always been valuable, even before it was commodified by eurocentric thought. Political philosopher and psychiatrist Frantz Fanon expressed this point: "For a colonized people the most essential value, because the most concrete, is first and foremost the land: the land which will bring them bread and, above all, dignity."[4] Although valuable for its relationship to all dependent on land for survival, the colonial venture reimagined it as solely a profit-generating commodity worth nothing apart from how it is developed by man (specifically white men). This privatizing of land became responsible for much of the social, economic, and political violence this world has experienced and continues to experience. Building fences and walls to protect the land that was appropriated, or coveting the land of neighbors beyond fences and walls, fosters injustices. The eurocentric philosophical privatization and commodification of land—making it into something that can be bought and sold, something requiring walls to protect—has turned what exists for common usage into a source from which power, profit, and privilege are derived at the expense of others, specifically those who originally inhabited said land.

Locke's commodification of land reduced its value and importance to nothing more and nothing less than a unit of capital, overlooking that the land, as a living entity, requires respect in the form of not being dominated by any one species of earthly creature. Land has come to be valued as the physical site for

---

[4] Frantz Fanon, *The Wretched of the Earth*, trans. Constance Farrington (Grove, 1963), 44.

exploitation of resources—location, location, location—and not as the source of all life. Failing to see land in relationship with those dependent on it for their existence and subsistence, Locke views it as passive and worthless until the active principle of human labor is applied.[5] He specifically argues,

> God and his reason commanded him to subdue the earth, i.e., improve it for the benefit of life, and therein lay out something upon it that was his own, his labour. He that in obedience to this command of God, subdued, tilled and sowed any part of it, thereby annexed to it something that was his property, which another had no title to, nor could without injury take from him.[6]

By this Lockean logic, failure of the original inhabitants to develop the land forfeited their legal claim to the land. The colonial pursuit of the most profitable use of the land demonstrated a lack of concern for the general welfare, contributing to the negation of the original community and their communal values.

An individualistic and capitalist-based society functions best when private property is protected and open markets are preserved. This philosophy is spiritualized through eurochristianity's artificial linkage to laissez-faire economics. This connection creates ethical spiritual truths concerning freedom and rights, allowing the dominant culture to prosper freely without guilt. Because those who are economically privileged can acquire immense tracts of land, they can, through their holdings and position within the ruling class, impose laws through politicians, who they keep in their pockets like loose change, and on those whose basic subsistence is land-dependent. The dispossessed can use the land as tenants if they recognize the supreme legal and moral authority of the land*lord*. Society constructed upon the cornerstone of

---

[5] Locke, *The Second Treatise of Government*, 26.
[6] Locke, *The Second Treatise of Government*, 31.

private ownership requires that the protection of property against trespassing and theft supersedes basic human rights.

Eurocentric property rights trump human rights as land becomes subjected to the colonial introduction of private property rights. Economist Franz Hinkelammert reminds us that the unconditional recognition of the right to private property deprioritizes all other rights, leading to global disenfranchisement and dispossession. Protecting private property exists at the expense of rights "to satisfy basic needs in food, shelter, medical attention, education, and social security."[7] If one jumps a fence to retrieve a fallen apple rotting on the ground to feed a hungry child, the trespasser can be arrested and charged with home invasion and theft regardless of the human right to eat. Advocating private property rights masks the concentration of wealth in the hands of a few, threatening democracy as those privileged with property control the direction and policies of society. Because economic power is directly linked to political power, the fight is not necessarily for the land but for who gets to reserve the right to use, enjoy, and profit off the land.

Mexican philosopher Enrique Dussel reminds us that private property has three origins: one works for it, steals it, or inherits it. If one works for it, the amount of land acquired is relatively small. If much property is owned, then it was undoubtedly stolen, sometimes without one's realization. Stealing land renders the land-thief responsible for the impoverishment or murder of the dispossessed. When property is inherited, the original sin of stealing and murder is transmitted to the next generation, who, through complicity with their progenitors' acts, continue to benefit from land ownership.[8] Maybe the Christian doctrinal concept of original

---

[7] Franz J. Hinkelammert, *The Ideological Weapons of Death: A Theological Critique*, trans. Phillip Berryman (Orbis, 1986), 120.

[8] Enrique Dussel, *Ethics and the Theology of Liberation*, trans. Bernard F. McWilliams (Orbis, 1978), 25.

sin is not transmitted from one soul to another as some medieval theologians would have us believe. Maybe the transmission of original sin occurs from one parcel of land to another. The original sin connected to the misuse of land and its unlimited acquisition has become the primary source of massive oppression and misery throughout history, best illustrated by the colonial venture. Maybe atonement for the original sin of land theft was best expressed by Mexican Emiliano Zapata's often quoted revolutionary cry: *La tierra es de quien la trabaja con sus manos.*[9]

Subduing Virgin Land

Colonial conquest becomes an erotic eurocentric fantasy, entailing a performance of taking and ravishing, whether it be land or the indigenous female bodies signifying the land. Historian Magnus Mörner argues that the conquest of the Americas began with the literal male sexual conquest and domination of the native indigenous woman.[10] Anthropomorphizing the land with the body of an indigenous woman allows for the simultaneous conquest of each. Fanon captures this link when he writes, "If we want to destroy the structure of [Native] society, its capacity for resistance, we must first of all conquer the woman."[11] Within the colonizer's imagination, indigenous female bodies, fused and confused with land, anxiously lay bare, awaiting the colonizer's forward-thrust of civilization and Christianization. Merging the body of an indigenous woman with land in the colonizer's imagination engenders the domestication of the original inhabitants of the land and deprives them of their aboriginal territorial claim. Inserting

---

[9] The land belongs to those who work it with their own hands.

[10] Magnus Mörner, *Race Mixture in the History of Latin America* (Little, Brown, 1967), 22–23.

[11] Frantz Fanon, "Algeria Unveiled," in *A Dying Colonialism*, trans. Haakon Chevalier (Grove, 1965), 37–38.

his pole upon which hangs the colonizer's flag, the colonizer claims ownership of both land and bodies, each longing, in the colonizer's mind, for their sadomasochistic domestication. Walls and fences become the means of domesticating both land and female bodies.

Postcolonialist thinker Anne McClintock reminds us how "the world is feminized and spatially spread for male exploration.... The myth of the virgin land is also the myth of the empty land ... awaiting the thrusting, male insemination of history, language, and reason."[12] The defined passivity of the native women—and, through her, the entire indigenous population—becomes synonymous with the passivity of virgin land. As a woman supposedly finds her value and self-worth through the dominating man who "owns" her and her body as husband or lover, so, too, does land require the action of man to develop its worth. This misogyny toward the land is poetically captured by global activist Mark Gerzon:

> Once the land had been won, it was treated like a fallen woman.... The wilderness, once conquered, was no longer wild, the virgin land, once used, lost her innocence.... We treat the land neither reverently, as our mother, nor chivalrously, as a virgin, but contemptuously, as if she were no better than a whore. We rape her. And when we are done, we leave her—and our wastes—behind.[13]

Virgin land is undeveloped and empty, in need of the insemination of the colonialist seed called progress; as McClintock notes, "the sexual and military insemination of an interior void."[14] Progress entails making land profitable because eurocentric thought

---

[12] Anne McClintock, *Imperial Leather: Race, Gender and Sexuality in the Colonial Contest* (Routledge, 1995), 23, 30.

[13] Mark Gerzon, *A Choice of Heroes* (Houghton Mifflin, 1982), 20–21.

[14] McClintock, *Imperial Leather*, 30.

legitimizes private property as belonging to the one who can develop virgin wilderness to its fullest potential. Under this worldview, land need not be respected while those who possess *her* claim for themselves certain inalienable rights. Her value lies in anticipating how the colonizer intends to domesticate her. Ravishment of virgin land / of the indigenous woman extends to the oppression of the land's original inhabitants by effeminizing them within the patriarchal order so that they, too, can be raped and assigned their proper subservient space. Once owned, the possessor is always threatened with loss of what was acquired. To prevent the possible shame caused by trespassers, which might result in loss, the land (woman) requires protection from any risk to the colonizer's honor. Walls are erected to demarcate what the settler owns or to keep out so-called savages.

The Hills Are Alive

During the 1980s, an ecological movement developed that recognized planet Earth as a self-regulatory functioning superorganism.[15] Known as the Gaia hypothesis (named after the Greek goddess for earth), this controversial theory among some eurocentric scholars argued that living and nonliving components that constitute a homeostatic Earth belong to a complex interacting system best understood as a single living organism. While celebrated within some eurocentric academic circles as a groundbreaking contribution to humanity's understanding of planet Earth, concepts such as these existed for millennia before their appropriation by a dominant eurocentric culture. Regardless of any traction a Gaia hypothesis might have upon a eurocentric worldview concerning land, land will continue to be commodified and owned as private

---

[15] See James Lovelock, *Gaia: A New Look at Life on Earth* (Oxford University Press, 1979).

property. At best, our relationship to land might now entail environmental responsibilities. While much has been written about our stewardship of the earth, especially among eurochristians, the word "stewardship" still connotes ownership. A steward, after all, seeks to manage that which they have dominion over, that which is subjugated to their skills as a manager of the property's resources.

The imposition of the eurocentric worldview of private property extends oppressive structures that enrich a global minority who confuse their unearned riches with advanced civilization, defining those on their margins as primitive. A more indigenous worldview questions if anyone can actually own the land, for land is alive and upon it all life depends, not just human life who eat cattle, but the cattle that eats grass, and the grass itself.

Not only does the earth live, thus requiring respect, but it also has its own spirit. What does it mean for land to be alive, to be a spiritual entity? Contrary to the eurocentric worldview, which defines land as a commodity that can be privatized for the purpose of exploitation, a more indigenous worldview recognizes land as life with which all creatures, including humans, have a relationship. If indeed land is a living and spiritual entity as opposed to the mere commodity to be used, sold, and traded through neoliberal economic concepts, then owning land becomes a form of slavery and building walls upon it becomes a form of imprisonment.

According to Osage scholar Tink Tinker, converting land—what he calls "our Grandmother"—into private property is the first order of business for a colonialist. This move is in line with the eurocentric notion that the cosmos exists to meet the needs and desires of humans, specifically eurocentric humans. Once the cognitive idea of property is established, the profitable venture of extraction of fossil fuels, mining, and establishing monocrop agriculture can begin for those seeking fortune. Tinker goes on to elucidate the consequences of this eurocentric way of thinking, "This [European] immigration and its imposition of a new worldview with its own idealized cognitive models has left our world in what my *wazhazhe* ancestors called *ganitha*, a world out of balance, in chaos, out of order."[16] Over a century prior to Tinker's assessment, Smohalla of the Wanapum voiced a similar understanding concerning one's relationship with the land. Repudiating eurocentric pressure to commodify land, he responded,

> You ask me to plow the ground. Shall I take a knife and tear my mother's bosom? Then when I die she will not take me to her bosom to rest. You ask me you dig for stone. Shall I dig under her skin for bones? Then when I die I cannot enter her body to be born again. You ask me to cut grass and make hay and sell it, and be rich like white men. How dare I cut off my mother's hair?[17]

Land is not about private property. Land is about relationship—relationship with a living entity, complete with spirit, which is, thus, due respect. For example, among the Yoruba people of West Africa, Oko is the Lord of agriculture lands while Osain rules in the forest, both responsible for their fecundity. The Egyptian God Geb is the earth God whose laughter causes earthquakes. In the Americas, Mother Earth for the Aztec is Tonantzin; Pachamama for the Incas. Dimū is Mother Earth, Goddess of all land and earth within Chinese religions; among Hindus, the earth Goddess is known as Prithvi. It would be too simplistic to simply dismiss these peoples' worldviews as a primitive form of apotheosizing the planet.

---

[16] Tink Tinker, "How the Eurochristian Invasion of Turtle Island Created Our Environmental Crises," in *Shifting Climate, Shifting People*, ed. Miguel A. De La Torre (Pilgrim, 2022), 21.

[17] James Mooney, "The Ghost-Dance Religion and the Sioux Outbreak of 1890," in *Fourteenth Annual Report of the Bureau of Ethnology to the Secretary of the Smithsonian Institution 1892–93, Part 2* (US Government Printing Office, 1896), 721.

By understanding the earth as "being" with spirit, a relationship can be established. This relationship requires creating a harmonious bond with all of creation. The hubris that humans, specifically cis-gender males, are the pinnacle of creation is highly problematic. Eurochristianity may expound that God occupies the central spot in the created order, but all of creation exists for the purpose of glorifying man, specifically cis-gender white males, who are even above the angels. Such a proposition understands man's raison d'être as being to rule, to have dominion. Tinker provides a counter argument when he reminds us that, within an indigenous worldview, "a chief is not valued above the people; nor are two-legged valued above the animal nations, the birds, or even trees and rocks."[18]

Land is not to be privatized. Privatization creates enslavement, not just of the living spiritual entity associated with land, but upon all who depend on the land for their existence. Once the land is stripped of its spiritual entity and reduced to a simple tradable commodity, it can be manipulated to benefit the global eurocentric minority at the expense of the global majority. A non-eurocentric worldview understands every living creature and every component of what constitutes Earth, whether it contains life or not, as requiring respect and protection. Hence, liberation is not limited to just the earth's marginalized but is extended to the earth itself. The exploitation of Earth's land and the exploitation of Earth's disenfranchised are interconnected, making it difficult to speak of one without mentioning the other.[19] Brazilian liberationist theologian Leonardo Boff connects the cry of the oppressed with the cry of the

---

[18] Tink Tinker, "Spirituality, Native American Personhood, Sovereignty and Solidarity," in *Spirituality of the Third World: A Cry for Life*, ed. K. C. Abraham and B. Mbuy-Beya (Orbis, 1994), 126.

[19] Miguel A. De La Torre, *Doing Christian Ethics from the Margins*, 2nd ed. (Orbis, 2014), 138–39.

earth, insisting that the structures and philosophy that justify the exploitation of the global disenfranchised are the same structures and philosophy that justify plundering the earth's wealth.[20]

Tinker provides us with a more holistic indigenous worldview. "In the Native American world," he writes, "we recognize that interrelatedness as a peer relationship between the two-legged and all others—four-legged, winged, and other living things. This is the real world within which we hope to actualize the ideal world of creational balance and harmony."[21] Harmony connotes coexistence. Harmonious human relationship with land is a matter of life and death, balancing our place and our needs within the world while seeking to preserve this planet for one's descendants who will live seven generations from now. If we wish to stay in a healthy relationship with the land, we reciprocate whenever we appropriate. This worldview of living in creational balance cannot coexist with the eurocentric, profit-generating anthropocentrism that justifies exploitation due to the belief of the superiority of man (specifically white men). To choose harmony requires rejecting private property and the hierarchies that subjugate land and people. Why? Because the hills are alive! Man (and here again I specifically mean cis-gendered males) is not the pinnacle of creation, nor the center, but just another component, no greater and no lesser than the trees, the hills and mountains, or even the stones that cry out the glories of the Creator (Isa. 55:12). Unfortunately, to maintain androcentric supremacy, walls are built to prevent others from trespassing.

---

[20] Leonardo Boff, *Cry of the Earth, Cry of the Poor*, trans. Phillip Berryman (Orbis, 1997), xi.

[21] Tink Tinker, "The Bible as a Text in Cultures: Native Americans," in *The People's Bible: New Revised Standard Version with the Apocrypha*, ed. Curtiss Paul De Young et al. (Fortress, 2009), 50.

Forgive Us Our Trespass

States, duty bound to protect private property, will employ the full physical, economic, and political force at their disposal to ensure "their" land is not threatened by a less civilized culture, those on the other side of the erected wall. Likewise, states, operating within a global zero-sum rule, are duty bound to seek new opportunities to increase their collective power, privilege, and profit by expanding their walls to encompass the land, resources, and labor of others, but not the others' perceived impure bodies. Well-constructed walls are porous enough for the wealth associated with bodies to seep through but thick enough to prevent the physical bodies from traversing. In the minds of the builders of physical or invisible walls, the best defense (a wall) is a strong offense (a wall). Those who are marginalized by the existence of the wall pay the price for this constant state of violence. Those for whom society has been constructed to benefit, the actual or ontological descendants of the original colonizers, reap the profits derived from walls.

Constructing a wall across land is not just a violation of the rights of the land. It is an unmitigated violence directed at those deemed inferior to eurocentrism. If we are to believe that one of the components of the United Nations' definition of "genocide" includes efforts to bring about the extermination and eventual disappearance of another's culture, then most walls become a genocidal technological tool. These walls can be a physical scar across the land like the Israeli separation wall or invisible posttraumatic scars upon the soul like the wall separating whiteness from Blackness in the United States. Walls can blockade a people, as with the US embargo against Cuba, or they can be extended to annex a people, like China's attempt to incorporate Hong Kong and Taiwan. They can separate a people who are hostile to each other like the Korean DMS or a people seeking to be reunited like the O'Odham straddling the US-Mexico wall.

Walls recount their own materialist narrative. Contrary to the modernist project, the human and the thing (walls) are woven together while reversing subject and object. Decentering anthropocentrism reveals that, rather than our building walls, walls build our identities. Constructed as a transcultural disenfranchising structure, walls objectify those living in their shadow. The global market economy, which creates massive profits for those on the "right" side of the wall, has historically been and continuously is responsible for much of the misery and death experienced by the vast majority of the world's dispossessed, who are located on the "wrong" side of the wall. Wall as a thing has its own importance and agency without depriving humans, specifically those objectified through the denial of their humanity, of concepts like justice. Exploring the weaponization of walls that separate provides an analytical prism through which to better grasp and understand how injustices of humans and nonhumans, of culture (understood as human activity), and of nature (which encompasses humans) is legitimized and normalized.

Gloria Anzaldúa poetically captures what it means to live within the shadow of walls, describing this border demarcation as

> *una herida abierta* [an open wound] where the Third World grates against the First and bleeds. And before a scab forms it hemorrhages again, the lifeblood of two worlds merging to form a third country—a border culture. Borders are set up to define the places that are safe and unsafe, to distinguish *us* from *them*.... A borderland is a vague and undetermined place created by the emotional residue of an unnatural boundary. It is in a constant state of transition. *Los atravesados* [the trespassers] live here: the squint-eyed, the perverse, the queer,

the troublesome, the mongrel, the *mulato*, the half-breed, the half dead, in short, those who cross over, pass over, or go through the confines of the "normal." ... Do not enter, trespassers will be raped, maimed, strangled, gassed, shot. The only legitimate inhabitants are those in power, the whites and those who align themselves with whites. Tension grips the inhabitants of the borderland like a virus. Ambivalence and unrest reside there and death is no stranger.[22]

Walls built to protect and secure the cultural advancements brought about by eurocentric so-called civilization, with its promises of freedom from the savage barbarism of the natives, advance the savagery of barbaric eurocentric civilization. As I have witnessed and as this book testifies, we who are a border people—living on the borders of acceptance and rejection, legitimacy and illegality, privilege and disenfranchisement—carry in our bodies what Anzaldúa notes to be *una herida abierta*.

The barbaric eurocentric civilization that is peddled as progress is, as cultural philosopher and literary critic Walter Benjamin (1892–1940) described, built upon the broken bodies of those relegated to the underside of history. Benjamin, who commits suicide at the border wall rather than fall into the hand of German eurocentric so-called civilization, remained skeptical of the concept of historical progress, noting, "There is no document of civilization which is not at the same time a document of barbarism."[23] Barbarism is not a threat to culture,

---

[22] Gloria E. Anzaldúa, *Borderlands / La Frontera: The New Mestiza* (Aunt Lute, 1999), 25–26.

[23] Walter Benjamin, "Thesis on the Philosophy of History," in *Illuminations*, trans. Harry Zohn, ed. Hannah Arendt (Schocken, 1968 [1940]), 256 § VII.

rather culture is entangled with the sadistic cruelty of eurocentric barbarism.[24]

For those on the other side of walls, no manifestation of eurocentric civilization exists absent of exploitation and domination. "Progress" becomes a term employed to legitimize the present in spite of the human wreckage left in its wake. A neat dialectical materialism, à la Hegel, that tracks the upward linear movement of time as if it is a chain of events is, instead, an illusion that masks, per Benjamin, "a single catastrophe which keeps piling wreckage upon wreckage and hurls it in front of [the Angel of History's] feet."[25] What dialecticians signal as eurocentric progress is but a pile of rotting human bodies belonging to those who have no right to occupy the land nor the history.

At US rallies, yelling, "Build That Wall!" creates unity among those privileged or believed-to-be-privileged by the walls they seek to build, for it creates an "us" to exist in contrast to a "them": a neat, simplistic dichotomy of those "civilized" in opposition to those "uncivilized." "Build that wall" becomes a defensive cry, warning of the false existential threat of the so-called possible loss of privilege, power, or profit. In fact, it is an offensive strategy designed to deprive their others of their privilege, power, or profit. For walls to succeed, the barbarism of wall-builders must be projected upon whomever is constructed as their other. Those who are the object of walls are stereotyped as primitives who threaten progress by seeking to take "our" lands, "our" jobs, "our" women. Because these walls keep people from seeing those on the other side dance with their lover or hearing the laughter of the children playing on the other side, others become unseen and unheard

---

[24] Walter Benjamin, *The Arcades Project*, trans. Howard Eiland and Kevin McLaughlin [based on German volume, ed. Rolf Tiedemann] (Belknap, 1999 [unfinished volume written between 1927 and 1940], 167–68—N5a, 7.

[25] Benjamin, "Thesis on the Philosophy of History," 257 § IX.

enemies who are easier to fear, hate, and decimate. This fear benefits political demagogic leaders, who manipulate these fears to stay in power or to increase their profits.

US president Donald Trump's one-time chief strategist Stephen K. Bannon is a useful example. Bannon was indicted for swindling funds from a private group called We Build the Wall that solicited funds to build a wall along the US-Mexico border. Although pardoned by the president during the waning days of his first administration, two of the other three people who were charged in the conspiracy to defraud the public admitted to embezzling funds that were supposed to go toward wall construction.[26] If land belongs to all for the good of all creatures that are dependent on land, then no one's presence can ever be illegal. There are no illegal aliens, only illegal walls—walls like the one Bannon and company tried to privately build or the one Trump tries to publicly build.

Contrary to the salient hyperindividuality of euroamerican culture and society, so-called primitive societies tend to be more communal.[27] The eurocentric concept of private property and its commodification had to be taught to the colonized to justify the violent theft of their lands. How then, to use anthropologist Ruth Behar's imagery, do we turn these vertical walls horizontal, transforming them into bridges?[28] How do we learn to say, *¡Mi casa es su casa, su causa es mi causa!*[29] A more liberative philosophical approach to land—recognizing its rights, its spirituality, its

---

[26] Benjamin Weiser, "After Pardon for Bannon, 2 Admit Bilking Donors to Border Wall," *New York Times*, April 21, 2022.

[27] See Robert N. Bellah, Richard Madsen, Ann Swidler, William M. Sullivan, and Steven M. Tipton, *Habits of the Heart: Individualism and Commitment in American Life* (University of California Press, 1985).

[28] Ruth Behar, "Introduction," in *Bridges to Cuba—Puentes a Cuba*, ed. Ruth Behar (University of Michigan Press, 1995), 5.

[29] My house is your house, your cause is my cause!

existence for the whole community—requires moving away from the eurocentric modernist definition of land and toward what has been called a primitive understanding of so-called undeveloped virgin land. A model for this "primitive" approach that we can possibly emulate might be found in a story of how a nascent religious cult, contrary to the laws of the civilizing empire of its time, organized itself along the belief that no one owned property because property existed for the benefit of all. This radical sharing eliminated anyone going without, for to each was given according to their needs (Acts 4:33–37).

2

The Wall of Impunity

Mitri Raheb

Some walls are clearly visible: the apartheid wall built by Israel to grab Palestinian land, or the Berlin Wall that once separated East Germany and the Eastern communist bloc from Western Europe, or the Great Wall of China that separated the Han people from "outsiders." Yet, many invisible walls also separate people—according to ethnicity, religion, or culture. In this chapter, I highlight a different kind of invisible wall that the genocide on the Palestinian people in Gaza has made visible. The genocide unfolding in Gaza has acted like a magnifying glass that has enabled Palestinians to see things much more clearly. It has revealed a wall of impunity constructed by the West to protect Israel at the expense of the Palestinian people, a wall that enables Israel to continue its settler colonial project without any repercussions. For the past one hundred years, the West has provided Israel with the necessary hardware in terms of military equipment and technology, in addition to the religious software that bestows a theological veneer and rationalization for the State of Israel. The wall of impunity that we highlight here goes further by providing Israel with political and cultural impunity.

Impunity at the UN Security Council

Palestinians have issues with United Nations Security Council (UNSC) resolutions in general. The bias that exists is nothing new but has increased and accumulated over the years. Since 1947, the United Nations (UN) has issued 189 resolutions on Palestine that were supposed to uphold peace and security for Palestinians. However, after seventy-seven years, the Palestinian people have never been as far from peace and security as they are now. UNSC Resolution 181 on the partition of Palestine did not prevent the Nakba from happening, and UNSC Resolutions 242 and 338, which called upon Israel to withdraw from the territories that it occupied in 1967, proved to be no more than empty words. After thirty years of a "peace process," Palestinians have achieved neither peace nor process, and six months of a genocidal war on Gaza were insufficient for the UNSC to agree on a ceasefire—a mere ceasefire! Three ceasefire resolutions were vetoed by the United States, three out of a total of eighty-five vetoes intended to grant Israel impunity and to prevent Palestinians from having a secure life, statehood, or even sufficient humanitarian aid. The UNSC endorses security for the occupier and not for the occupied. It was hurtful to see the US ambassador to the United Nations, Linda Thomas-Greenfield—an African American woman whose ancestors experienced slavery, oppression, racism, and rape—be the one raising her hand at the UNSC meetings against a permanent ceasefire.

The Security Council resolutions contain noble statements, but the entire UN system, an accomplishment of the post–World War II era, is, in essence, a colonial system that grants the right to veto to four European and settler-colonial countries out of the five permanent members. The UN structure thereby ensures a position of privilege for European colonial powers at the expense of the Global South, and this veto was exploited by exactly those powers. Is there not a conflict of interest if those entrusted with international peace and security are the same global superpowers that were and still are the main arms producers and dealers responsible for over 90 percent of military exports worldwide? How ironic that at least one of these five powers entrusted with international peace and security has opened its arms arsenal to Israel to choose whatever they want and supplied them with over twenty-one thousand dumb bombs that cause large-scale destruction rather than precision. Another two powers have provided political impunity for Israel's genocidal war and enabled the destruction of the entire Gaza Strip, rendering it uninhabitable.

When South Africa, a nation that endured apartheid, settler colonialism, and genocide, came to the aid of Palestinians by addressing the International Court of Justice, it was no surprise that only former settler-colonial states that had themselves committed genocide came to defend Israel. Even after months of constant bombardment in Gaza, the UNSC has been unable to ensure adherence to the principles of its own International Humanitarian Law or to secure sustainable access to food, clean water, and medical supplies, effectively allowing Israel to weaponize starvation as a genocidal tool.

The UN Human Rights Charter was another accomplishment of the post-WWII era but the Palestinian experience over past years, and especially recent months, poses the question of whether this universal charter was primarily geared toward white Europeans. A simple comparison of the West's stance toward Ukraine versus Palestine makes such a question legitimate. One might term it a clear double standard by Western politicians who apply colonial standards to provide impunity for colonial powers and their allies, and who espouse "human rights" selectively to promote their own colonial ambitions and goals. How ironic that the many Western countries that invested billions of dollars in Palestine to promote human rights and strengthen civil society have since abandoned Palestinians by cutting funding to Palestinian human rights organizations. The cuts in funding followed immense Israeli pressure in response to reports by these organizations of crimes of apartheid by Israel on both sides of the Green Line, as defined by the United Nations itself. Apartheid was defined in the UN Convention as the "implementation and maintenance of a system of legalized racial segregation in which one racial group is deprived of political and civil rights."[1]

Impunity in the Media

No genocide has received as much coverage as the genocide in Gaza. Al Jazeera Live TV channel has covered the genocide 24/7 as it unfolded despite the situational difficulties. During the first 18 months, the Israeli military murdered 165 journalists and media workers, injured 59 others, and arrested 75 in an attempt to conceal Israeli atrocities in Gaza following the October 7 attack by Hamas. Reporters Without Borders has filed several complaints with the International Criminal Court for plausible war crimes committed by Israel against Palestinian journalists in Gaza.[2] So far, no Western journalists have been allowed to enter Gaza, except for a few selected journalists who were allowed to enter Gaza for an hour or two, accompanied by the Israel military to specified locations only. Unfettered coverage by the Western media has been prohibited. Furthermore, Israeli *hasbara* and propaganda have exploited the October 7 attack by fabricating a story about beheaded babies that went viral and depicted Palestinians as barbarians and "human animals" in order to manufacture consent

---

[1] United Nations, *International Convention on the Suppression and Punishment on the Crime of "Apartheid."* See G.A. Res. 3068 (XXVIII), 28 U.N. GAOR Supp. (No. 30) at 75, U.N. Doc. A/9030 (1974), 1015 U.N.T.S. 243, entered into force July 18, 1976.

[2] Christophe Deloire, "RSF Files Second Complaint with ICC for War Crimes against Journalists in Gaza since 7 October," Reporters Without Borders, December 22, 2023, https://rsf.org/en/rsf-files-second-complaint-icc-war-crimes-against-journalists-gaza-7-october.

for the genocide that followed. What is striking is not so much Israeli policy in suppressing freedom of the press but the bias of the Western media as seen in this case study of CNN.

The Guardian newspaper conducted an investigation of CNN coverage of Gaza and published its findings on February 4, 2024, under the title "CNN Staff Say Network's Pro-Israel Slant Amounts to 'Journalistic Malpractice.'"[3] Based on the accounts of six CNN staffers in multiple newsrooms and dozens of internal memos and emails obtained by *The Guardian*, CNN editorial policies have led to "a regurgitation of Israeli propaganda and the censoring of Palestinian perspective in the network's coverage of the war in Gaza."[4] A CNN staffer put it this way: "The majority of news since the war began, regardless of how accurate the initial reporting, has been skewed by a systemic and institutional bias within the network toward Israel."[5] This bias included tight restrictions on quoting Hamas while Israel military spokesmen's statements were taken at face value.

Another CNN journalist put it more bluntly:

Many [CNN journalists] have been pushing for more content from Gaza to be alerted and aired. By the time these reports go through Jerusalem and make it to TV or the homepage, critical changes—from the introduction of imprecise language to an ignorance of crucial stories—ensure that nearly every report, no matter how damning, relieves Israel of wrongdoing.[6]

---

[3] Chris McGreal, "CNN Staff Say Network's Pro-Israel Slant Amounts to 'Journalistic Malpractice,'" *The Guardian*, February 4, 2024.

[4] McGreal, "CNN Staff Say Network's Pro-Israel Slant Amounts to 'Journalistic Malpractice.'"

[5] McGreal, "CNN Staff Say Network's Pro-Israel Slant Amounts to 'Journalistic Malpractice.'"

[6] McGreal, "CNN Staff Say Network's Pro-Israel Slant Amounts to 'Journalistic Malpractice.'"

CNN staffers were instructed by the editor-in-chief and CEO, Mark Thompson, to continuously remind viewers of "the immediate cause of *this current conflict*, namely the Hamas attack and mass murder and kidnap of civilians."[7] Another CNN journalist described how the network editors were acting as a surrogate censor on behalf of the Israeli government: "The system results in chosen individuals editing any and all reporting with an institutionalized pro-Israel bias, often using passive language to absolve the [Israel Defense Forces] of responsibility, and playing down Palestinian deaths and Israel attacks."[8] The *Guardian* investigation described several examples of this bias, including how CNN presenter Sar Sidner adopted the Israeli story of the beheaded babies and claimed to have video evidence of it, although this proved to be a lie. This is just one example of how Israeli *hasbara* was "promoted in an emotional way with very little scrutiny by someone who is supposed to be a neutral news presenter."[9] If this is the case with CNN, one must imagine the type of reporting at other US channels like Fox News.

What is true for CNN is true for most of the Western media outlets who silence Palestinian stories, ignore Palestinian suffering, and avoid the historical context.[10] On November 9, 2023, over nine hundred journalists condemned Israel's killing of journalists in Gaza and urged for integrity in Western media coverage of Israel's atrocities.[11] They accused US newsrooms of bias against

---

[7] McGreal, "CNN Staff Say Network's Pro-Israel Slant Amounts to 'Journalistic Malpractice.'"

[8] McGreal, "CNN Staff Say Network's Pro-Israel Slant Amounts to 'Journalistic Malpractice.'"

[9] McGreal, "CNN Staff Say Network's Pro-Israel Slant Amounts to 'Journalistic Malpractice.'"

[10] Media Monitoring, "CfMM Report 'Media Bias: Gaza 2023–24,'" Centre for Media Monitoring (blog), March 6, 2024.

[11] Melissa Koenig, "More Than 750 Journalists Sign Letter Condemning 'Israel's Killing of Journalists in Gaza,'" *New York Post*, November 10, 2023.

Palestinians in their reporting of the war on Gaza and stated, "We also hold Western newsrooms accountable for dehumanizing rhetoric that has served to justify the ethnic cleansing of Palestinians. Double standards, inaccuracies and fallacies abound in American publications and have been well documented."[12] The letter goes on to say that newsrooms have "undermined Palestinian, Arab, and Muslim perspectives, dismissing them as unreliable, and have invoked inflammatory language that reinforces Islamophobic and racist tropes. They have printed misinformation spread by Israeli officials and failed to scrutinize the indiscriminate killing of civilians in Gaza."[13] They ended their letter by calling on journalists to tell the full truth without fear or favor, and urged them to use precise terms that are well-defined by international human rights organizations, including "apartheid," "ethnic cleansing" and "genocide." They concluded by stating that hiding evidence of war crimes in Gaza is "journalistic malpractice and an abdication of moral clarity."[14]

What is true for the American media is also true for European and other Western media, which provide Israel with a wall of public impunity.[15] In one of the largest statistical analyses of media coverage, the Centre for Media Monitoring laid out the empirical evidence for significant bias by the British media in its coverage of the war on Gaza. The report[16] shows that emotive language describing Israelis as victims of attacks was used eleven times

---

[12] Koenig, "More Than 750 Journalists Sign Letter Condemning 'Israel's Killing of Journalists in Gaza.'"

[13] Koenig, "More Than 750 Journalists Sign Letter Condemning 'Israel's Killing of Journalists in Gaza.'"

[14] Koenig, "More than 750 Journalists Sign Letter Condemning 'Israel's Killing of Journalists in Gaza.'"

[15] Michael Neureiter, "Sources of Media Bias in Coverage of the Israeli-Palestinian Conflict: The 2010 Gaza Flotilla Raid in German, British, and US Newspapers," *Israel Affairs* 23, no. 1 (January 2, 2017): 66–86.

[16] Media Monitoring, "CfMM Report 'Media Bias: Gaza 2023–24.'"

more than for Palestinians; most television channels promoted Israel's "right" to self-defense five times more than Palestinian rights; broadcast television referred to Israeli perspectives almost three times more than Palestinian ones; and pro-Palestinian voices faced misrepresentation and vilification that perpetuated harmful stereotypes. Palestinian interviewees on Western channels were first asked to condemn Hamas, but no journalist dared to ask an Israeli if they condemned indiscriminate Israeli airstrikes on civilians in Gaza.

In the German media in particular, Axel Springer, the media giant and Europe's largest publisher, who owns the *Bild* and *Die Welt* daily newspapers, has the support of Israel enshrined in its mission statement. Journalists working there must sign a letter declaring that they will refrain from criticizing Israel. The *Bild* newspaper is known for smearing pro-Palestinian voices. After an interview I gave to *Der Spiegel*, Germany's most serious weekly magazine, was published online on October 29, 2023,[17] the *Bild* newspaper launched a smear campaign against me that can best be described as character assassination.[18] Alongside these smear tactics, critical voices who dare to push for a balanced perspective risk losing their jobs. Employees who questioned the bias in their own media outlets were fired, not only in Germany,[19] but in Canada,[20] the United States,[21] and Australia.[22]

---

[17] Monika Bolliger, "(S+) Israel-Hamas-Krieg: Ein palästinensische Pastor Mitri Raheb spricht über den Konflikt," *Der Spiegel*, October 29, 2023.

[18] "Er hetzt gegen Israel: 'Spiegel' kuschelt mit Hass-Pastor," *Bild.de*, October 30, 2023.

[19] Daniel Boguslaw, "Axel Springer Fires Lebanese Employee Who Questioned Pro-Israel Stance," *The Intercept*, October 26, 2023.

[20] "Palestinian-Canadian Journalist Fired by Major Canadian Network for Pro-Palestine Stance," *Middle East Monitor*, November 29, 2023.

[21] Aleks Phillips, "Full List of Journalists Fired over Pro-Palestinian Remarks," *Newsweek*, October 25, 2023.

[22] Tiffanie Turnbill, "Antoinette Lattouf: ABC Presenter Sacked over Gaza Post Ignites Row in Australia," BBC, January 26, 2024.

The genocide in Gaza has also exposed bias in major social media platforms. When Palestinians who felt excluded from mainline media started sharing images, videos, and hashtags exposing evidence of human rights violations and war crimes, Facebook, Instagram, Twitter, TikTok, and others responded by censoring pro-Palestinian content. The global digital rights organization Access Now has documented hundreds of cases where social media platforms suppressed pro-Palestinian posts.[23] The exclusion of Palestinian voices perpetuates a form of digital apartheid in which the Palestinian narrative is marginalized, free speech is violated, and platforms are complicit in genocide.

The war on Gaza has exposed the sad reality of the myth of a Western free press because, when it comes to coverage of Palestine, studies of Western media repeatedly show a lack of integrity and professionalism. Alternative media resources are available, and *Democracy Now!* is a great example of credible investigative journalism.[24] The award-winning journalist Amy Goodman,[25] born to secular Jewish parents, is engaged in progressive, serious, and independent journalism in her coverage of Gaza and other global issues.

Impunity in Academic Settings

The silencing of free speech regarding Palestine has a long history but reached unprecedented levels in academic circles after October 7. Following the attack by Hamas, many US university presidents were urged by pro-Israel groups to issue statements condemning the attack and to show that they stand with Israel. Major donors threatened to withdraw their financial support from academic

---

[23] Kelly Lewis, "Social Media Platforms Are Complicit in Censoring Palestinian Voices," *The Conversation*, May 24, 2021.

[24] "About Democracy Now!" https://www.democracynow.org/about.

[25] "Staff: Amy Goodman," Democracy Now!, https://www.democracynow.org/about/staff.

institutions if they did not issue such statements. It is little wonder that many of these statements were one-sided, with no reference to the larger context, and used inflammatory language that lacked academic reasoning.

However, the Israeli airstrikes, ongoing bombardment of Gaza, and the pictures of thousands of murdered Palestinians aired on al Jazeera did not leave young people unaffected. Challenges emerged to the pro-Israel hegemonic situation on campuses when students demonstrated and spoke up for Palestine. University campuses became the epicenters for clashes between pro-Palestinian and pro-Israeli groups. Harassment intensified against pro-Palestinian scholars, students, and groups. Governor Ron DeSantis ordered colleges across Florida's university system to "deactivate" Students for Justice in Palestine (SJP) from campuses and claimed that this group "knowingly provide material support" to Hamas.[26] On October 25, two pro-Israel groups, the Anti-Defamation League and the Brandeis Center, wrote to nearly two hundred university presidents urging them to investigate their chapters of Students for Justice in Palestine. In the days that followed, several universities, including Brandeis, Columbia, and George Washington University, suspended and criminalized those SJP chapters.[27] Columbia went even further, suspending the chapter of Jewish Voices for Peace.[28]

Universities that did not follow this line faced significant repercussions. The presidents of Harvard, the University of Pennsylvania, and the Massachusetts Institute of Technology were grilled as they testified before a House committee and attempted

---

[26] Ari Blaff, "DeSantis Directs Florida State Universities to 'Deactivate' Students for Justice in Palestine Group," *National Review*, October 28, 2023.

[27] Vimal Patel, "A.C.L.U. Sues DeSantis over Crackdown on Pro-Palestinian Campus Group," *New York Times*, November 16, 2023.

[28] CBS New York Team, "Columbia University Suspends Student Groups Students for Justice in Palestine & Jewish Voice for Peace for Allegedly Violating School Policies," CBS News New York, November 10, 2023.

to walk a fine line between free speech, allowing protests to take place, and combating antisemitism.[29] A member of the House Committee used the working definition of antisemitism published in 2016 by the International Holocaust Remembrance Alliance (IHRA),[30] which defines antisemitism as "a certain perception of Jews, which may be expressed as hatred toward Jews. Rhetorical and physical manifestations of antisemitism are directed toward Jewish or non-Jewish individuals and/or their property, toward Jewish community institutions and religious facilities."[31] The problem is that when "Jewish community institutions" include the State of Israel, making any critique of the State of Israel becomes antisemitic. Israel's genocidal response to the events of October 7 has triggered massive criticism of the State of Israel, and this was felt across US universities. Israel, with all its lobbying arms, has tried to weaponize antisemitism to silence this criticism. When pro-Palestinian students at Harvard chanted, "Long live Palestine; long live the intifada" (the Arabic word for uprising), these chants were described by the Harvard Hillel group as "abhorrent antisemitic calls."[32] While Israel's genocidal attack on Gaza was in full swing, chanting "from the river to the sea ... Palestine shall be free" at campuses was interpreted by pro-Israel groups and New York Republican Elise Stefanik as calling for the genocide of Jews. The pressure on university presidents who refused to silence student voices or ban student groups from expressing

---

[29] "WATCH: Harvard, MIT, Penn Presidents Defend Efforts to Combat Antisemitism on Campus," *PBS NewsHour*, December 5, 2023.

[30] John Morgan, "IHRA Antisemitism Definition 'Undermining Academic Freedom,'" *Times Higher Education (THE)*, September 13, 2023.

[31] Global Jewish Advocacy, *The Working Definition of Anti-Semitism: What Does It Mean, Why Is It Important, and What Should We Do with It?* (American Jewish Committee, n.d.), 6.

[32] Madeleine A. Hung and Joyce E. Kim, "Harvard Pro-Palestine Groups Organize 'Week of Action,' Drawing Criticism for 'Intifada' Chants," *Harvard Crimson*, December 3, 2023.

their support for Palestine finally led to the resignation of Penn president Liz Magill on December 10, 2023, and of Harvard's first black president, Claudine Gay, on January 2, 2024. The MIT president, Sally Kornbluth, was supported by the MIT governing board and was able to remain in office. These were not exceptions, and hundreds of scholars in many countries were suspended for refusing to adopt a pro-Israeli stance.[33]

The situation in Israeli universities was worse. In a recent study, Maya Wind exposed how Israeli academia is complicit in Israel's settler colonial project and how Israeli universities serve as pillars of Israel's system of oppression against the Palestinian people. Academic disciplines, degree programs, campus infrastructure, and research laboratories all serve the colonization of Palestinian land and people.[34] For years, Israeli nationalist groups had focused on seeking the dismissal of some faculty members, urging donors to withdraw funding unless the faculty member be removed. These groups published blacklists with a ranking of political correctness.[35] After October 7, Palestinian scholars teaching at Israeli universities came under attack, and Palestinian students had to deactivate their social media accounts after pro-Palestinian posts were criminalized. The renowned Palestinian scholar Nadera Shalhoub-Kevorkian was asked to resign after she distributed a petition accusing Israel of genocide. For weeks, she was under constant attack with threats on her life from Israeli right-wing groups. Ultimately, Shalhoub-Kevorkian was suspended, then reinstated before resigning.[36]

---

[33] Gemma Ware, "Israel-Gaza War Is Having a Chilling Effect on Academic Freedom—Podcast," *The Conversation*, December 18, 2023.

[34] Maya Wind, *Towers of Ivory and Steel: How Israeli Universities Deny Palestinian Freedom* (Verso, 2024).

[35] Dahlia Scheindlin, "Academic Freedom under Attack? Interview with Prof. Neve Gordon," *+972 Magazine*, April 19, 2011.

[36] MEE Staff, "Hebrew University Suspends Prominent Palestinian Academic," *Middle East Eye*, March 12, 2024.

The Tale of Two Academic Societies

In the wake of October 7, pressure to release a statement was also felt by other academic institutions. As examples, we look here at two organizations: the Society for Biblical Literature (SBL) and the American Academy of Religion (AAR). Founded in 1880, the SBL is the oldest and largest learned society devoted to critical investigation of the Bible from a variety of academic disciplines, with the mission to "foster academic scholarship in biblical studies and cognate across global boundaries."[37]

Following pressure from a group organized by (among others) Duke professor Marc Brettler and Bar-Ilan professor Nili Samet, the SBL Council approved the following statement by majority vote on October 16:

> The Society of Biblical Literature (SBL) vigorously condemns the terrorist attacks in Israel initiated by Hamas on October 7, 2023. The slaughter of innocents, taking of hostages, wanton destruction, and the ongoing atrocities against civilian non-combatants are horrific and opposed to the values we espouse as human beings and as a professional society dedicated to the advancement of scholarship on the Bible. We are concerned by the subsequent upsurge in anti-Semitic violence in the United States and globally, and encourage each one of you, our scholarly community, to stand firm against such actions in your own academic institutions. As a professional organization, we stand in solidarity with the people of Israel and wish to support all impacted by these tragic events, especially our members and their families. SBL resolves to develop appropriate educational media, publications, and conferences challenging the use of biblical and other

---

[37] "About SBL," Society of Biblical Literature, https://www.sbl-site.org/aboutus/mission.aspx.

authoritative texts to justify hatred and intolerance in any form. As SBL's governing board, we pledge our support and send strength to members of our organization in Israel whose family members are missing or held hostage by Hamas in Gaza, and we mourn with our colleagues impacted by these tragic events and all other innocent victims of the conflict.[38]

Many SBL members felt that this was a one-sided statement, and on October 19 they wrote to the council, urging them to "take a principled, thoughtful, and moral position, and to right this 'one-sided' statement with an equally passionate public statement that decries the Israeli war crimes of apartheid and ethnic cleansing, and also expresses solidarity with the highly endangered population of Palestinians."[39] In this letter they raised many important issues that are true for other similar statements. They wrote,

> While we condemn all violence perpetrated on Palestinian or Israeli civilians, we are appalled by SBL's complete silence on the question of the massive human rights violations being carried out relentlessly by the Israeli military against an entire civilian population trapped in place by borders they cannot cross and by the internationally attested war crimes being carried out by the Israeli government, a government which deprives an entire population of civilians of the essential resources of life (food, water, electricity, and fuel). We are equally disturbed by SBL's inability to condemn the ongoing and massive war crimes

---

[38] Society of Biblical Literature, "SBL Council Statement on the Hamas Attacks in Israel," October 16, 2023, https://www.sbl-site.org/assets/pdfs/council/SBLSTATEMENT10.16-20.pdf.

[39] Open Response to Statement by SBL Council, October 20, 2023, https://sites.google.com/view/response-to-sbl-council/home?authuser=1.

committed by the Israeli military in the Gaza Strip that have so far claimed the lives of more than 3,500 Palestinians, the majority of whom are children, including, as it at very least appears, the recent Al-Ahli Baptist hospital bombing that led to the death of around 500 patients and medical staff. In addition, we are shocked that you find it impossible to name the root causes of this war, as of so many wars preceding it, in the ongoing 56-year-and-counting settler-colonial military occupation of the Palestinian people by the State of Israel. We are shocked by your refusal to condemn the systemic Israeli oppression that is enforced on Palestine and has again come to international attention because of the events during the past two weeks. We would like to believe that you, as the leadership of the Society of Biblical Literature, are both aware enough and mature enough to hold multiple, complex, and difficult truths in your minds and hearts at the same time. We are profoundly disappointed to discover that this does not become evident in your present statement. By not mentioning Palestinians by name, you are not only committing an academic ethnic cleansing of an entire people, but you are also using propagandist language that is inappropriate for a respected academic organization. Any materials published by the SBL that do not adhere to international law and the biblical concepts of justice, peace, and human dignity for all serve as pure propaganda for the State of Israel. They are detrimental to SBL's credibility.[40]

This letter and the dissatisfaction of many members pushed the council to issue a second statement on October 20 that was slightly more nuanced but that equated the oppressors with the

---

[40] "Open Response to Statement by SBL Council."

oppressed. Even this watered-down statement was denounced by an Israeli-based organization declaring that "the distinction between good and evil is straightforward and must be acknowledged clearly in the strongest terms possible," and demanded that "the leadership of the SBL stand unequivocally with Israel."[41] A few days later, several (mostly Jewish Israeli) SBL members disaffiliated themselves from the SBL because it had "actively engaged in outrageous false equations."[42] These reactions demonstrate that many Israeli scholars were accustomed to having an unquestioned monopoly in many academic settings and were not used to being challenged. The SBL Council issued a further statement on October 30 "to clarify that both of its recent statements stand side by side," and that the second statement was meant to supplement the first statement rather than replace it. The statement went on to say,

> Council expresses sympathy with all members of the Society who continue to be deeply affected by the lack of clarity in our statement making. Even if we have not gotten our wording right in every instance, be sure that we remain committed to our values of inclusivity, transparency, equity, accountability, diversity, critical inquiry, scholarly integrity, and openness to change. We are a plural society, and a single statement will never capture all facets of our diversity.[43]

This last statement looks like a cheap way out.

---

[41] Seth Sanders, "Flagship Biblical Studies Group Faces Bitter Divide over Statements on Israel/Palestine," *Religion Dispatches*, November 20, 2023; Vered Noam, "Why I Resigned the Society of Biblical Literature," academia.edu, October 24, 2023.

[42] Athalya Brenner-Idan, Dan'el Kahn, Aren M. Maeir, Raanan Eichler, et al., "Public Letter of Disaffiliation from SBL," accessed February 11, 2025, https://tinyurl.com/SBLResignOpen.

[43] James F. McGrath, "Society of Biblical Literature Statement #3 on Gaza, Israel, and Hamas," *Religion Prof: The Blog of James F. McGrath*, October 31, 2023.

Fortunately, not all academic institutions bow to pressure from the Israel lobby, and some maintain their integrity. In contrast to the SBL, the statement of the American Academy of Religion (AAR) adopted a different stance. With roots dating back to 1909, the AAR is the largest scholarly society dedicated to the academic study of religion. AAR is not a faith-based organization but has the mission to "foster excellence in the academic study of religion and enhance the public understanding of religion."[44] The AAR Board of Directors issued a statement on October 24, 2023, "on the crisis in Israel and Palestine."[45]

The statement started by recognizing that no public statement adequately expresses the empathy and solidarity with those who are heartbroken and outraged. Then it went on to condemn "the killing of Israeli civilians and the taking of Israeli hostages by Hamas" as well as "the lethal violence against Palestinian civilians and the decades-long occupation and denial of human rights to Palestinians by Israel's government." As a scholarly organization "that values the critique of constellations of power, the AAR rejects all forms of colonialism, dispossession, occupation, hegemony, and violence." The statement goes on to highlight the danger of "dehumanizing others," and while it recognizes the importance of grief and mourning, it insists on human rights and the dignity of all people. The statement concludes by stating,

> We call for freedom of information and caution against the dangers of too-easily spread disinformation. We strive to promote free inquiry and critical examination for all scholars, and to create space for listening to those who

---

[44] "About AAR," American Academy of Religion, https://aarweb.org/AARMBR/AARMBR/About-AAR.aspx.

[45] "AAR Statement on the Crisis in Israel and Palestine," American Academy of Religion, https://aarweb.org/AARMBR/AARMBR/About-AAR-/Board-of-Directors-/Board-Statements-and-Endorsements-/AAR-Statement-Crisis-Israel-Palestine.aspx.

historically have been ignored, exploited, and silenced. Specifically, we are in solidarity with scholars and students who face retaliation for speaking out against government-inflicted terror and oppression.[46]

The difference between the SBL and AAR statements is like day and night.

Conclusion

The genocide in Gaza was an eye-opener for many as it became clear that Palestinians are not confronting the Israeli settler-colonial state as such but the entire Western Empire. Zionism was the nexus of European colonialism and Jewish nationalism that resulted in a settler-colonial state called Israel. Since the Balfour Declaration of 1917, Western empires have fully supported the creation and consolidation of this state while ignoring the legitimate right of self-determination of the indigenous Palestinian people. Western countries have continuously shielded the State of Israel with a wall of impunity. The genocide on Gaza has like never before exposed this complicity and lack of credibility. Freedom of media, academic freedom, and international legitimacy are neither universal nor applicable to those in the Global South. Scholars in the Global South have raised questions of trust in Western historiography as has been seen during the Gaza coverage. If the media is so biased in the case of Palestine, does that not mean that a free press is simply a Western myth? All Western knowledge production is now being reevaluated. The genocide in Gaza made the cracks in the Western wall visible like never before. This is a call to decolonize Western academia, to rethink Western epistemology, and for scholars from the Global South to continue to write and share their story until all walls fall.

---

[46] "AAR Statement on the Crisis in Israel and Palestine."

3

About the Berlin Wall and the Iron Curtain

Building and Deconstructing Walls

JOHANNA ERZBERGER

Besides common features concerning their function and impact, the visual similarity calls for a comparison between the Israeli so-called Separation Wall and the Berlin Wall. Both monuments limit(ed) freedom of movement. Both divide(d) a society. Both are connected by contradicting narratives. Both have/had real-life impact as well as symbolic potential.

Henri Lefebvre's terminology of space allows us to discuss their comparison and its possible deconstruction. The Berlin Wall divided a nation and two political systems. Its architecture's "conceived space," which specified it as a "rampart against fascism," clashed with the "lived space" of people who experienced it as a measure of their ruling political system to keep them under and in their area of control. Regarding the "Separation Wall," the "conceived space" of two nations being kept apart to protect one against the other, is questioned not only by the "lived space" of those affected and by "conceived spaces" negated by its construction, but by it being undermined by other "conceived spaces," touching on questions of identity and land upheld in circles defending the wall. The demarcation line does not follow any given reality (e.g., the Green Line), but defends a division of space that it foremost creates. It serves as an example for the interplay of perceived and conceived space. The fall of the Berlin Wall, having become a metaphor for the rejection and the overcoming of an ideological narrative by history, might be a reference point not to be underestimated. Notwithstanding all differences—that are not restricted to their difference in height[1]—the Berlin Wall indeed illustrates the potential of lived space to question conceived space and to lead to change.

Henri Lefebvre, The Production of Space

Henri Lefebvre published his *La production de l'espace* in 1974. It was translated into English under the title *The Production of Space* in 1991.[2] Lefebvre, a sociologist by formation and profession, was heavily influenced both by his ideological background as a Marxist and by where he lived and worked, first in Strasbourg (1961–1965), then Paris (1965–1973), during a period of heavily felt urbanization in which the population of the metropolitan area of Paris grew faster than in any other period during the twentieth century.[3]

Lefebvre's epistemology of space focuses on three aspects of space: the geographical dimension of space, the cultural evaluation of space, and the human experience of space. The geographical

---

[1] Being eight to nine meters high, wherever it takes the form of a wall, the Separation Wall doubles the height of the Berlin Wall. See www.btselem.org/separation_barrier.

[2] Henri Lefebvre, *La production de l'espace* (Éditions Anthropos, 1974); Lefebvre, *The Production of Space* (Blackwell, 1991).

[3] Christian Schmid, *Stadt, Raum und Gesellschaft: Henri Lefebvre und die Theorie der Produktion des Raumes* (Steiner, 2005); and Edward W. Soja, *Postmodern Geographies: The Reassertion of Space in Critical Social Theory* (Verso, 1989).

dimension of space, the *perceived space* refers to the space that is experienced, the mere materiality of physical space. The cultural evaluation of space refers to the *conceived space*, space as it is imagined or pictured in a specific cultural setting. Conceived space refers to space as it is represented in language and metaphor, as well as in maps and drawings. Conceived space refers to the cultural meaning of space, to the ideology that expresses itself in a particular meaningful image of space. The human experience of space or lived space is the space as it is experienced by its inhabitants. If the conceived space is dominating, lived space is the dominated space.

All three dimensions or aspects of space are constantly interacting. All perceived space is already the product of cultural activities, of architecture or agriculture, cultural activities that are building on and are implementing conceived space. Perceived space is accessible only as lived space. And lived space, as much as it experiences perceived space and opposes and questions conceived space, is also always already informed by the interaction.

A Short History of the Berlin Wall

On August 13, 1961, the sector borders surrounding western Berlin were closed by movable blockades. Later, those movable installations were gradually replaced by more permanent types of barriers. One year after the closure of the sector border, only 12 *kilometers* of border installations consisted of an actual wall.[4] In the middle of the 1970s, those border installations had reached a total length of approximately 150 *kilometers*. The section of the border that divided the eastern and the western parts of the city had a length of about 50 *kilometers*,[5] consisting of a 50- to-

---

[4] Alexandra Hildebrandt, *Die Mauer. Zahlen. Daten* (Verlag Haus am Checkpoint Charlie, 2001), 38.

[5] The exact numbers vary, sometimes within the same publication.

250-meter-wide border strip, composed of barbed wire, safety strips, and other installations. In 1989, this safety strip covered a surface of 330 hectares or 3,300,000 sq. meters.[6] About 100 *kilometers* of additional border separated West Berlin from its nonurban neighborhoods. Sources vary slightly regarding the exact numbers as the exact course of the border installations varied over time.[7]

In order not to infringe on the rights of the Western allies that were occupying West Berlin, the government of the German Democratic Republic erected the border installations exclusively on its own territory. These installations, however, cut through and destroyed grown city structures such as buildings, factories, gardens, and cemeteries, in addition to four railroad lines, five suburban train lines, two metro lines, five rivers or water canals, as well as water, sewage, gas, and electricity supply systems.[8]

The makeup of and outlook on the border installations from both East and West changed over time. Whereas, at the beginning, visual contact between people on both sides was still possible, later versions of the border installations comprising massive walls and a broader border strip made visual contact impossible.[9] At the same time, there was an interest on the part of responsible parties within the German Democratic Republic to camouflage the border installations on their Eastern side as well as to aestheticize the sight of the wall and border installations as seen from the

---

Klaus Dietmar Henke, "Die Berliner Mauer," and Günther Schlusche, "Stadtentwicklung im geteilten Berlin," both in *Die Mauer: Errichtung, Überwindung, Erinnerung*, ed. Klaus-Dietmar Henke (DTV, 2011), 17, 419. The first refers to 143.6 kilometers, the second has 156.4 kilometers.

[6] Schlusche, "Stadtentwicklung," 419.
[7] Hildebrandt, *Die Mauer*, 32.
[8] Schlusche, "Stadtentwicklung," 419.
[9] Anke Kuhrmann, "Die Mauer in Malerei und Graphik," in *Die Mauer: Errichtung, Überwindung, Erinnerung*, ed. Klaus-Dietmar Henke (DTV, 2011), 302.

West. The barbed wire that had crowned the wall disappeared in the late 1960s.[10] House facades that could be seen from the West were modernized. Demolition of buildings that were situated on the border strip allegedly to create a "clean sight" (following the official line)—might have served less visibility of the disruption of city structures and an operational border system.[11] Among those buildings were several important cultural and historical landmarks, such as the Reconciliation Church (Versöhnungskirche) and the Hotel Adlon.

The Separation Wall and Separating Narratives: Conceived Spaces

Eastern and Western narratives interpreted the border installation that constituted the Berlin Wall in different ways. Those narratives changed over time. In the Federal Republic of Germany, they were subject to a public discourse conducted by the civil society, political parties, and government institutions. That discourse resulted in a relative public consensus and informed the official stance that political and government institutions took. In the German Democratic Republic, the official narrative—though undoubtedly written referring to, and thus informed by, a broader public's lived space—was primarily authored by the authorities of the state.

The East

An essential characteristic of the conceived space of the "antifascist barrier"—as it was promoted by East Germany—was that it was directed against the alleged infiltration of capitalists, warmongers,

---

[10] Kuhrmann, "Die Mauer in Malerei und Graphik," 303.

[11] Gerhard Sälter, "Die Sperranlagen, oder: Der unendliche Mauerbau," in *Die Mauer: Errichtung, Überwindung, Erinnerung*, ed. Klaus-Dietmar Henke (DTV, 2011), 132, 134–35.

fascists, and so on from the West. The officially declared goal was as follows:

> The fulfillment of the mandate of the working class given by the Socialist Party on behalf of the people: to protect against every enemy the inviolability of the borders of the state, our socialist order and the peaceful life of the citizens.[12]

The public iconographic presentation of the wall in the sphere of influence of the German Democratic Republic mirrored this conceived space. Within official presentations, the antifascist barrier itself was—with few exceptions—hardly ever depicted.[13] Recurrent motifs were soldiers and workers defending it. Via its iconographic presentation, the underlying narrative claimed to speak for the entirety of the people—represented by those population groups to which this role was ascribed by the social and political system.

A second element of the conceived space that was promoted by East German narratives, which surpassed the geographic borders of Berlin or even of both German states, was its peacekeeping function in separating two conflicting powers.[14] The peacekeeping

---

[12] *Die Erfüllung des von der Sozialistischen Einheitspartei im Namen des Volkes erteilten Klassenauftrags, die Unverletzlichkeit der Staatsgrenze, unserer sozialistische Ordnung und das friedliche Leben der Bürger gegen jeden Feind zu schützen.* Politische Hauptverwaltung der Nationalen Volksarmee Deutschen Demokratischen Republik, *Vom Sinn des Soldarseins: Ein Ratgeber für den Grenzsoldaten* (VEB, 1987). Quoted in Winfried Heinemann, "Die Sicherung der Grenze," in *Die Mauer: Errichtung, Überwindung, Erinnerung*, ed. Klaus-Dietmar Henke (DTV, 2011), 144.

[13] Elena Demke, "'Antifaschistischer Schutzwall'—'Ulbrichts KZ' Kalter Krieg der Mauerbilder," in *Die Mauer: Errichtung, Überwindung, Erinnerung*, ed. Klaus-Dietmar Henke (DTV, 2011), 99, 102.

[14] Sebastian Richter, "Die Mauer in der deutschen Erinnerungskultur," in *Die Mauer: Errichtung, Überwindung, Erinnerung*, ed. Klaus-Dietmar Henke (DTV, 2011), 259.

function of the wall was, at times, seconded by Western minority voices.[15] The German Democratic Republic thus took credit for having prevented a military conflict by having erected those border installations of which the Berlin Wall was part.

The West

A relative consensus that was formed by the public discourse within the Federal Republic of Germany opposed the wall. Based on this consensus, two topics were predominant from the start: the disruption of (national) unity and the lack of freedom (of movement). They were reflected by two types of images that dominated the depiction of the wall: the separation of people—often depicted by the separation of members of one family—and scenes of escape.[16] Unity and freedom (of movement) were portrayed as values directly attacked by the wall. Over time, West German policy introduced a certain "normalization" in its relationship to the other German state, though never to the point of an official recognition of the German Democratic Republic by the Federal Republic of Germany. The official stand of the Federal Republic remained one of nonacceptance. A de facto acceptance of a permanently divided city on the part of the municipality of West Berlin showed only in 1984, five years before the fall of the wall, in city plans that conjectured a permanently independent West Berlin entity.[17]

According to both Eastern and Western narratives, including those Western narratives that had no interest in justifying its existence, the wall not only separated two territories or two groups of people. It separated two distinct political and social models. The wall that came to represent the separation of those social models

---

[15] Richter, "Die Mauer in der deutschen Erinnerungskultur," 265.
[16] Demke, "Schutzwall," 97.
[17] Schlusche, "Stadtentwicklung," 423.

and the political powers behind them had a structural, but less tangible and less iconic equivalent in the "iron curtain" separating the spheres of influence of NATO and the Warsaw Pact, of which the Berlin Wall was part.[18]

Lived Spaces

Since the beginning, the lived space of Berlin inhabitants was affected by the destruction of city structures that occurred because of the setup of the border installations and, consequently, the building of the wall. As long as movement was limited by the border installations but visual contact between people on both sides was not prevented by those installations, the other side of the wall stayed visible and present. Later generations of the border installations made the other side invisible. The disruption that was created by the border installations was notably less felt after newly built city structures had adapted to it. Efforts were made on the side of the East Berlin authorities to minimize clashes between conceived and lived space and to prevent lived space from undermining conceived space by means of camouflage and aestheticization. As the separation of social and political systems by the wall came to be accepted as a matter of fact, if not in principle—by a majority within both civil societies, as well as by those politically responsible—lived space accepted and adapted to conceived space.

What remained was the limitation of movement. The conceived space of the antifascist barrier clashed with and was undermined by the lived space of those citizens of the German Democratic Republic whose freedom of movement was limited not exclusively and not even foremost by the Berlin Wall or other

---

[18] *Octopussy* (1983) from the James Bond series features the wall and the Checkpoint Charlie as the transition point between East and West.

border installations around Berlin, but by the inner German border and the Iron Curtain. For those whose freedom of movement was limited by the installations, the border installations were experienced as directed against themselves and not against the West. The conceived space of the antifascist barrier was eventually also undermined by the lived space of those who were supposed to impose limitations of freedom of movement on their fellow citizens. Different lived spaces that came to be in tension with the conceived space created fractures among citizens of the German Democratic Republic.

The narrative behind the antifascist barrier was further undermined by the lived spaces of the citizens of the Federal Republic of Germany although, or even because, their freedom of movement was not limited to the same degree. Political normalization resulted in facilitations of border crossings from the West that—at least to a certain degree—had the effect of enabling exactly those encounters between East and West that the wall was supposed to prevent. The easing of border crossings and the increased semipermeability of the wall for citizens of the Federal Republic of Germany and inhabitants of West Berlin, which was bought by strongly needed economic support, undermined the idea of a peace that ensured separation of systems. Given that the wall had indeed created a closed and secured space in which a separated Eastern society was able to develop, its semipermeability undermined this effect. The increased semipermeability of the wall also effectively contradicted the narrative of the wall being directed against the West. In review, the acceptance of the wall by the Western world created the conditions that allowed it to be undermined. The semipermeability of the wall resulted in bringing Germans from the German Democratic Republic in contact with the West while continuing to limit their freedom of movement.

A certain acceptance on a political level was accompanied by a certain level of adaption in everyday life on both sides. Adaption and acceptance diminished the role that the wall played in the inner landscapes of citizens of the Federal Republic of Germany. Twenty years after August 13, 1961, the date of the division of the city of Berlin, half of the population of Western Germany could not connect this date to any historical event.[19] Even in 1989, civil rights activists in East Germany initially fought for a reformed German Democratic Republic, not for reunification.[20] Whereas the political division of Germany had been more or less accepted by both sides, the restrictions of movement had not.

Thirty years after the fall of the wall, not only has it disappeared, newly built city structures have also made the former separation of the city practically invisible. The wall, whose physical representation survives only in memories, photography, and displaced and displayed bits and pieces, has been fully transformed into and reduced to an icon.

The Wall as a Figure of Speech: Synecdoche, Metonymy, and Metaphor

The role that the wall plays (or played) particularly in conceived space, but also in lived space insofar as lived space opposes, questions, or undermines conceived space, is not sufficiently covered in terms of the perception of its materiality. The wall points beyond itself and its perception. The border installations that were erected on August 13, 1961, did not form a wall at all.[21] From their installation to their dismantling in the aftermath of the events of 1989, a concrete wall made up only part of the border installations that divided the city. That August 13, 1961, came to be known as "der Tag des Mauerbaus," the day on which the Berlin Wall was built, in retrospect shows that the Berlin Wall

---

[19] Richter, "Die Mauer," 258.
[20] Richter, "Die Mauer," 261.
[21] Sälter, "Die Sperranlagen," 122.

had become a synecdoche for the border installations that divided Berlin. The representation of those border installations by one (later) part of it was inscribed into the prehistory of the wall when referring to the day of their first construction.[22] In a similar way, the "fall of the wall" refers to the opening of the inner German border as a whole.[23] But it also stands for the end of a regime and for the end of German division, for freedom of movement and travel. The visibility and tangibility of the wall, its easy visualization, predestined the wall to turn into a metonymy—a form of nonactual speech that has a reference point in a reality that is part of what that form of nonactual speech represents.

The aftermath of the metonymy of the wall is a reception history, in which the wall stands for an ongoing separation after its fall and the end of the German division. "Die Mauer ist nach ihrem Fall fast ganz verschwunden, als eine der großen politischen Ikonen der Menschheit ist sie gegenwärtiger denn je."[24] Originating from the story "Der Mauerspringer" (1982) by the author Peter Schneider—who was born in what later was to become East Germany, but grew up in the West—the "wall in one's head" (*Mauer im Kopf*) became a figure of speech.[25] The wall took a metaphorical meaning.

---

[22] It was the latest version of the wall that became iconic, the so-called Grenzmauer 75, which was crowned by a tube. Sälter, "Die Sperranlagen," 122.

[23] The term "Mauertote" [dead at the wall], which refers to those who died while trying to escape by surmounting the Berlin Wall, has no equivalent reference for those who died while trying to leave the sphere of influence of the German Democratic Republic via another route.

[24] "The Wall has almost completely disappeared since its fall, but as one of the great political icons of humanity it is more present than ever." Henke, "Berliner Mauer," 31.

[25] *Die Mauer im Kopf einzureißen wird länger dauern, als irgendein Abrissunternehmen für die sichtbare Mauer braucht.* Doris Liebermann, "Die Mauer in der Literatur," in *Die Mauer: Errichtung, Überwindung, Erinnerung*, ed. Klaus-Dietmar Henke (DTV, 2011), 277.

The Metonymization or Metaphorization of the Fall of the Wall

The wall not only plays a specific role in perceived, conceived, and lived space. In the interplay of these three spaces, it points beyond itself. To put it differently, the fall of the wall—if interpreted as the breakdown of both a regime and its narrative—can be described as the overcoming of the perceived space by lived space and points beyond itself, becoming a metonymy and, in the end, even a metaphor for overcoming (other) unjust power structures. Part of the power of the metonymy (or the metaphor) derives from the fact that what was the symbol of an overcome conceived space and an overcome narrative connected with that conceived space was literally removed and broken down, and the space was physically transformed by this breakdown. The actual disappearance of the Berlin Wall after its fall has significantly contributed to its metaphorization. Within the setting of a new conceived space, the no-longer-existing wall serves as a counterhorizon that represents an overcome past and, thus, a remembered space that cannot be contradicted or conflicted by lived space anymore.

The conceived space of the so-called antifascist barrier, and with it the physical reality of the Berlin Wall itself, the perceived space, seems to have crumbled in the face of it being persistently questioned and contradicted by a lived space that was characterized by a limitation of movement and individual freedom. However, if read with a historical-critical eye, the underlying narrative of the overcoming of one conceived space by lived space implies some shortcomings. It tends to forget an economic and political reality that surpasses the geographical borders of Berlin and even both German states. It also surpasses the parameters of space. The political system that the Berlin Wall stood for and was part of might not have come down if the economic situation of both the Soviet Union and the German Democratic Republic had not been so desolate. It also ignores the role of third parties, the Federal

Republic of Germany, similar developments in neighboring countries, and most importantly the Soviet Union, whose leading politicians chose not to interfere.

The Paintings on the Wall

The paintings that have been attributed to both the Berlin Wall and to the so-called Separation Wall have become an integral part of their respective iconography. The paintings on both walls are or have been read as means of creative resistance. However, at least in the case of the Berlin Wall, the situation is complex.

Only the Western side of the wall proved accessible to artists. As the wall was built on the territory of the German Democratic Republic, the painting did not—strictly speaking—take place on the territory of West Berlin. Paintings on the Berlin Wall took place in a legal vacuum. For that reason, paintings were not taken down, even when they were not unequivocally applauded by a Western German civil society.[26] Neither were they univocally seen as a means of resistance at the time. Paintings could be meant or understood as mere graffiti in a public space and, as such, be applauded or condemned.[27] Not every painting carried a political message. On the other hand, the wall built on the German Democratic Republic's territory meant that every performance at or on the wall had at least the potential to be understood as a political act.[28] At the same time, paintings on the wall were repeatedly under dispute as the means of trivialization

---

[26] Ronny Heidenreich, "Eine Mauer für die Welt. Inszenierungen außerhalb Deutschlands nach 1989," in *Die Mauer: Errichtung, Überwindung, Erinnerung*, ed. Klaus-Dietmar Henke (DTV, 2011), 442.

[27] In this respect they did not prove different from those, for example, on the New York City subways.

[28] Lutz Henke, "'Mauerkunst,'" in *Die Mauer: Errichtung, Überwindung, Erinnerung*, ed. Klaus-Dietmar Henke (DTV, 2011), 317.

and belittlement of the wall.[29] They could be understood as an act of acceptance and adjustment to its injustice. In the end, the evaluation of the paintings lay largely in the eye of the observer. Moreover, for its greater part, the wall stayed paint free.[30]

After the fall of the wall, the meaning of the paintings became the subject of disambiguation, increasingly read as means of its creative erasure. This might have been because, foremost, painted sections of the wall were chosen as memorials, which—bereaved of their former function—worked as a piece of art. The transformation of pieces of the wall into icons or even metaphors put the painting into the service of the iconic meaning of the wall. Occasionally paintings have even been subsequently added to exhibited parts of the Berlin Wall that had originally been without them.

The wall functions as an icon, representing a conceived space that was overcome by lived space: the narrative of the antifascist barrier was undermined by the desire for freedom of those living on its East. However, what has become iconic is the wall as it could be seen from the West, as it was decorated by painters and artists living in the West. Their outlook on the wall came to illustrate the winning narrative.

The Separation Wall, the Berlin Wall, and the Question of Comparability

To understand a basic difference concerning the way in which conceived and lived space refer to each other and eventually contradict each other regarding the Separation Wall and the Berlin Wall, it is helpful to add another category, namely that of the authors and the addressees of the underlying narrative of the conceived space. Regarding the Berlin Wall, those responsible for

---

[29] Henke, "Die Berliner Mauer," 30.
[30] Heidenreich, "Eine Mauer," 442.

building the wall and the authors of the narrative justifying it, allegedly and according to this narrative, acted in the interest of those whose lived space was most noticeably affected and whose lived space most obviously contradicted the conceived space. It thus created fractures and troubled loyalties within one society, among citizens of the German Democratic Republic.

Those responsible for the building of the Separation Wall and the authors of its justifying narrative are speaking in the name of a group whose lived space is less directly affected by the wall, notwithstanding the fact that some of their members might not be convinced by this narrative and might not identify with those speaking in their name. The international community is another addressee of the narrative whose lived space is likewise not compromised by the Separation Wall. No matter if Israeli citizens or an international community do or do not agree to the security reasons given to justify the construction of the wall, it is not their freedom of movement that is limited, and neither is the space to which they lay claim limited. Those who have the political power to break down the wall by no longer justifying it or by overcoming its conceived space are not those whose lived space the wall compromises. Consequently, they will have to allow their conceived space to be questioned by the lived spaces of others.

The breaking down of the Berlin Wall—representing a conceived space undermined, questioned, and in the end transformed by lived space—became a metaphor of hope that has been applied to other walls, physical and metaphorical, in the aftermath. However, the Berlin Wall itself turned foremost into this metaphor after its breakdown and disappearance. The narrative that became a metaphor implies simplifications and disambiguation. Economic factors and the role of third parties have no counterpart in the metaphor, as there have been ambiguities and disagreements about dealing with the wall while it stood. A metaphor, by definition, does not share all characteristics with its subject of application. The power of the metaphor lies in its depiction of a positive outcome and the inspiration of hope. For example, most of the paintings on the Separation Wall are comments on the occupation, often by referring to the materiality of the wall on which they are painted, making it part of their form as well as of their content. Although meaningful, reference to the paintings on the Berlin Wall in the eye of the observer, rightfully so or not, provides an additional layer of meaning, anticipating their success in overcoming the wall, notwithstanding the fact that those on the Berlin Wall were not necessarily sharing in that intention—and could not before the fact.

The metaphorization of the Berlin Wall and of its fall has laid the foundations for it being inscribed into alternative conceived spaces that reflect on other walls—the so-called Separation Wall being one prominent example. Keeping in mind that references to the Berlin Wall refer to a metaphor that itself refers to a metonym, those references might indeed help to formulate the perspective of a peaceful transformation of space and serve as an inspiration. However, direct comparisons fall short and need to be considered if translated into political action.

Postscript

This chapter was written before October 7, 2023, and the subsequent Gaza War. The fence around Gaza is and was part of both conflicting lived and conceived spaces. Its overcoming was not peaceful. It was not inspired by a transformation of conceived space due to its incompatibility with lived space, but by brutal force. For now, the overcoming and the destruction of the fence and the following atrocities committed by members of Hamas has assured an Israeli majority of a conceived space that implies the necessity of that fence. Neither has the subsequent military reaction that turned the lived space of the Gazans into a largely uninhabitable space, deconstructed their conceived space. However, there is a minority—in both Palestine and Israel—that not only questions the benefit of the fence under the impression of recent events but asks for the renegotiation of the conceived space under the condition of the recognition of every lived space, their own and that of the others. In plain words, they ask for an end of the occupation. The discussion only starts there.

4

The Great Wall and Eggs

A Hong Kongers' Social-Spiritual Movement in the Post–National Security Law Era

Lap Yan Kung

Receiving the Jerusalem Prize for the Freedom of the Individual in Society in 2009, Haruki Murakami used the egg-versus-wall metaphor in his address: "Between a high, solid wall and an egg that breaks against it, I will always stand on the side of the egg."[1] This metaphor became a symbol widely used by Hong Kong protesters in the 2010s.[2] It not only showed solidarity with the vulnerable but also resisted adopting a pessimistic view. Since the implementation of the National Security Law in Hong Kong in June 2020, open demonstration has rarely occurred in the city. The government considers the law as an effective means to restore Hong Kong "from chaos to order, from stability to prosperity,"[3]

---

[1] Haruki Murakami, Acceptance Address, Jerusalem Prize, February 2009.

[2] Michael Tsang, "Who's the Egg? Who's the Wall?: Appropriating Haruki Murakami's 'Always on the Side of the Eggs' Speech in Hong Kong," in *Modern Japanese Political Thought and International Relations*, ed. Felix Roesch and Atsuko Watanabe (Rowman and Littlefield, 2018), 221–40.

[3] The Hong Kong Special Administrative Region of the People's

but Hong Kongers have a different perception.[4] They consider that it has fundamentally ruined the values, ethos, and way of life in Hong Kong. Dissident voices are no longer freely heard in media, civil society, and other spheres.

The principle of "one country, two systems" has been jeopardized because the emphasis on the "one country" has become more prominent. In order to resist the hegemony of the system, symbolized by Murakami as the Great Wall, those who choose to stay in Hong Kong have initiated a new social-spiritual movement characterized by transitioning from organization of mass social movement to *Wai^4 Lou^4*, which means gathering together and supporting one another, shifting their focus from strategy and action to *Co^{1}Sam^1*, protecting their original impetus and developing a lifestyle politics instead of depending upon an electoral system. An example of this is the yellow economic circle, which involves supporting shops that share democratic values and standing with the young protesters. This social-spiritual movement goes beyond the traditional forms of political activism and incorporates elements of friendship, personal transformation, and everyday life politics. This chapter reflects on the nature of the Great Wall in terms of ontological security, the lived experiences of Hong Kongers as fragile eggs, and the social-spiritual movement of Hong Kongers, exploring the theological relevance and cultural framing of this movement.

Republic of China, "II. Build a Solid Foundation for Security While Upholding the Principle and Leveraging the Advantages of 'One Country, Two Systems,'" in *The Chief Executive's 2022 Policy Address*, Hong Kong government, October 2022.

[4] The term "Hong Kongers" refers to people who have a strong Hong Kong identity, distinguishing them from both the people of Hong Kong and the Chinese.

The Great Wall and Ontological (In)Security

"One who fails to reach the Great Wall is not a hero," said Chairman Mao Zedong in 1935. This statement suggests that admirable individuals must overcome difficulties. Apart from being a symbol of a great obstacle, the Great Wall historically served as a means of protection against foreign invasions. Over time, it has gradually transformed into a Chinese national symbol, representing sovereignty, unity, defense, stability, and power.[5] In 1984 Deng Xiaoping declared, "Love our China, restore our Great Wall."[6] The Great Wall has become a site of identity politics. Interestingly, the nickname of the Chinese women's volleyball team is the "Great Wall of Women." However, some Chinese people have different experiences and perceptions of the Great Wall. Some view it as a symbol of the suppression of freedom. For example, popular platforms like Google, Facebook, YouTube, and certain overseas websites are inaccessible in China, which is commonly referred to as the "Great Firewall." This restriction stems from the Chinese government's lack of trust in its people and fear of foreign influence and interference, driven by the inherent instability of its authoritarian structure. As a result, the Great Wall symbolizes a paradox, representing both national pride and national low esteem.

Anthony Giddens, in his sociological analysis of high modernity, defines "ontological security" as a basic need of individuals for "a sense of continuity and order in events, including those not directly within the perceptual environment

---

[5] Arthur Waldron, *The Great Wall of China: From History to Myth* (Cambridge University Press, 1990); William A. Callahan, "The Politics of Walls: Barriers, Flows and the Sublime," *Review of International Studies* 44, no. 3 (2018): 456–81.

[6] Cited in Carlos Rojas, *The Great Wall: A Cultural History* (Harvard University Press, 2010), 135.

of the individual."⁷ He explains that "to be ontologically secure is to possess, on the level of the unconscious and practical consciousness, answers to fundamental existential questions which all human life in some way addresses."⁸ Ontological security pertains to "security as being" rather than "security as survival."⁹ At the core of the concept of ontological security is the confidence generated by the basic trust an individual has in other members of society, which helps reduce existential anxiety. This trust system, in turn, functions as a "protective cocoon" that filters out dangers that could threaten the individual's ability to maintain a stable continuity of identity.[10]

Built on Giddens's original articulation, Jennifer Mitzen sees ontological security related not only to individuals but to states. In her theory, ontological security is gained over time through the routinizing of relationships between states and their significant others, enabling states to anticipate how to act and what actions to expect in return. States strive to maintain this routine behavior to avoid becoming ontologically insecure, which would result in unfamiliar expectations of their own actions and the actions of others. In order to alleviate ontological insecurity, a state may engage in behavior that is detrimental to its physical security if it reinforces the state's conception of its own identity.[11]

Brent Steele further develops the principle of ontological security and argues that it is not solely derived from interactions with others. Instead, ontological security is rooted in the relationship of identity with a state's "biographical narrative,"

---

[7] Anthony Giddens, *Modernity and Self-Identity: Self and Society in the Late Modern Age* (Polity, 1991), 243.

[8] Giddens, *Modernity and Self-Identity,* 47.

[9] Giddens, *Modernity and Self-Identity,* 52.

[10] Giddens, *Modernity and Self-Identity,* 55.

[11] Jennifer Mitzen, "Ontological Security in World Politics: State Identity and the Security Dilemma," *European Journal of International Relations* 12, no. 3 (2006): 341–70.

which provides the basis for its sense of security.¹² The biographical narrative constitutes the stories or justification through which a state gives meaning and relevance to an event and is constructed through the state's reflexive monitoring of its own behavior. According to Steele, ontological insecurity can arise from interactions with other states as well as from internal changes to national identity resulting from "the internal dialectic that arises from the ontological security seeking process."¹³ Therefore, national identity needs to be understood not only as the identification of the state in relation to others, but also as the internal understanding of the state's self and the expectations of behavior that result from it (both of the self and the other). When nationalism is embedded in a biographical narrative, relevant policies can serve as powerful identity signifiers, conveying unity, security, and inclusiveness, particularly in times of crisis. Hence, in the face of potential uncertainty and its impact on self-identity, nationalist rhetoric becomes an effective strategy for identity maintenance, as it protects society members from strangers and outsiders and safeguards the state against ontological insecurity.

What is the status of China's ontological security? How does China construct its ontological security? According to Feng Zhang, three distinct historical manifestations of China's experience can be identified throughout the twentieth and twenty-first centuries: the imperial China, the revolutionary People's Republic of China, and the contemporary People's Republic.¹⁴ These periods are characterized by imperial sino-centricism, benevolent pacifism, and magnanimous inclusionism in the imperial period; revolutionary sino-centricism, great power entitlement, and moralism during the revolutionary

---

¹² Brent J. Steele, *Ontological Security in International Relations: Self-Identity and the IR State* (Routledge, 2008), 10.

¹³ Steele, *Ontological Security in International Relations*, 32.

¹⁴ Feng Zhang, "The Rise of Chinese Exceptionalism in International Relations," *European Journal of International Relations* 19, no. 2 (2011): 305–28.

period; and great power reformism, benevolent pacifism, and harmonious inclusionism during the contemporary period. Zhang's analysis reflects two important aspects of China's ontological security. First, it is the understanding of China as *Zhongguo*, the central state, or more commonly known as the "central" or "middle kingdom," in which the Chinese perceive themselves as the morally and culturally superior center of the known world.

The Great Wall of China, thus, was employed to operationalize another dynamic dyad—the civilization/barbarism distinction—that governed China's political, moral, and literary discourse. The Belt and Road Initiative, adopted in 2013, reveals the self-image of the Chinese government. It emphasizes the *Daguo Waijiao* (major country diplomacy), promoting the building of "a community with shared future for humanity."[15] It emphasizes "China's peaceful rise" and that "China has never invaded any other country—and never will." However, the Western world may see the rise of China as the "China Threat." The hindrance of the development of China caused by the Western world undermines China's ontological security.

Second, the Chinese government uses the concept of *Bainian Chiru* (the century of humiliation) to spread the consciousness of crisis.[16] This period began with the Opium Wars with the British Empire in 1839 and ended with the founding of the People's Republic of China in 1949. It asserts that the decline of Chinese power during the nineteenth and early twentieth centuries was the result of China's division and exploitation by oppressive imperial powers and corrupt domestic elites.[17] The Chinese Communist

---

[15] Weixing Hu, "Xi Jinping's Major Country Diplomacy: The Role of Leadership in Foreign Policy Transformation," *Journal of Contemporary China* 28, no. 115 (2019): 1–14.

[16] Zheng Wang, *Never Forget National Humiliation: Historical Memory in Chinese Politics and Foreign Relations* (Columbia University Press, 2014).

[17] William A. Callahan, "National Insecurities: Humiliation, Salvation, and Chinese Nationalism," *Alternatives* 29, no. 2 (2004): 199–218.

Party is the savior that ended the *Bainian Chiru* of the Chinese and restored dignity to the Chinese people. However, the *Jingwai Shili* (foreign forces) have not stopped their invasion and always want to weaken China. The Chinese government considers that the *Jingwai Shili* is exploiting issues related to Hong Kong, Taiwan, Tibet, and Xinjiang to destabilize China. First, the discourse of *Bainian Chiru* gives the Chinese government a reason for developing and consolidating an ideology of *Aiguo* (patriotism), but this is more about diverting domestic attention and preventing challenges to its legitimacy. Second, the Chinese government is adopting a more aggressive defense strategy to protect China from potential invasion. It sees its actions in the South China Sea as a defensive strategy more than an extension of its power. The next issue is how the Chinese government's concern for ontological security affects Hong Kong and vice versa.

Hong Kong: A Promise or a Threat

The Chinese government resumed its exercise of sovereignty over Hong Kong in 1997 and implemented the "one country, two systems" model to manage the political, economic, and social differences between China and Hong Kong. This can be seen as an innovative attempt in world politics, as it allows for the coexistence of two contrasting ideologies—socialism and capitalism, continental law and common law. Although some people in Hong Kong were skeptical about the integrity of the Chinese government, as reflected in the number of emigrations, the Chinese government made efforts to prove that it, as a socialist state, could be trusted, and the Sino-British Joint Declaration on the Question of Hong Kong would be respected. As a resident of Hong Kong, I can say that, from 1997 to 2020, the Chinese government showed a high degree of tolerance toward Hong Kong's politics.

For instance, Hong Kong, along with Macau, was the only place on Chinese soil where the commemoration of the 1989 Tiananmen Incident was tolerated. Protesters were allowed to hold mass demonstrations on July 1 and October 1. The former marks the establishment of the Hong Kong Special Administration Region while the latter is China's National Day. Former president Jiang Zemin (1993–2003) famously quoted a literary saying, "Well water [Hong Kong] does not mix with river water [the mainland]," signifying that Hong Kong should not interfere in China and that China would also not interfere in Hong Kong. Did the Chinese government adhere to not mixing the waters? The answer was not simply yes or no. The Chinese government exhibited self-control on Hong Kong issues, and therefore the extent and scope of interference were relatively limited.[18]

As a dissident, I was occasionally invited by the Chinese government to participate in their activities. On one occasion in the late 2000s, I was asked to deliver a lecture to researchers at the Chinese Academy of Social Sciences (Beijing). The government requested that I first submit a full manuscript of my lecture for inspection. Later, a Chinese official invited me to dinner and informed me that nearly 50 percent of the content in my manuscript had not been approved. He explained, "There is nothing wrong with you, but our country, at this stage of development, is not able to accept your views. I hope that one day our country will progress. I hope you can understand our situation. Please amend your manuscript accordingly, and you are welcome to come to our country." This was my first experience of listening to a senior government official asking to give China time to progress. I did not believe such conversations happened to me alone. It was a sign that the

---

[18] Jennifer Eagleton, *The Mixing of Well and River Water: Hong Kong under the One Country, Two Systems*, China Policy Institute, December 2, 2014.

Chinese government had a relatively healthy self-image reflected in its degree of toleration. Perhaps this was related to the period of the Beijing Olympics in 2008.

On the other hand, I would say that Hong Kong provided a platform for the Chinese government to engage with others, learn to coexist with dissenting views, and initiate communicative rationality, all of which contributed to its ontological security. However, a notable change has taken place in Chinese politics since Xi Jinping assumed power in 2012. In short, under Xi's leadership, China has witnessed a consolidation of power and a shift toward a more assertive and centralized governance model.[19] At the same time, the rise of Hong Kong localism in the early 2010s, such as the anti-Hong Kong Express Rail Link movement (2010), the anti-patriotic education movement (2012), the Umbrella Movement (2014), and the anti-extradition bill protest (2019) confronted Xi's centralized governance indirectly and unintentionally. The Chinese government interpreted the protests in Hong Kong as an extension of color revolutions and the conspiracy of *Jingwai Shili* to destabilize China. All these incidents one way or another shook the ontological security of the Chinese government, which finally led to application of the National Security Law to Hong Kong on June 30, 2020.

Some people questioned why Hong Kongers were so naïve as to initiate the 2019 protest, because the scale of the protest exacerbated the ontologically insecure sense of the Chinese government. They held that Hong Kongers should be realistic and pragmatic. In fact, the people of Hong Kong were more used to being concerned about their material than their public life. However, they were not able to remain indifferent to public life in 2019 because they were moved by young protesters. They could not let young protesters suffer for Hong Kong alone.[20] Indeed,

---

[19] Arthur S. Ding and Jagannath P. Panda, eds., *Chinese Politics and Foreign Policy under Xi Jinping* (Routledge, 2021).

[20] Lap Yan Kung, "Crucified People, Messianic Time and Youth in

Hong Kongers have paid a very high price for the 2019 protest. Many of them have left Hong Kong and a few thousand are imprisoned. I have talked to many Hong Kongers; almost all had no regrets.

According to the Chinese government, the National Security Law was intended to restore stability and security to Hong Kong following the 2019 protest.[21] However, it raised concerns about the erosion of rights and freedoms in the region. Many media outlets and newspapers have been closed, civil organizations deemed politically sensitive have faced restrictions or closure, and politically sensitive books have been removed from libraries. There have been numerous arrests of protesters, activists, and former opposition lawmakers.[22] In order to support national security, a strong version of patriotic education was introduced.[23] Sinicization of religion (Christianity) one way or another is promoted in Hong Kong. Election candidates face stringent censorship, allowing only those deemed patriots to run for office.[24]

The academic index of Hong Kong, which measures academic freedom and autonomy, has seen a significant decline.[25] The

---

Protest," in *Hong Kong Protests and Political Theology*, ed. Pui Lan Kwok and Francis Ching Wah Yip (Rowman and Littlefield, 2021), 133–47.

[21] Siu-Kai Lau, "National Security Law for Hong Kong Has Positive Impact," *China Daily*, July 25, 2021; Hualing Fu and Michael Hor, eds., *The National Security Law of Hong Kong* (University of Hong Kong Press, 2022).

[22] Thomas Kellogg and Charlotte Yeung, "Three Years in, Hong Kong's National Security Law Has Entrenched a New Status Quo," *ChinaFile*, September 6, 2023; "Explainer: Hong Kong's National Security Crackdown—Month 34," *Hong Kong Free Press*, May 23, 2023.

[23] Mercedes Hutton, "Hong Kong Welcomes Passing of China's Patriotic Education Law, Which Covers City and Macau," *Hong Kong Free Press*, October 25, 2023.

[24] Peter Lee, "Democratically-Elected Seats to Be Slashed to 20% for Local Hong Kong Elections; Candidates Vetted," *Hong Kong Free Press*, August 21, 2023.

[25] "The Academic Freedom Project," V-Dem, Varieties of Democracy: Global Standards, Local Knowledge, 2025.

departure of more than three hundred thousand people (4 percent of the population) from Hong Kong, as indicated by surveys, reflects the concerns and uncertainties surrounding the changes in the territory. The international community has expressed its concern about human rights in Hong Kong, but the Chinese government shows no sign of restricting its grip, because its ontologically insecure sense does not provide it with confidence to allow the two systems of "one country, two systems" more freedom to develop.

A Social-Spiritual Movement

Since the implementation of the National Security Law, those who have chosen to remain in Hong Kong are faced with the question of how to live behind the Great Wall, which, according to Murukami, is "too high, too strong, and too cold." In recent years, I have observed a social-spiritual movement characterized by $Wai^4 Lou^4$, $Co^1 Sam^1$, and the yellow economic circle emerging among Hong Kongers. It was not organized but rather occurred in a fragmentary manner. It appears to be a retreat driven by frustration and political suppression, but it is also a process of reorientating relations, values, and actions for agents involved in social transformation.

$Wai^4 Lou^4$ and Solidarity

$Wai^4 Lou^4$ is a term widely used by Hong Kongers in the post–National Security Law era. It literally means "to stay around the fireplace with family and friends, usually having hotpot," which is a common practice in Hong Kong residents' everyday life, especially during winter. In 2019, the protesters employed the term $Sau^2 Zuk^1$, which literally means hands and feet to address one another. They needed a strong brotherhood and sisterhood in order to counter enemies.[26] A shift from $Sau^2 Zuk^1$ to $Wai^4 Lou^4$

---

[26] Lap Yan Kung, "Is God Our $Sau^2 Zuk^1$, Comrade or Friend, with

reflects that Hong Kong has moved from a state of conflict to a state of the so-called *Fuk⁶ Seong⁴* (returning to normal). But a state of *Fuk⁶ Seong⁴* has nothing to do with healing and reconciliation because the issue of justice has not been properly addressed. Contrarily, the state is filled with brokenness and mistrust.

A survey released in early 2020 found that nearly one in three adults in Hong Kong reported symptoms of posttraumatic stress disorder (PTSD). Prevalence of PTSD symptoms was six times higher than after the Umbrella Movement in 2014, rising from about 5 percent in March 2015 to almost 32 percent in September–November 2019.[27] *Wai⁴ Lou⁴* is a practice of Hong Kongers caring for one another. It can involve simple activities like going out for a drink or meal, having a chat, or living with another. People say *Gaa¹ Yau⁴* (add oil, power up) to greet one another. These gatherings aim to support one another, ensure each other's safety, and avoid arrest. Specifically, *Wai⁴ Lou⁴* includes supporting protesters who are in prison as well as ex-prisoners. For prisoners, this support can take various forms, such as organizing visits, posting letters, providing material assistance, attending court hearings, and taking care of their families and other needs. *Wai⁴ Lou⁴* intends to send a message that the prisoners are not forgotten, and they look forward to a day when they can be *Wai⁴ Lou⁴* in person. For ex-prisoners, this support focuses on seeking employment. Furthermore, *Wai⁴ Lou⁴* involves providing counseling services to Hong Kongers with PTSD. As of December 2023, the service was still ongoing. However, many individuals with PTSD hesitate to seek help due to concerns that their information will be released to the police, leading to potential

---

Reference to the 2019 Hong Kong Anti-Extradition Law Amendment Movement and *Fratelli Tutti*?" *Lumen: A Journal of Catholic Studies* 10 (2022): 33–57.

[27] Michael Y. Ni et al., "Depression and Post-Traumatic Stress during Major Social Unrest in Hong Kong; A 10-Year Prospective Cohort Study," *Lancet* 395, no. 1020 (January 25, 2020): 273–84.

repercussions. An atmosphere of mistrust spreads among people, so most of counseling services are carried out secretly.

Wai⁴ Lou⁴ is an act of solidarity, giving time to and taking care of one another. *Wai⁴ Lou⁴* is a lay, unorganized, and spontaneous movement addressing everyday life. Everyone can do something for others. It introduces an important element to the political landscape, emphasizing that political effectiveness and success should not overshadow passion and caring for humanity. I would say that *Wai⁴ Lou⁴* is very similar to the Christian practice of communion, characterized by trust, reciprocal care, the celebration of difference, and open exchange of communication,[28] and it provides concrete examples of communion for churches in the post–National Security Law era. However, *Wai⁴ Lou⁴* can also lead to the formation of exclusive small cliques that disregard others. This is why protesters have their own *Wai⁴ Lou⁴*, and the pro-establishment has its own. Besides, different groups of protesters have their own *Wai⁴ Lou⁴*; they may have no overlap between them and even be against one another due to different political views. While *Wai⁴ Lou⁴* is about communion and solidarity, it can also inadvertently foster exclusivism and reinforce differences in beliefs. People suffering from frustrations and PTSD understandably need *Wai⁴ Lou⁴*, but people in *Wai⁴ Lou⁴* should be more self-aware and self-critical of *Wai⁴ Lou⁴*, ensuring that it does not boost dualism, demonize enemies, and exclude diversity.

Co¹ Sam¹ and Existence

Co¹ Sam¹ is another term that Hong Kongers commonly used during the 2019 protest and in the post–National Security Law era. It literally means "the true heart, the original intention, the wish made at the beginning." During the protests, the protesters

---

[28] Anne-Marie Ellithorpe, *Towards Friendship-Shaped Communities: A Practical Theology of Friendship* (Wiley Blackwell, 2022), 183.

challenged the police by asking what their *Co¹ Sam¹* was. "Aiding the distressed, fighting against evil, and punishing the wicked" was the police's motto, but what the police were doing during the 2019 protest was not protecting the people. They were simply an extension of the authorities' power and had lost their conscience. In this era, Hong Kongers use *Co¹ Sam¹* to encourage one another in order to overcome their frustration and powerlessness to effect change. How to protect and sustain one's *Co¹ Sam¹* is an existential issue for Hong Kongers, particularly those in Hong Kong.[29] However, *Co¹ Sam¹* can become a kind of emotional and moral bondage because someone who changes their mind would be condemned as betraying *Co¹ Sam¹*. This condemnation can be very damaging because it targets one's existence. We appreciate the concern of *Co¹ Sam¹*, but understanding how it is to be interpreted remains an issue.

According to Zen Buddhist thought, *Co¹ Sam¹* refers to the beginner's mind (heart) when they first encounter things. It is characterized by curiosity, openness, and a nonprejudiced mindset. *Co¹ Sam¹* entails dropping one's expectations and preconceived ideas about something, allowing one to be more flexible, grateful, present, and open.[30] It reminds Hong Kongers not to cling to their past experiences but rather approach each moment as something new. The here and now transforms karma, not the past. Moving on is not betraying *Co¹Sam¹*; instead, it is a responsible life, taking the present seriously, not living in the past. However, some Hong Kongers hesitate to adopt a Buddhist view. They claim that it may serve as an excuse for not persisting in the pursuit of social justice.

The Bible's Sermon on the Mount provides Hong Kongers with another reference for *Co¹ Sam¹*. It is purity of heart. Jesus

---

[29] Lap Yan Kung, "A Politics of Re-Existence: Christianity and Social Protest in Hong Kong," in *Political Theology in Chinese Societies*, ed. Joshua Mauldin (Routledge, 2024), 185–206.

[30] Shunryu Suzuki, *Zen Mind, Beginner's Mind* (Shambhala, 2011).

said, "Blessed are the pure in heart, for they shall see God" (Matt. 5:8). Seeing God in Jewish tradition was dependent upon one living with the religious traditions of purity and impurity, but Jesus offered a different path. For instance, even the disabled (considered impure by religious law) could see God if they were pure in heart. People are accustomed to interpreting purity of heart ethically,[31] but this can easily devolve into moralism, which is simply another form of the religious traditions of purity and impurity. Furthermore, it can easily lead to self-righteousness based on behavior, a concern of the Reformation. I would argue that being pure in heart simply means maintaining faith in God. This is not purely an inward journey, but a spiritual journey that opens one to the exteriority of existence. Faith in God is not to focus on oneself but brings one to transcend oneself. This faith in God allows one not to lose hope and love.

Neither the beginner's mind (heart) in Buddhist understanding nor the purity of heart in Christian understanding can replace *Co¹ Sam¹* but can liberate it from potential emotional and moral bondage. *Co¹ Sam¹* is to preserve one's existence as an echo to Jesus's words, "[The power] can kill the body but cannot kill the soul" (Matt. 10:28).

Yellow Economic Circle and Everyday Life

The yellow economic circle is the idea and practice of Hong Kongers wherein businesses within the circle receive support and patronage while those outside the circle, seen as unsupportive of the protest movement, are boycotted or worse. This extends to various aspects of daily life, including dining, shopping, media and news outlets, transportation, payment methods, services, artists,

---

[31] Pawel Wygralak, "'Blessed Are the Pure in Heart, for They Shall See God' (Matt 5:8) as Interpreted by the Church Fathers (4th–5th Cent.)," *Verbum Vitae* 38, no. 2 (2020): 579–91.

and brands. The objectives of the yellow economic circle are to counter the blue economic circle initiated by state power and to generate counterpolitical pressure on businesses, compelling them to reconsider supporting the government.[32] However, we should not romanticize the practice of the yellow economic circle. For instance, some so-called yellow businesses competed among themselves to prove that they were more yellow than others. Besides, not all yellow restaurants focused on providing good quality food and services. Ironically, some of them betrayed the trust of Hong Kongers as their primary interest was to earn money. Despite these weaknesses, the yellow economic circle helps to consolidate discursive and symbolic resources for maintaining the solidarity and collective identity of Hong Kongers.

The yellow economic circle is a form of political consumerism. Unlike expressing their political views and demands through the conventional electoral systems, political institutions, and organized political movements, people involved in political consumerism exercise their political power through their wallets and their role as consumers. First, this shopping for change signifies a more conscientious action. Second, it is the politicization of everyday life choices, including ethically, morally, or politically inspired decisions. Third, lifestyle politics can be both individual and collective, encompassing lifestyle change, mobilization, and politics. Finally it serves as a relatively soft form of political activism in the post–National Security Era. The yellow economic circle demonstrates that individuals can make a difference, regardless of how small their actions or

---

[32] Protesters in 2019 used yellow as their color while the pro-establishment used blue. Hannah Poon and Tommy Tse, "Enacting Cross-Platform (Buy/Boy)Cott: Yellow Economic Circle and the New Citizen-Consumer Politics in Hong Kong," *New Media and Society*, June 7, 2022; M. Y. H. Wong, Ying-ho Kwong, and Edward K. F. Chan, "Political Consumerism in Hong Kong: China's Economic Intervention, Identity Politics, or Political Participation?" *China Perspectives* 3 (2021): 61–71.

impacts may be. It is a movement driven by self-awareness and personal lifestyle change.

Theologically, I find that the yellow economic circle bears some connection to the Christian idea of a messianic lifestyle. This theme is frequently found in the theology of Jürgen Moltmann.[33] The term "messianic" essentially means "Christological"; the Christological foundation always points toward the eschaton, the future reign of Christ. A "messianic lifestyle" refers to the church as the people of hope, living between the remembrance of Christ's history and the hope for his kingdom. In this interim period, they express a life characterized by openness, equality, freedom, friendship, and peace. The yellow economic circle enriches the imagination of the Christian messianic lifestyle through its concrete consuming practice, and in return, the Christian messianic lifestyle deepens the belief of lifestyle politics.

Cultural Framing Perspective

The way that Hong Kongers live in this post–National Security Law era is, to me, very similar to the context that Jesus's parable of the wheat and the weeds intends to address (Matt. 13:24–30), a parable about living in between. First, when good deeds are performed, there are those who deliberately engage in wrongdoing. The wrongdoing is not accidental, but a deliberate choice, which can be frustrating. However, second, the master in the parable chooses not to remove immediately the weeds that represent bad deeds and bad people, not because there is a possibility for the weeds to become wheat or because the wheat needs the weeds to grow better. Rather it is because removing the weeds might

---

[33] Jürgen Moltmann, *Theology of Hope: On the Ground and the Implications of a Christian Eschatology* (SCM, 1967); Moltmann, *The Passion for Life: A Messianic Lifestyle* (SCM, 1978); Moltmann, *The Church in the Power of the Spirit* (SCM, 1977); Moltmann, *The Way of Jesus Christ* (SCM, 1990); and Moltmann, *The Spirit of Life: A Universal Affirmation* (SCM, 1992).

accidentally harm the wheat. In the early stage, wheat and weeds closely resemble each other in appearance. Third, the coexistence of wheat and weeds is a reality of life. How to be patient, how to not lose hope, and how to persist in good are qualities that servants need to nurture. Last, when the time comes, the master will separate the wheat from the weeds. This represents the fulfillment of the eschatological hope. How may Jesus's parable enrich Hong Kongers' experience?

I consider that both Jesus's parable and the experiences of Hong Kongers in *Wai⁴ Lou⁴, Co¹ Sam¹*, and the yellow economic circle are primarily concerned with cultural framing rather than a politics of accommodation. The cultural framing perspective of a social movement is defined as "conscious strategic efforts by groups of people to fashion shared understandings of the world and of themselves that legitimate and motivate collective action."[34] Cultural frames encompass "metaphors, symbols, and cognitive clues that cast in issues a particular light, and suggest possible ways of responding to these issues."[35] Jesus's parable is a kind of cultural framing, for it not only provides language and symbols for understanding that a problem exists—that is, the wheat and the weeds—but also offers hope for salvation, as depicted in the belief that "when the time comes, the master will separate the wheat from the weeds." Conversely, *Wai⁴ Lou⁴, Co¹ Sam¹*, and the yellow economic circle provide frames for shared understanding, recognizing a window of opportunity and establishing goals. People engaging in *Wai⁴ Lou⁴* may be a group of disparate individuals, but they draw encouragement from one another

---

[34] Doug McAdam, John D. McCarthy, and Mayer N. Zald, "Introduction: Opportunities, Mobilizing Structures, and Framing Processes: Toward a Synthetic, Comparative Perspective on Social Movements," in *Comparative Perspectives on Social Movements*, eds. Doug McAdam, John D. McCarthy, and Mayer N. Zald (Cambridge University Press, 1995), 6.

[35] G. Davis, D. McAdam, W. R. Scott, and M. Zald, *Social Movements and Organization Theory* (Cambridge University Press, 2005), 48–49.

to protect their *Co¹ Sam¹*. *Co¹ Sam¹* fuels their thirst for justice, passion for peace, and unwavering resolve. The yellow economic circle serves as an example of establishing a goal and identifying a pathway for action. Hong Kongers' experiences provide a lens through which the meaning of Jesus's parable is concretized, and in turn, Jesus's parable resonates with the experiences of the people of Hong Kong, as captured in the saying "*An⁴ Zoi⁶ Zou⁶, Tin¹ Zoi⁶ Hon³*" [Whatever you do, God is watching you]. Both Jesus's parable and the practice of *Wai⁴ Lou⁴*, *Co¹ Sam¹*, and the yellow economic circle contribute to the cultural framing of the social-spiritual movement of Hong Kongers. One of the features of the social-spiritual movement is its addressing emotions such as anger, fear, grief, indignation, and hope more than merely focusing on political opportunities and mobilizing structures. Benjamin Shepherd reminds us that "changing entrenched systems of oppression requires shifts in emotional as well as intellectual attitudes,"[36] and the social-spiritual movement of the Hong Kongers is a response to the shift.

Conclusion

The experiences of Hong Kongers resonate with Murakami's address at the 2009 Jerusalem Prize for the Freedom of the Individual in Society:

> A solid wall [is] called the System. To all appearances, we have no hope of winning. The wall is too high, too strong and too cold. If we have any hope of victory at all, it will have to come from our believing in the utter uniqueness and irreplaceability of our own and others' souls and from the warmth we gain by joining souls together.[37]

---

[36] Benjamin Shepard, "Play, Creativity, and the New Community Organizing," *Journal of Progressive Human Services* 16, no. 2 (2005): 52.

[37] Murakami, *Acceptance Address*.

Whether the wall (the system) will be torn down is not an issue, because seeds can grow in the cracks or on the surface of the wall. The wall is strong, but it does not hinder the growth of seeds. The victory lies in becoming and protecting one another without being divided or assimilated by the system. The community possesses a vision as well as a power of cultural framing: the social-spiritual movement in which Hong Kongers are currently engaged. Nevertheless, this social-spiritual movement is not God's kingdom itself and is not without its flaws. Whether the Hong Kong government perceives it as a form of "soft resistance" or not,[38] St. Paul testifies that "faith, hope, and love will endure" (1 Cor. 13:13), providing a solid theological resource for the cultural framing of this movement.

---

[38] Jeffie Lam and Harvey Kong, "Hongkongers Must Stay Vigilant against People with Ulterior Motives and Foreign Forces Trying to Sow Discord, City Leader John Lee Says," *South China Morning Post*, November 18, 2023.

5

Peace at the Korean Demilitarized Zone

A Feminist Praxis of De-Imperialization, Decolonization, and Demilitarization

BOYUNG LEE

Since the war between Israel and Hamas, as most media call it,[1] broke out on October 7, 2023, Korean media allotted a significant amount of time and pages to report on it. However, I found only one distinctive thing in Korean news media, particularly conservative ones. Highlighting Hamas militants' use of motorized paragliders to breach the Gaza-Israel border, Korean conservative media critics and politicians invoked likely attacks by North Korea using a similar method to cross the world's most heavily militarized[2] and ironically

---

[1] A simple Google search yields countless news reports, including from al Jazeera, Haaretz, CNN, AP News, Reuters, the *Washington Post*, the *New York Times*, etc., with the title "Israel-Hamas War," "War between Israel and Hamas," or "Israel-Gaza War."

[2] The area is littered with active land mines and the remains of Korean War casualties, with the most heavily armed guards on both sides of the border. Christine Hong, "The Unending Korean War," *Positions: Asia Critique* 23, no. 4 (2015): 597.

named Demilitarized Zone (DMZ).³ Computer-generated images of North Korean soldiers flying over the Korean DMZ (KDMZ) to the South were repeatedly shown on TV screens and other media. While this method of attack was considered highly probable at the time, political pundits suspected that it was a strategic threat by the now-impeached president, a member of the conservative party, and his minority ruling party to boost their meager approval ratings ahead of the general election in early 2024.

Supporters of the conservative party government emphasize that the Israel-Hamas War gives more reason to maintain the National Security Law, which the progressives have lobbied for decades to outlaw. In other words, the current crisis in the Middle East, which appears to have nothing to do with Korean affairs, made inter-Korean divisions across the DMZ even more explicit, as well as further intensified conflicts at its southern border. Ideologies of the Cold War that had divided the country into two along the 38th parallel, redrawn as the current DMZ during the Korean War, are now much more than a territorial marker separating North Korea and South Korea.

The DMZ is a political, ideological, kinship, moral, and psychological wall that separates the nations and their people, forcing them to choose their affiliation. According to Suk-Young Kim, a Korean American performance and cultural studies scholar, Koreans have long been developing close-knit ties and communities through familial and cultural kinship. However, since the division, they have been forced to distance themselves from the other Korea as a prerequisite for ideal citizenship, thus shaping a social culture that encourages people to choose their affiliation not by what they support but by what they oppose, even within South Korea.⁴

---

³ Da-gyum Ji, "Hamas Weapons, Tactics Resemble Those of NK: JCS," *Korea Herald,* October 17, 2023.

⁴ Suk-Young Kim, *DMZ Crossing: Performing Emotional Citizenship along the Korean Border* (Columbia University Press, 2014), 6.

Divisive policies of successive anticommunist dictatorial governments backed by the United States and its colonial interests, acts of violence and massacres by the state against those with opposing voices and views, political and social retribution to the families of victims, justification of ordinary people's sacrifice for the nation's economic development, irreconcilable gaps between haves and have-nots—and more—all have created and intensified such cultures of affiliation-by-opposition throughout Korea's modern history.[5] In sum, the KDMZ is much more than the only remaining physical front line of the Cold War, as traditionally understood. From the perspectives of many Koreans living with its history and consequences, it is a literal and symbolic space replete with accumulated emotion, trauma, open wounds, and tension deeply tangled with colonial interests and projects of the United States and other global superpowers. It requires critical analysis of how it came about from the machinations of foreign powers like the United States, Soviet Union, and China, which were more concerned with their own Cold War agendas, rooted in the logic of colonialism, than the fate of the people on the Korean peninsula.[6]

To reorient the KDMZ discourse, I first locate it in its somewhat broader historical context by sketching how American hegemonic battles for its interests in the Asia-Pacific region are directly connected to the division of the Korean peninsula. This critical examination of the region's history points to the need to understand the Cold War, including the Korean War, in the larger imperial and colonial schemes of the United States and its competition and intersection with the hegemonic interests of other global superpowers like the Soviet Union / Russia and China. I argue

---

[5] For a comprehensive presentation of this point, see Heonik Kwon, *After the Korean War: An Intimate History* (Cambridge University Press, 2020).

[6] Nami Kim and Wonhee Anne Joh, "Introduction," in *Critical Theology against US Militarism in Asia,* ed. Nami Kim and Wonhee Anne Joh (Palgrave Macmillan, 2016), xii.

that the KDMZ and the division it creates will remain unless we approach peace in the Korean peninsula with a new paradigm or framework based on de-imperialization and decolonization. I conclude the chapter by exploring the feminist praxis of demilitarized peace to collapse both the physical and metaphorical walls of the KDMZ. I concretely offer how peace can be pursued through grassroots mobilization, transnational collaboration, and solidarity building that center on the lived experiences of the people most impacted by the war, violence, and division rather than on politics and the absence of violence by force.

The Cold War and Two Koreas as an Imperial Project of the United States

The KDMZ or DMZ is a land strip that spans the Korean peninsula near the 38th parallel north. As a border barrier, the DMZ effectively divides the peninsula into North and South Korea. With a length of 250 kilometers (160 miles) and a width of approximately 4 kilometers (2.5 miles), the metaphorical wall is often referred to as the oldest continuous front line of the Cold War.[7] It was initially conceived as a buffer zone for a temporary ceasefire during the Korean War, ironically still dividing the peninsula seventy years later. The complex spatial region was defined by the Armistice Agreement between the United Nations, North Korea, and China, excluding South Korea, in 1953, redrawing the original partition line along the 38th parallel north.

The formation of the inter-Korean border along the 38th parallel north was begun by the superpower Allies at the end of World War II. Anticipating their defeat of Japan, the United States, China, and Great Britain met in Cairo in November

---

[7] Hyun Kyung Lee and Dacia Viejo-Rose, "The Eclectic Heritage-Scape of a Tense Border in the Paju DMZ, South Korea," *Korea Journal* 63, no. 2 (Summer 2023): 46.

1943 to discuss Japan's fate and these powers' trusteeship over Japan's former colonies, including Korea. They agreed that Japan should forfeit all territories acquired through force to prevent it from gaining excessive power. In the subsequent joint statement following the conference, Korea was mentioned for the first time:

> It is their purpose that Japan shall be stripped of all the islands in the Pacific which she has seized or occupied since the beginning of the first World War in 1914, and that all the territories Japan has stolen from the Chinese, such as Manchuria, Formosa, and The Pescadores, shall be restored to the Republic of China. Japan will also be expelled from all other territories which she has taken by violence and greed. The aforesaid three great powers, mindful of the enslavement of the people of Korea, are determined that in due course Korea shall become free and independent.[8]

Many Koreans who have devoted their lives to their country's independence since the Japanese colonization were dismayed that the conference was held and the statement was written without consulting any Korean experts, Koreans themselves, or inviting various Korean exile governments.[9] They were afraid of their fate being determined again by new foreign powers after their occupation by Japan. Many Koreans on the peninsula, as well as those serving in exile governments and fighting against Japan on the frontline of the war, proposed plans for Korea's future.

As the conclusion of the war loomed in August 1945, Allied leaders remained divided on the future of Korea. However, two

---

[8] "The Cairo Declaration," in *Foreign Relations of the United States, Diplomatic Papers, The Conferences at Cairo and Tehran, November 26, 1943* (US Government Printing Office, 1961), 448–49.

[9] Theodore Jun Yoo, *The Koreas* (University of California Press, 2022), 41–42.

days after the atomic bombing of Hiroshima on August 6, 1945, Soviet leaders, following Stalin's agreement with Roosevelt at the Yalta Conference, invaded Manchuria. American leaders feared that the Soviet Union might occupy the entire Korean peninsula.[10] To prevent this, the US military assigned two young colonels, Dean Rusk and Charles Bonesteel, under the guidance of Brigadier General George Lincoln, to define the American occupation zone. Reviewing a small *National Geographic* map of Asia (not Korea) for about half an hour, they proposed the 38th parallel as the administrative line for the two armies, dividing the country approximately in half while keeping the capital, Seoul, under American control. The Soviet Union agreed to this proposal. It was incorporated into General Order No. 1 for the administration of postwar Japan.[11] Soon after, Lieutenant General John R. Hodge established a military government to administer the southern region, until 1948 when Harvard-educated Syngman Rhee was handpicked by the United States as the first president of South Korea. This was the start of two nations in Korea: the US-occupied Republic of Korea (South Korea) and the Soviet Union–backed Democratic People's Republic of Korea (North Korea). Korea was liberated from one foreign power and then immediately occupied and controlled by the other two superpowers with opposite political views.

The Koreans, having not secured victory by their own power, found themselves unprepared to facilitate the transfer of political power. The rapid disintegration of the Japanese empire after the victory of the allied powers led to a significant power vacuum, creating potential civil unrest and political instability for the Korean

---

[10] Arthur L. Grey, "The Thirty-Eighth Parallel," *Foreign Affairs* 29, no. 3 (1951): 483.

[11] Marie Lee, "The Violence of Forgetting: On the Anniversary of the Korean War Armistice, Here's Why America Finally Needs to Remember the Forgotten War," *Boston Globe*, July 27, 2022.

people over the next several years. This lack of readiness resulted in competition and conflicts among Korean leaders over establishing a new government—its ideological foundation, leadership, and so on. Amid struggles, certain leaders started earnestly formulating plans to reconstruct their nation, collaborating even with people on the other side of the 38th parallel for one Korea.[12] However, the United Nations passed the resolution to establish two separate governments on the Korean peninsula. The North and the South, backed by the Soviet Union and the United States, respectively, both claimed to be Korea's sole legitimate government, and neither accepted the border as permanent.

While Syngman Rhee's government welcomed the UN decision and claimed legitimacy, some Korean people resisted through demonstrations and uprisings. Large-scale protests erupted across Jeju Island in the south from March 1948 onward, followed by uprisings in other areas. Demonstrators called for the withdrawal of US troops from Korea. The local police began perpetrating atrocities against demonstrators, collaborating with the Northwest Youth Group, a paramilitary organization composed of anticommunist Korean refugees from the North dispatched by the US Army Military Government in Korea (USAMGIK). The protesters, their families, anyone hiding them, and other innocent civilians, including children and women, were accused of being communists.

According to the National Committee for Investigation of the Truth about Jeju Island on April 3, which defined the event as a genocide, about 10 percent of the island's population was killed, and even more people fled for their lives to Japan.[13] The Rhee administration's brutality and suppression against people in

---

[12] Yoo, *The Koreas*, 41.

[13] The National Committee for the Investigation of the Truth about the Jeju April 3 Incident, *The Jeju 4-3 Incident Investigation Report*, December 15, 2003.

Jeju and throughout South Korea were notorious. Anyone with opposing views was accused of being a communist, and martial law was constantly enacted. Some historians, thus, call the Jeju uprising the beginning of the Korean War, which ruptured millions of families and killed about five million soldiers and civilians.[14] Beyond physical division between north and south across the 38th parallel, Koreans started having ideological and political divisions and wars even within South Korea, and such division intensified during and after the war.

The Korean DMZ and the US Empire Building

The DMZ is an adjusted border of the existing inter-Korean division line, the 38th parallel, set at the end of the Korean War. Understanding the nature of the Korean War, which began on June 25, 1950—when North Korea invaded South Korea, following years of hostilities between the two Koreas—is critical to redefining the meaning of the KDMZ as more than the only remaining Cold War site. Several distinctively different definitions of the Korean War are available, depending from which perspective the conflict is interpreted. The most common understanding is that the war was a proxy war in the Cold War, as China and the Soviet Union supported North Korea, while the United States and allied countries supported South Korea.[15] Although the numbers do not do justice to the lives lost in the war, the data are still useful for understanding the extent to which both Koreas were devastated and how costly the Korean War was on many levels.

---

[14] Ji-Yeon Yuh, "Beyond Numbers: The Brutality of the Korean War," *Presbyterian Mission*, April 19, 2018.

[15] Joo Ok Kim, "Untelling the Tales of Empire: Intimate Epistemologies of the Korean War" (PhD dissertation, University of California, San Diego, 2013), xii.

Here are some statistics that Ji-Yeon Yuh compiled from various sources, including the US Department of Defense:[16]

- The United States dropped 635,000 tons of bombs, including 32,557 tons of napalm. This tonnage is greater than bombs dropped during the entire Pacific campaign of World War II or the Vietnam War.
- About 1.2 million soldiers from 19 countries were killed: 217,000 from South Korea, 406,000 from North Korea, 600,000 from China, 36,000 from the United States, and 5,000 from the other UN nations.
- More than 3 million Korean civilians (about 10 percent of the population) were killed.
- The war displaced 2 million children under the age of eighteen.
- About 2 million Koreans are either part of a separated family or know someone who is.

The impact of the war, especially the human cost that people paid for personally and collectively, cannot be calculated. However, these statistics show the extent of how destructive the Korean War was to everyone. Thus, after almost three years of fighting, an armistice agreement was signed by the United Nations, North Korea, and China, excluding South Korea, on July 27, 1953. The DMZ was created as a temporary buffer zone for a ceasefire, slightly redrawing the 38th parallel north, the original division line of 1945.

An interesting fact is that the agreement was for an armistice, not for peace. It also did not include South Korea, the subject of the war. South Korean president Rhee yielded operational control of the Republic of Korea's armed forces to General Douglas

---

[16] Yuh, "Beyond Numbers." The National Archives of Korea report similar statistics.

MacArthur, the initial UN forces commander. The Korean military conducted the war under UN command. Rhee, a strong anticommunist, also refused to sign the armistice agreement for the war that failed to expel communists from the Korean peninsula.[17] The armistice, designed as a temporary military truce pending a final peace deal, led to peace discussions in Geneva in 1954, but they concluded without a formal peace treaty. As a result, the Korean peninsula technically remains in a state of war, divided by a heavily fortified provisional border.

After the war, President Rhee sought a defense treaty with the United States, and the officially signed Mutual Defense Treaty between the United States and the Republic of Korea right after the war in 1953 legitimized the continued presence of US military forces in South Korea. This arrangement transformed Korea into a crucial militarization center in the Asia Pacific for the United States. Consequently, not only is the Korean DMZ a symbol of ongoing conflict, but all of Korea has evolved into one of the world's most militarized regions. The persistent state of war, symbolized by the DMZ, has justified both South Korea and the United States in increasing their military capabilities within Korea. Regarding this, Christine Hong, a Korean American scholar, assesses, "The structure that holds the 'peace' is thus itself agonistic—profoundly militarized and perilous. Militaries armed with nuclear weapons enforce the cease-fire along the most heavily mined strip of land in the world, ironically referred to as the 'demilitarized zone.'"[18]

Hong further argues that the Korean War was critical for the United States to become an imperial state with global hegemony.[19]

---

[17] Jooseop Keum, "Korean War: The Origin of the Axis of Evil in the Korean Peninsula," in *Peace and Reconciliation: In Search of Shared Identity*, ed. Sebastian Kim, Pauline Kollontai, and Greg Hoyland (Ashgate, 2008), 111.

[18] Hong, "The Unending Korean War," 597.

[19] Hong, "The Unending Korean War," 601.

It has given rise to a robust institutional framework that consistently generates crises that justified building the national security state, the military-industrial complex, and a perpetual war economy. The Korean War specifically served as a pretext for the United States to establish and maintain a substantial military footprint in South Korea and other parts of Asia, significantly influencing regional politics and security dynamics. Echoing Hong, Nadia Kim insists that the United States' division of the Korean peninsula, involvement in the war, and maintaining a substantial military presence should be seen as a part of a broader pattern of US imperialism where American military and political power was projected to assert influence and control over other regions.[20] It is not a benevolent act, as many Koreans would think.

Since the nineteenth century, the United States, a new global rising power, competed for global supremacy with the established European imperial powers, such as the British and Spanish Empires. From the late nineteenth to the early twentieth century, US capitalism and industrial expansion led to resource- and labor-focused colonialism and imperialism in Asia and the Pacific. Starting with involvement in China during the Opium Wars, the United States acquired regions like Hawaii, Cuba, Guam, Puerto Rico, and the Philippines after the Spanish-American War and engaged in the US-Philippines War. American influence expanded across the Pacific Islands until the mid-twentieth century.[21] In this context, the United States used South Korea as a platform to spread capitalism and counter communist influences from the Soviet Union and, later, China. Korea has been and continues to

---

[20] Nadia Kim, "What Americans Need to Know about the Korean War," *Scholars Strategy Network*, April 1, 2019.

[21] Kieu Linh Caroline Valverde and Wei Ming Dariotis, "Introduction," in *Fight the Tower: Asian American Women Scholars' Resistance and Renewal in the Academy*, ed. Kieu Linh Caroline Valverde and Wei Ming Dariotis (Rutgers University Press, 2019), 41.

be a crucial strategic point for the United States to promote its interests in Asia Pacific. Despite the nature of the Korean War, deeply entangled with the US imperial project, historian Bruce Cumings assesses that, due to a failure to grasp the nuanced factors driving the conflict connected to racist and colonial worldviews, many Americans oversimplified the situation, perceiving it merely as a noble US reaction to supposed Soviet imperial ambitions in Northeast Asia.[22] To most Americans, the Korean War, a proxy Cold War they did not win or defeat, has been forgotten. However, many scholars like Cumings and others, who study the Korean War and US militarism in global contexts from decolonial perspectives and pay attention to the grassroots experiences of the people, argue that such a view comes from US-centric worldviews, lack of knowledge of other cultures, and the racial and colonial worldviews embedded in most Americans' minds.[23]

Cynthia Enloe argues that common perceptions of ordinary US citizens regarding US militarism are grounded in several beliefs: (1) the existence of US military bases holds material value for the communities near these installations; (2) the presence of US military bases occurs at the invitation of the local governing authorities; (3) the mission of US military bases is benevolent, representing the most civilized form of militarism; and (4) the pervasive militarized concepts of "threat," "enemy," and "security" naturally call for a militarized response, aligning with the long-standing "peace and security" motif ingrained in the US logic of domination.[24]

---

[22] Bruce Cumings, *The Korean War: A History* (Modern Library, 2010), 77–100.

[23] Please see Christine Hong's, Nadia Kim's, Heonik Kwon's, and Bruce Cumings's works that deconstruct the Western notion of the Korean War as a forgotten war from decolonial and postcolonial perspectives.

[24] Cynthia Enloe, "Foreword," in *The Bases of Empire: The Global Struggle against U.S. Military Posts*, ed. Catherine Lutz (New York University Press, 2009), ix–xii.

The KDMZ as a Military and Colonial Border

Unfortunately, similar perceptions are also prevalent among South Koreans, rooted in Korea's indebtedness toward the United States as a liberator.[25] According to Christine Hong, the unending Korean War situation, officially backed by the armistice agreement and the defense treaty, set the tone for the ongoing unequal relationships between the United States and Korea. It created among many South Koreans attitudes of indebtedness toward the United States, a benevolent savior, generous friend, and blood ally: Americans liberated Koreans from brutal Japanese colonization, protected them from communists during the war with unfathomable sacrifices, helped to build a democratic country, and continue to provide security through its military presence and other supports. Hong observes that the concept of "liberation" that South Koreans have regarding the United States is linked to lasting obligation or a "debt of honor," by which she means "an apparently dischargeable debit on a geopolitical balance sheet that stems not only from the 1945 US Pacific War defeat of Japan but also US 'sacrifice' in the Korean War."[26]

The perception of indebtedness toward the United States—particularly prevalent among older generations, people with anticommunist perspectives, and conservative Christians[27]—fostered a belief that any criticism of the United States equates to supporting communism. Under the severe National Security Law

---

[25] Hong, "The Unending Korean War," 601. Also see Joo Ok Kim, "Untelling the Tales of Empire," 2–6.

[26] Hong, "The Unending Korean War," 601.

[27] Namhee Lee notes that "the "red hunt" in the South was carried out with added ferocity when Christians fleeing from the North joined in. Christians in North Korea had suffered severe persecution in the early stages of the North Korean regime, giving rise to Christians' vehement anticommunism. Namhee Lee, "The Korean War, Anticommunism, and the Korean American Community," *Presbyterian Mission*, April 30, 2018.

and the Anticommunist Law of South Korea, anyone who spoke out against economic disparities in a capitalist system, the limited political freedoms in the country, South Korea's imbalanced relationship with the United States, or even those advocating for the reunification of Korea were labeled as communists.[28] This belief underscores the perceived duty to ensure that the Korean government maintains and strengthens its close ties with the United States by aligning with American values in Korean society. This alignment is often interpreted as both the maintenance of anticommunist policies and the exclusion of groups seen as societal disruptors, such as the LGBTQ+ community, Muslim immigrants, feminists, labor union members, and others with leftist viewpoints.[29] It is widespread to see conservative protesters in the streets of Seoul who carry their signboards in one hand and the national flag of the United States in the other. As stated above, the DMZ is not only in the middle of the country but also exists among citizens of the same country. The notion of liberation, which could ideally signal the beginning of a process of decolonization, is, unfortunately, reduced to a colonial and colonized mindset and practice.

The impact of the war that Koreans felt from such an unimaginable loss of lives and livelihoods is unmeasurable, and it has been continuing for generations with suffering, separation, grief, fear, trauma, tension, ongoing divisions, and more. Unlike the Korean War as a forgotten war by most Americans and Westerners, to Koreans, it is an unforgettable war that is still ongoing on psychological, societal, political, and cultural levels. As both Koreas, the UN Forces, and US militaries heavily guard the DMZ, people live with unforgettable memories and open wounds of war; ideological

---

[28] Lee, "The Korean War, Anticommunism, and the Korean American Community."

[29] Nami Kim, *The Gendered Politics of the Korean Protestant Right: Hegemonic Masculinity* (Palgrave Macmillan, 2016), ix–xvii.

debates and conflicts over relationships with North Korea are still dividing Koreans in the South. Their various stories told, untold, or silenced are still shaping their relationships, ideological and political perspectives, and worldviews. Moreover, the differences between the war generations, which prioritize anticommunism and militarization for self-defense, and subsequent generations, which pursue democratization and reunification, are becoming much more comprehensive than probably the uncrossable DMZ.[30]

The KDMZ as a Political, Ideological, and Kinship Border

The Korean War has a lasting legacy that continues to shape inter-Korean, South Korean, and geopolitical dynamics. The war's impact extends to the families separated by the conflict and opposite ideologies, the political relationships in the region, and the ongoing discussions around reunification and peace on the Korean peninsula, including families that have not lost anyone to the war. In the summer of 2023, I visited my elderly parents in Korea. My father is a Korean and Vietnam War veteran and a retired Korean Marine Corps officer. In his retirement, he is actively involved in several veterans' organizations, such as the Korean War Veterans Association, providing active leadership. He firmly believes in the necessity of the US military presence in Korea for national security, anticommunist law enforcement, and a powerful government for social order. In other words, he is one of those staunch conservative Christian older people. My father and I, a postcolonial feminist theologian who advocates for democracy, freedom, human rights, and reunification, hardly share common ideological and political perspectives, especially on Korean politics. At home,

---

[30] Sook Jong Lee, "Generational Divides and the Future of South Korean Democracy," in *Demographics and Future of South* Korea, ed. Chung Min Lee and Kathryn Botto (Carnegie Endowment for International Peace, June 29, 2021).

we have been practicing the "Don't Ask, Don't Tell" approach on Korean political issues. However, an incident led us to cross the long-respected boundaries in 2023.

A close friend, who knows about my love for arts and co-curatorial experience on Asian/American arts to do public theology work, gifted me with two large art exhibit posters that she had gotten from the curator. The 2021 exhibit, titled *Promise*, showed North Korean and South Korean artists' paintings and photographs featuring the beautiful nature of the Korean peninsula. It was grant-funded by the South Korean government's Ministry of Culture, Sports and Tourism, and sponsored by the National Inter-Korean Exchange and Cooperation Local Government Council and the Foundation of Inter-Korean Cooperation, two progressive previous government-created organizations to promote reunification. Later, I learned that both the organizations and their leaders have long been accused of being pro-communists and followers of North Korea by conservatives, particularly Christian anticommunists like my father. Without that knowledge, due to the size of the posters in a long tube that did not fit in my suitcases, I asked my father to ship it to my home in Denver, Colorado.

Two nights before my return trip to the United States, my father opened the poster tube while I was asleep to make a postal and customs label. The first thing he noticed was the background of the post, a painting of Heaven Lake, a volcanic crater lake atop Baekdu Mountain, the tallest mountain in North Korea, which often shows up in North Korean leaders' political propaganda about their chosen bloodline. Then, he saw the two "pro-communist" organizations' names as sponsors. After that, his mind was running rapidly to write multiple versions of fiction about how and why his beloved daughter had become a follower of North Korea, thus completely betraying him and his anticommunist country.

Early the following day, I woke up to a heated debate between my parents about who and what I had become: their daughter, raised by patriotic military parents on military bases with the proper ideological education, is now a North Korea–praising communist, and thus they failed both as parents and citizens of South Korea. Then he started scrutinizing me, their almost sixty-year-old theologian daughter, about her dangerous ideologies and worldviews. I respectfully challenged him and this thinking with my wealth of knowledge. However, I could not make any difference in his anticommunist and dualistic worldview formed in the context of the Japanese colonization and the US intervention to "save" Korea, fighting as a soldier in the Korean War, and the anticommunist education and formation he received throughout his adult life. We ended the conversation with his declaration that I, a non-Korean citizen, should not be involved in matters of his country, constantly threatened by uneducated younger progressive generations. I realized once again that we have an uncrossable DMZ in our family. Although my entire extended family on both sides is from the southern part of the peninsula and did not lose anyone to the Korean War, there is an invisible but almost unbreakable wall existing between the older and younger generations, progressives and conservatives, and anticommunists and decolonialists.

I share this family story to highlight what I have argued throughout the chapter: the DMZ is not just a physical marker that divides the two Koreas in the heavily militarized zone. It is also a political, ideological, moral, kinship, and theological border. The Korean War caused devastating loss of life, with millions of Korean civilians and soldiers, as well as numerous foreign troops, killed or wounded. The division left deep psychological and cultural scars on the Korean people. The trauma of war, division, and the ongoing military tensions have shaped the collective consciousness of North Koreans and South Koreans. Despite this ongoing and, at times, escalating tension between the two Koreas and within the same side of the border, the Korean War is often labeled as "the Forgotten War" by dominant historical narrators and by most Americans and Westerners. Instead, I, along with other decolonial scholars and activists, argue that it should be remembered as an unforgettable chapter in modern history, particularly when examined through the lens of US imperialism and militarization.

A Feminist Praxis of Decolonial and Demilitarized Peace-Building

As a part of the US imperial project, the war played a significant role in shaping postwar international relations, influencing US foreign policy in Asia, the dynamics of the United Nations, and the strategies of major powers like China and Russia in the region. The war and its aftermath contributed to the nuclear proliferation issue on the Korean peninsula, with North Korea developing nuclear capabilities partly in response to the military threat it perceives from the United States and its allies. Thus, the DMZ must be seen as a continuation of the colonial legacies in Asia, where external powers played a decisive role in controlling the destinies of nations. This aspect underscores the intersection of imperialism, colonialism, and militarization in shaping the region's history. Envisioning justice at the physical and symbolic DMZ means that a multifaceted approach is required to address the historical, political, and social complexities of the ongoing war in Korea and the region. For this, I argue the following:

First, it is critical to redefine regional power dynamics by moving away from the United States' hegemonic approach in Asia. Achieving peace requires a shift from a strategy centered on maintaining US dominance to one that promotes transnational cooperation and mutual respect. This includes reevaluating military exercises and alliances that exacerbate tensions. On

October 22, 2023, the United States, Japan, and South Korea conducted their first joint air exercise. This military drill followed a meeting at Camp David in August, where US president Joe Biden, Japanese prime minister Fumio Kishida, and South Korean president Yoon Suk Yeol initiated a new phase of trilateral cooperation. While North Korea is often cited as a regional threat justifying increased military presence, the strategic alliance of the United States, Japan, and South Korea primarily, in fact, serves to counter China's influence. The escalation of military presence in Northeast Asia to serve the United States' intense competition with China risks creating hostile regional divisions and potentially disrupting long-standing economic collaborations. This situation draws neighboring, so-called saved nations like South Korea and Japan into disputes through interconnected alliances. Deescalating tensions necessitates a shift from strategies focused on preserving US supremacy.

Vijay Prashad insists that leaders for this change should come from those in grassroots movements who are already actively resisting, including people in Jeju Island, opposing a US naval base since 2007; Okinawans challenging their role as a strategic US location; and the citizens of Taiwan, who face significant risks in the event of regional warfare. Transnational solidarity and cooperation are necessary to tear down the wall. Fostering a transnational sense of solidarity includes recognizing the interconnected nature of regional struggles and working toward a collective effort in decolonization, de-imperialization, and ending the residual Cold War mentality.[31]

Second, given the "hidden" history behind the Cold War and the Korean War, it is crucial to recognize and address the historical impacts of colonialism and imperialism in Korea and

---

[31] Vijay Prashad, "War Looks Just as War Looks: Dismal and Ugly," *The Forty-Fourth Newsletter (2023) of TriContinental*, November 2, 2023.

the broader region. This involves understanding the psychological and societal scars left by these histories and fostering a collective effort toward healing and reconciliation. For this, it is critical to question and dismantle militarized narratives and practices. This includes critically examining the military's role in society and its impact on regional dynamics. Especially in South Korea, where a military dictatorship with anticommunist views and policies was in power for decades, thus creating military cultures in all corners of the society, undoing military worldviews and practices is essential. Even though democracy by the people's movement has been present since 1987, the legacy of militarism is still deeply embedded in governments, policies, and many citizens' minds. Especially when conservatives seize power, military practices are often reenacted, particularly in their approach to North Korea, often nullifying reconciliation talks and treaties made by previous progressive governments with North Korea. They are often framed in US-centric, nationalistic, and consumerist approaches. Renarrating Korea's modern history through the lens of decolonization and de-imperialization is urgent and essential.

One of the concrete actions toward tearing down the wall is establishing a peace agreement to replace the armistice. Because the Korean peninsula is technically still at war, both Koreas spend astronomical amounts of money for further militarization. In 1991, South Korea's defense budget totaled 7,452 billion KRW. By 2011, this figure had escalated to 31,403 billion KRW, marking a fourfold increase over two decades. By 2019, defense expenditures had risen to 46,697 billion KRW, equivalent to approximately US$42.5 billion. This substantial growth in defense spending was primarily attributed to mitigating threats from North Korea, especially following its declaration as a nuclear-armed state in 2017. In 2019, North Korea's total gross domestic product (GDP) was recorded at $33.504 billion, notably lower than South Korea's defense budget for the same year. Despite the disparity in economic scales, South

Korea has persistently augmented its military capabilities and spending, ascending to the world's sixth-largest military power, and achieving the tenth position globally regarding defense spending.[32] These figures show the need to formally end the Korean War by replacing the armistice agreement with a peace treaty. This symbolic and practical step can pave the way for more stable and peaceful relations on the peninsula.

The conditions for peace in Korea are not limited to national politics but extend across borders. Incorporating transborder aesthetic practices, feminist critiques, and interdisciplinary approaches can provide a more holistic and effective path toward peace. Feminist scholars and activists, such as Women Cross DMZ (WCDMZ),[33] have been building a solidary movement among women in South Korea and North Korea, and others in global contexts, to end the Korean War and to build peace in the Korean peninsula through relationship-building and collective support.[34] Recognizing peace as an active, dynamic process rather than just the absence of conflict or suppression of violence through heavily militarized confrontation, like in the KDMZ, the feminist approach pursues demilitarized peace. According to Suzy Kim, truly demilitarized peace is realized not merely through the cessation of hostilities but through active engagement in face-to-face interactions and the building of personal relationships. This approach is inherently feminist, as it values interdependence and mutual support, traits often undervalued or seen as weaknesses in a patriarchal society that

---

[32] Youkyoung Ko, "End the Korean War and Stop the US-China Arms Race," *Foreign Policy in Focus*, July 14, 2022.

[33] WCDMZ is an organization formed in 2014 to mobilize women globally for peace in Korea through education, advocacy, and organizing. They undertook a historic crossing of the DMZ in 2015: https://www.womencrossdmz.org/about-us/.

[34] Suzy Kim, "Women as 'Dupes,' 'Stooges,' and 'Armies of Beauties,'" *Periscope: Social Text Online*, December 21, 2018.

typically glorifies individualism and competition. By emphasizing the importance of personal connections and collective support, the feminist perspective reframes peace-building as a process grounded in shared experiences, empathy, and the fostering of communal bonds.

Scholars like Crystal Mun-hye Baik and Jane Jin Kaisen further expand on this by critiquing the concept of militarized peace, which is often underpinned by hypermasculine notions of power and control.[35] In this context, peace is maintained through military strength and dominance, an approach that inherently marginalizes and renders vulnerable those bodies and spaces deemed less powerful or significant, often feminized entities. They point out the irony of a peace that is maintained through the threat or presence of militaristic force, which often perpetuates a cycle of fear and aggression. In proposing a solution, Baik and Kaisen advocate for demilitarized peace, which moves beyond national borders and politics. This peace is built on feminist principles, emphasizing aesthetic practices and activist critiques that challenge and transcend traditional nationalistic and militaristic frameworks. They argue that genuine peace in regions like Korea cannot coexist with a dominant military presence, especially one that is foreign and operates on principles contrary to those of feminist peace. The feminist approach to peace thus calls for a radical rethinking of how peace is understood and achieved. It suggests moving away from a model that relies on power dynamics and militaristic strength, advocating for peace built on empathy, mutual respect, and transnational solidarity. This perspective emphasizes the importance of grassroots movements, personal relationships, and the empowerment of marginalized voices, all crucial elements in fostering a peace that is equitable, sustainable, and genuinely reflective of the needs and desires of all communities involved.

---

[35] Crystal Mun-Hye Baik and Jane Jin Kaisen, "Introduction: Korea and Demilitarized Peace," *Periscope: Social Text Online*, December 21, 2018.

A feminist approach to peace is also helpful in bringing healing to the Korean people who are living with wounds and trauma. The war and division have had profound effects on Korean society, disrupting kinship and family structures and relationships, shaping national identities, and influencing domestic and foreign policies. Many people are enduring trauma and cultural shifts resulting from the conflict and division. If we continue to understand the Korean War and division from traditional perspectives focused on militarization, healing is not possible. Healing calls for a reimagining of peace and reconciliation that is centered on the experiences and aspirations of the Korean people rather than the strategic interests of external powers.[36] Narratives of the personal and communal impact of the war, the voices and perspectives of those most affected by the conflict and division, including the deep emotional and social scars that persist across generations of Koreans, should be at the center.

Achieving peace in Korea requires a concerted effort that involves redefining power dynamics, healing historical wounds, demilitarizing society and borders, fostering transnational solidarity, challenging militarized narratives, formalizing peace agreements, embracing feminist praxis, addressing nationalism and consumerism, and adopting transborder and interdisciplinary perspectives. This comprehensive approach can help address the deep-rooted causes of conflict and pave the way for a more peaceful and cooperative future in the region.

For this, any peace-building work in Korea should also be theological. As briefly mentioned earlier, Korean Protestant Christians, especially those who fled from North Korea after being persecuted for their faith, significantly contributed to building an anticommunist society with militarized peace in South Korea. As a result, a substantial portion of the Christian community in South Korea has tended to align with nationalistic, militaristic, and

---

[36] Kwon, *After the Korean War*, 135.

consumerist values, often positioning themselves in opposition to North Korea. In other words, fighting against North Korea, rather than predominantly advocating for peace and reconciliation, has become a critical marker of having a deep faith in God.[37] Korean American feminist theologian Anne Joh argues that it is because dominant Christian theologies have often been intertwined with the logic of universal sovereignty and the civilizing mission, thereby contributing to the justification of colonial practices, which, according to her, include border-building.[38] Following Mbembe's point that "sovereignty means the capacity to define who matters and who does not, who is *disposable* and who is not,"[39] tearing down the wall becomes a theological anthropology question. In other words, demilitarized and decolonial peace work requires a theological shift.

Decolonial, de-imperial, and demilitarized peace-building requires a comprehensive and nuanced approach that acknowledges the complex interplay of colonial legacies, Cold War politics, regional dynamics, and the lived experiences of the Korean people. It challenges conventional narratives and seeks to center the voices and perspectives of those most affected by the conflict and division. It is a transnational solidary work. Only then will the military, political, ideological, moral, kinship, and theological border the DMZ has built be replaced with true decolonial and demilitarized peace.

---

[37] Tim Huber, "The Church's Role in South Korea's Militarization," *Anabaptist World*, June 28, 2023.

[38] Wonhee Anne Joh, "Walls/Borders: Visible Signs of Militarized Colonial Desires Past and Present," *Political Theology Network Blog*, June 24, 2019.

[39] Achille Mbembe, "Necropolitics," *Public Culture* 15, no. 1 (2003): 27.

6

Israel's Apartheid Wall

Mitri Raheb

Israel's apartheid wall is one of many manifestations of the Israeli settler colonial project in Palestine. The State of Israel is Europe's latest and last settler colonial project. Until the end of World War I, Palestine was part of the Ottoman Empire, a vast land mass that stretched from the Russian borders in the north to Yemen in the south, from the Mediterranean in the west to Iran in the east, without any internal borders or walls. In the mid-nineteenth century, as the Ottoman Empire weakened, key European powers saw an opportunity to divide regions of the empire among themselves.

The British had their eyes on Palestine with the aim of colonizing it and controlling key trade routes. However, the colonization of Palestine was to be implemented with Jewish labor and Jewish finance. Jews were seen as aliens in Christian Europe because of their religion, language, and social environments. To prevent impoverished Russian Jewish immigrants from flooding the United Kingdom, the British sought to channel these immigrants to Palestine and asked affluent British Jews to fund this project. The declaration signed on November 2, 1917, by Lord Arthur James Balfour, the British foreign secretary, to the Jewish banker Baron Walter Rothschild, paved the political way for the colonization of Palestine. This process of colonization has been implemented gradually over the past hundred years and continues to the present day.

The British mandate over Palestine paved the way for Jewish control of key cities and regions in Palestine and enabled Jewish military groups to occupy 77 percent of historical Palestine in 1948. Thus, the region was not only divided into nation-states (Jordan, Lebanon, Syria) with their own borders, but Palestine itself was divided into three parts: the State of Israel under Jewish control, the West Bank under Jordanian control, and the Gaza Strip under Egyptian control. Barbed-wire borders were erected within Palestine and military zones established between the different areas. Jerusalem itself was divided between a Jewish and an Arab section with the Mandelbaum Gate as the only passage point between the two.

In 1967, Israel occupied the West Bank and the Gaza Strip, among other areas. Thus, Palestine was geographically unified under Jewish control. Although Israel was able to conquer the land with ease, on this occasion it could not rid itself of the Palestinian occupants. Israel, therefore, decided to put the newly occupied areas and their population under the jurisdiction of the Israeli military. The existence of the indigenous population presents a major challenge to any settler colonial project intent on controlling both the geographical and demographic landscape.

On September 13, 1993, Palestine Liberation Organization (PLO) chairman Yasser Arafat and Israeli prime minister Yitzhak Rabin signed the Oslo Accords on the lawn of the White House. Prior to signing, the PLO recognized the State of Israel in exchange for Israel recognizing the PLO as the "representative of the Palestinian people." The Oslo Accords gave the PLO the right to interim Palestinian self-rule in limited areas of the West Bank and the Gaza Strip, pending a permanent settlement within five years. While densely populated areas were put under Palestinian self-rule, the less populated, water-rich agricultural areas were retained under full Israeli control. Thus, Israel rid itself of the population but controlled the geography within the structure of the Jewish settler colonial project.

On Settler Colonialism

The prevailing status in all of Palestine since the Balfour Declaration is one of settler colonialism. The main feature that distinguishes settler colonialism from classical or neocolonialism is the fact that settler colonialists come to settle permanently in an already occupied land, exercise state sovereignty and juridical control over the indigenous land, while ultimately aiming to eliminate the indigenous people.[1] The goal is to occupy, slowly but surely, the geography while removing the local demography. To this end, settler colonialism has developed a variety of mechanisms, ideological constructs, and social narratives. The indigenous land is described as *terra nullius*, empty or barren land waiting to be discovered that becomes the private property of the settlers. The native people are depicted with racist constructs as savages, violent human animals, or terrorists, while the settlers are portrayed as the civilized and brave pioneers. To defend the settled property from the savages, a police state is created and granted extraordinary power over the native people, including power over their civil affairs. Walls are one of the many means that a settler colonial power uses to grab more land—geography—while confining the indigenous people behind high walls under the pretext of "security."

The Apartheid Wall

Israel constructed walls in Palestine in the context of a highly celebrated peace process. Less than a year after signing the Oslo Accords, Israel started fencing in the Gaza Strip, and in 1996,

---

[1] Raheb Mitri, *Decolonizing Palestine: The Land, The People, The Bible* (Orbis, 2023), 2–5.

military checkpoints were erected in the West Bank as the only points of entry into Israel. A year later, these checkpoints were put under the jurisdiction of Israeli border police, and a system of permits was introduced to control Palestinians' access to Jerusalem and Israel. These permits were mainly given to Palestinian workers to fulfill the Israeli economy's need for laborers. In 2000, Ehud Barak approved a plan to establish a "barrier to prevent the passage of motor vehicles" into Israel.[2] Since then, I joined 5.5 million Palestinians residing in the West Bank and Gaza who are prevented from driving our cars in Jerusalem or Israel. Israel subsequently took additional measures designed to separate the West Bank from the Gaza Strip, thereby splitting the Palestinian population into two separate entities and cutting them off from each other.

The Apartheid Wall in the West Bank

The collapse of peace negotiations at Camp David and Sharon's provocative storming of al-Aqsa Mosque in September 2000 triggered the second Palestinian intifada (uprising). Following a series of Palestinian operations inside Israel, the Israeli military invaded several West Bank cities in 2002, and the Israeli cabinet announced its decision to "begin the immediate construction of a fence."[3] The Israeli military embarked on a process of confiscating Palestinian land, uprooting trees, and leveling the earth to enable the construction of the "fence."

The term "fence" is misleading, and Israeli human rights organizations use the term "separation barrier." The International Court of Justice in The Hague used the word "wall," and Palestinian organizations now refer to the "apartheid wall." In the past four years, several of the most credible human rights organizations, including Israeli human rights organization B'tselem, have

---

[2] Yehezkel Lein, *The Separation Barrier, Position Paper September 2002* (2002), 3.

[3] Lein, *Separation Barrier*, 3.

declared that the threshold has been crossed and apartheid is now a reality on both sides of the Green Line, the 1949 armistice line that separates Israel from the West Bank.[4] Human Rights Watch[5] and Amnesty International[6] have also identified the situation in historical Palestine as apartheid. The definition of "apartheid" was set out in the Geneva Conventions, the International Convention on the Suppression and Punishment of the Crime of Apartheid, and the Rome Statute of the International Criminal Court. Three decisive elements define the crime of apartheid: the implementation of a system of segregation based on race, religion, or ethnicity designed with the intent to maintain domination by one group over another; the use of diverse legislative measures to enforce and legalize segregation; and inhuman practices and violations to impose and enforce such segregation. These three components are found in the definition of settler colonialism; apartheid and settler colonialism are two sides of the same coin.

The apartheid wall is 712 kilometers (442 miles) in length, twice the length of the Green Line (320 kilometers, 200 miles). Although only 20 percent of the wall comprises 8-meter (26-foot) concrete blocks, twice the height of the Berlin Wall, the entire edifice is built as a military facility that "includes a system of fences ('preventive,' 'warning,' and 'delaying'), an anti vehicle component, patrol roads, a trace path on each side to disclose the footprints of infiltrators, plus warning and surveillance systems. The total width of the barrier, including all these components, ranges between 35 and 100 meters."[7]

---

[4] "Apartheid," *B'Tselem: The Israeli Information Center for Human Rights in the Occupied Territories.*

[5] Omar Shakir, "Israeli Apartheid: 'A Threshold Crossed,'" *Zentith*, July 19, 2021; republished at the Human Rights Watch website.

[6] Rania Muhareb et al., *Israeli Apartheid: Tool of Zionist Settler Colonialism* (Al-Haq, 2002).

[7] Eyal Hareuveni, "Arrested Development: The Long-Term Impact of Israel's Separation Barrier in the West Bank," B'Tselem: The Israeli Information Center for Human Rights in the Occupied Territories, 2012, 13–14.

Palestinians might have accepted a wall built along the Green Line as an internationally recognized border between the State of Israel and the State of Palestine as part of the so-called two-state solution in which Israel has the right to defend its borders. However, 85 percent of the wall is built not along the Green Line but deep inside the West Bank, de facto annexing 10 percent of West Bank land. This is also where half of the Israeli settlements in the West Bank (82 out of 159) and over 85 percent of the settler population are located.[8] The 11,000 Palestinians who reside west of the apartheid wall are confined within small enclaves cut off from the rest of the West Bank and controlled by restrictions on movement, building permits, and the cultivation of farmland. The goal of the Israeli state is to make the life of these Palestinians so intolerable that they ultimately abandon their land and relocate "voluntarily" east of the wall. The apartheid wall separates 1,590 Palestinian communities residing in the east from their farmland to the west of the wall, forcing residents to seek special permits or "prior coordination" to access their own land. Access is channeled through seventy-four gates, of which fifty-two open only during the olive harvest.[9]

The Wall Around Gaza

The situation in the Gaza Strip is much worse. Since 1994, it has been surrounded by a barrier that cuts the Palestinian residents off from the rest of the world within a 365-square-kilometer (140-square-mile) open-air prison, the largest in the world. After dismantling the Jewish settlements in the Gaza Strip in August 2005, Israel withdrew from Gaza but did not give up its control over the territory and destroyed the Gaza airport before leaving.

---

[8] Hareuveni, "Arrested Development," 13.
[9] United Nations Office for Coordination of Humanitarian Affairs (OCHA), "The Humanitarian Impact of the Barrier," July 9, 2013.

Israel continues to control the waters along Gaza's shore and does not allow the operation of a port, or fishing in the open seas beyond six nautical miles. The fence around the strip is 60 kilometers (37 miles) long on the Israeli side and 12.6 kilometers on the border with Egypt. In 2008–2009 a buffer zone of 300 to 600 meters was created inside the Gaza Strip alongside the barrier, with the result that 25 percent of Gaza's fertile land was no longer accessible to Palestinians. In 2019, Israel added a 6-meter (20-foot)-high galvanized steel fence to its military installation around Gaza.[10] There are two crossings into Gaza from Israel: one for people and a second for goods, in addition to a third crossing into Egypt. Israel controls all goods transported in and out of Gaza and has the last word even on the Rafah border with Egypt. An extensive list of raw materials is forbidden entry into Gaza, and 75 percent of Gaza's factories have been forced to shut down as a result.

The Ruling of the International Court of Justice

On December 3, 2003, the UN General Assembly requested an advisory opinion from the International Court of Justice on the "legal consequences arising from the construction of the wall being built by Israel, the occupying Power, in the Occupied Palestinian Territory."[11] Israel refused to cooperate with the proceedings and questioned the court's jurisdiction in this case. In a majority decision, the court denied Israel's argument and established that certain human rights instruments were applicable in the Occupied Territories where large stretches of the wall were being built.

The first issue discussed was the effect of the wall on the right of the Palestinian people to self-determination. The court expressed its fear that the barrier's route would create a fait

---

[10] "The Gaza Strip: One Big Prison," B'Tselem: The Israeli Information Center for Human Rights in the Occupied Territories, 2007.

[11] International Court of Justice, "Legal Consequences of the Construction of a Wall in the Occupied Palestinian Territory," The Hague, 2003.

accompli that would lead to the de facto annexation of territory west of the wall, and which would severely violate the right to Palestinian self-determination. The second issue was the legality of the wall in international humanitarian law. The court stated that the separation barrier is intended to alter the demographic composition of the annexed area, thereby replacing the local Palestinian population with Jewish settlers in violation of Article 49 of the Fourth Geneva Convention. In addition, the opinion stated that the confiscation of private land to build the wall was deleterious to the owners of private property and violated Articles 46 and 52 of The Hague Regulations of 1907, and Article 53 of the Fourth Geneva Convention. The third issue was the legality of the wall under international human rights law. The court ruled that the wall violates the right to freedom of movement, the right against invasion of privacy of home and family, the right to work, and the right to an adequate standard of living, health, and education. The court concluded, "Israel could not rely on a right of self-defense or on a state of necessity to preclude the wrongfulness of the construction of the wall," and that such construction is contrary to international law.[12]

In its conclusion, the court stated, "Israel must put an immediate end to the violation of its international obligations by ceasing the works of construction of the wall and dismantling those parts of that structure situated within Occupied Palestinian Territory and repealing or rendering ineffective all legislative and regulatory acts adopted with a view to construction of the wall and establishment of its associated regime." The court further made it clear that Israel must make reparation for all damage suffered by all natural or legal persons affected by the wall's construction.[13] The court reminded the other states of their obligation to refrain from assisting in maintaining the unlawful situation that has arisen following construction of the wall, and to take legal measures

---

[12] International Court of Justice, "Legal Consequences."
[13] International Court of Justice, "Legal Consequences."

to ensure enforcement of the Fourth Geneva Convention. To date, Israel and its Western allies have ignored this ruling of the International Court of Justice.

The Wall: A Matter of Life or Death

The human toll of the apartheid wall on Palestinians is severe; the wall not only separates Bethlehem from Jerusalem but prevents patients from reaching hospitals, children from attending schools, farmers from reaching their land, and Christians and Muslims from visiting their holy sites in Jerusalem. Here is just one example from our own family. Very early on January 4, 2004, my father-in-law experienced severe stomach pains. We called an ambulance to take him to the nearest hospital in Bethlehem. There we were told that there was no specialist to examine him, and he needed to be moved to one of the Christian hospitals in Jerusalem. My brother-in-law called the Red Crescent and was told that ambulances are not allowed to cross the checkpoint on the wall separating Bethlehem from Jerusalem until around 8 a.m.

When the ambulance arrived, the driver asked if the patient had a permit from the Israeli military authorities to enter Jerusalem. My brother-in-law replied that his father held a permit to enter from 5 a.m. until 7 p.m. but his mother did not. The driver said it would depend on the mood of the Israeli soldiers at the checkpoint whether the ambulance would be allowed to pass or not. My father-in-law was put into the ambulance, and my mother-in-law joined him. My wife and her siblings kissed their father goodbye, and the ambulance drove toward the main checkpoint at the northern entrance to the city.

The route from the hospital to the checkpoint is less than half a mile, and the ambulance arrived at the checkpoint in less than five minutes. No other cars were there, so the driver was optimistic that they would pass through quickly. However, the ambulance had to wait for the soldier to indicate that the driver should bring the vehicle forward for inspection. Fifteen minutes elapsed while they waited for a sign from the soldier, and finally the soldier signaled the ambulance to approach. The soldier asked the driver where he was going. "To the hospital in Jerusalem. I have a patient who is in great pain and needs to get there," the driver replied.

"Does the patient have a permit?" the soldier asked. "Yes, he has! Here it is." The soldier took the permit, a sheet of red paper about six by eight inches in size. At the top of the permit, issued by the Israeli military administration, was the title "Entry Permit to Israel," although under international law East Jerusalem is part of the occupied Palestinian territories and not part of Israel. The permit showed my father-in-law's name and his ID number. The permit was valid for three months and the reason stated was business. My father-in-law was a businessman operating a restaurant not far from the wall.

The Israeli soldier told the driver, "This permit is not valid." The driver asked my father-in-law, "I thought you told me that you have a valid permit for Jerusalem?"

My father-in-law answered, "It is valid. Read the date carefully. It is still good for a few more weeks. Can't you read?"

"I can read," the soldier replied. "There is no problem with the date, but it says that the purpose of entry is business. Today you are a patient and not a businessman, so the permit is not valid. You are not allowed to enter."

My mother-in-law was becoming more and more worried about her husband and said, "But we are American citizens. Here are our American passports. As such, we cannot be prevented from entering Jerusalem."

"Your American citizenship does not count in Israel if you are Palestinian," the soldier replied. "Go back, get a permit, and then return. Turn around quickly."

"Do you not fear God? Don't you see that this old man is in pain?" replied my mother-in-law.

It was clear by then that the soldier was in a bad mood and we had no chance of entering. The driver decided to try his luck at the other checkpoint to the west of Bethlehem, less than a mile away. At that checkpoint, the soldier asked for my father-in-law's permit, read it, and gave it back. "The patient can enter Jerusalem, but not this ambulance," the soldier said.

"But this isn't the first time that we've entered Jerusalem with this ambulance!" the driver retorted.

"No, today, the ambulance is not allowed."

As attempts to reason with the soldier were fruitless, the ambulance driver called another ambulance from Jerusalem with a yellow Israeli number plate. In half an hour, the Jerusalem ambulance arrived at the checkpoint, backed up, and stopped back-to-back with the Bethlehem ambulance with the blue number plate. The drivers carried my father-in-law from one ambulance into the other and the ambulance quickly left the checkpoint to Jerusalem. By then, it was close to 11 a.m. Two doctors were waiting at the hospital, and they performed a cardiogram and several other tests. "His situation is very serious. You are late. He had a severe heart attack a few hours ago. His heart muscles are severely damaged, and his chances of survival are very low," the doctor said. Twelve days later, on January 16, 2006, my father-in-law died in the hospital. He was seventy-four years old. His only son was not allowed to enter Jerusalem to see his father for the last time at the hospital.

Connection to Globalization

I studied in West Germany in the 1980s, when a wall still divided Berlin. All the people I knew hated walls because they are a sign of an oppressive regime that prevents people and nations from pursuing happiness and living in democracy. US president Ronald

Reagan gave a speech at the Berlin Wall on June 12, 1987, in which he called for the general secretary of the Communist Party of the Soviet Union, Mikhail Gorbachev, to "tear down this wall." That phrase became a political mantra for a hatred toward walls and what they represent. When the Berlin Wall fell in 1989, I never thought that another wall would be erected in my own country by the same powers that were eager to tear down the wall in Berlin.

The stance of the West started to change in 2003 when Israel began construction of its apartheid wall. To counter the illegality of building the wall on Palestinian land, Israel employed its *hasbara* (propaganda) machine to market the wall as an effective strategy for combating terrorism. In the context of the war on terrorism, Israel saw a golden opportunity to position itself as the expert in this field and to invest heavily in the security industry. The West that once hated walls fell in love with them after 2003. Construction of the wall along the US-Mexico border accelerated during the era of President George W. Bush, when over five hundred miles of a double-layered, reinforced barrier were completed.

> Hermes drones manufactured by Israel's Elbit Systems were the first unmanned aerial vehicles deployed at the (U.S.) southern border in 2004. A decade later, customs and border protection authorities awarded the company's subsidiary, Elbit Systems of America, a $145 million contract to construct its integrated fixed towers (IFT) system in Nogales, Arizona.[14]

However, it was President Trump who championed building the wall and encouraged his followers to chant, "Build the wall!" at his rallies. When border wall prototypes were exhibited in 2017 in San Diego, "the only foreign contractor on display was ELTA, a

---

[14] Britt Dawson, "Interview with Gabriel Schivone: U.S. Borderlands, Israel's Latest Surveillance Technology Laboratory," *Journal of Palestine Studies* 47, no. 4 (2018): 57–58.

subsidiary of Israel's Aerospace Industries."[15] In 2019, Trump stated, "A wall protects. All you have to do is ask Israel. They were having a total disaster and they had a wall. It's 99.9 percent stoppage."[16]

Israel prides itself in having over six hundred exporters of security technologies and services.[17] It markets its products as tested in combat, meaning on real people, the Palestinians. No wonder Israel has waged more than five wars on Gaza within the last fifteen years, as these conflicts enable Israel to keep testing its latest military equipment in real-world situations. Palestine has become the perfect laboratory for the Israeli military-techno industry that is exported globally and is Israel's largest export sector.[18] These exports include the training of border police and immigration and customs enforcement agents based on strategies developed by the Israeli military and employed against Palestinians. More than twenty Israeli companies are housed within the University of Arizona Tech Parks, another military industry laboratory that tests its prototypes in the Arizona desert, while manufacturing the appliances at low cost across the border in Sonora, Mexico. "Such a partnership not only enables them to turn high profits, it also keeps the United States and Mexico abreast of Israel's latest innovations in matters of security technology."[19] For these reasons, people started to refer to this cooperation as the "Palestine-Mexico border."[20]

---

[15] Dawson, "Interview with Gabriel Schivone," 58.

[16] Isabel Kershner, "Trump Cites Israel's 'Wall' as Model. The Analogy Is Iffy," *New York Times*, January 27, 2017.

[17] International Trade Administration, US Department of Commerce, "Israel: Safety and Security," October 6, 2023.

[18] See Antony Loewenstein, *The Palestine Laboratory: How Israel Exports the Technology of Occupation around the World* (Verso, 2023).

[19] Dawson, "Interview with Gabriel Schivone," 59.

[20] Jimmy Johnson, "A Palestine-Mexico Border," *NACLA* [North American Congress on Latin America] (blog), June 29, 2012.

Envisioning Justice

Since oppressors and settler colonial states cooperate in the border wall industry, those oppressed and affected by walls need to join forces. Soon after Israel started to build the wall around Bethlehem, we at Dar al-Kalima University started to explore how we could best use our know-how to creatively resist the wall. A visible expression of our deliberations was a project titled "Defacing the Wall," for which we invited three Mexican muralists to visit Palestine. Over three weeks in autumn 2004, Alberto Aragon Reyes, Gustavo Chavez Pavon, and Erasto Molina Urbina responded to our invitation to work in collaboration with local artists, art students, and internationals from Denmark, Sweden, Germany, the United States, England, Holland, Spain, and New Zealand to paint murals on the ugly concrete blocks surrounding cities in the West Bank. The paintings were very expressive and reflected the suffering, the pain, and the wounds that afflict oppressed people worldwide.

In 2017, Palestinian and Mexican grassroots movements launched an initiative called World without Walls, endorsed today by over four hundred movements worldwide. Their initial statement read, "From Israel's apartheid wall on Palestinian land to the U.S. Wall of Shame on indigenous land at the border with Mexico, walls are monuments of expulsion, exclusion, oppression, discrimination, and exploitation.... Walls have not only risen to fortify borders of state control but demarcate the boundaries between the rich, the powerful, the socially acceptable and the 'other.'"[21] Every year on November 9, which marks the anniversary of the fall of the Berlin Wall, these grassroots organization engage in popular resistance action to demand the dismantling of walls. Also, in 2017, the London-based artist Banksy opened a

---

[21] Stop the Wall: Palestinian Grassroots Anti-Apartheid Wall Campaign, "About Us," 2025.

boutique hotel by the wall in Bethlehem named The Walled Off Hotel, where the most expensive rooms are those facing the ugly apartheid wall directly.[22]

On October 7, 2023, a group of young Palestinian Hamas fighters succeeded in neutralizing the complex security along Israel's wall, including its long-range cameras, sophisticated sensors, and remote-control weapons, to breach the high-tech wall at thirty different points. Israel's pride in its high-tech security was shattered by the ease with which the security was overcome. The events of October 7 dealt a blow to Israeli military exports and the image of Israeli security expertise, as well as being the deadliest attack in Israel's history. It was also proof that walls cannot guarantee security and that security is not possible without justice and an end to the Israeli occupation.

Israel has exploited October 7 as an excuse to advance its settler colonial project by making the Gaza Strip uninhabitable for Palestinians. The ultimate goal is to see the people of Gaza displaced "voluntarily" and thereby empty the land. The Israeli *hasbara* machine fabricated stories about the beheading of Israeli babies and raping of women to create an image of the savage Palestinian, propaganda being an important tool of settler colonialism. Israeli politicians portrayed Palestinians as "human animals." Internationally, politicians describe the events of October 7 as "barbaric" but have little to say about the killing of over thirty thousand Palestinians, 70 percent of them women and children.

South Africa, a country that has experienced settler colonialism firsthand, brought the case of Gaza to the International Court of Justice on the basis of the Convention on the Prevention and Punishment of the Crime of Genocide. The court accepted the case and concluded that "at least some of the acts and omissions alleged by South Africa to have been committed by Israel in

---

[22] Raheb, *Decolonizing Palestine*, 2–5. See http://www.walledoffhotel.com/.

Gaza appear to be capable of falling within the provisions of the Convention."[23] It was no coincidence that the countries that came to aid Israel at the court all had settler colonial histories—namely, the United States, Germany, Canada, and the United Kingdom. This fact underlines that the Israeli wall, occupation, and settler colonialism are part and parcel of a Western settler colonial and imperial global structure.

Palestinians do not fight against a concrete wall but, as the apostle Paul put it, "against principalities, against powers, against the ruler of the darkness of this age" (Eph. 6:12). For the last hundred years, Western empires have been waging war through their Israeli proxy against the Palestinian people. Yet with all its military, economic, political, and ideological power, the West has not been able to suppress people's desire for freedom. This aspiration was echoed by the hundreds of thousands of demonstrators who flooded the streets of capital cities globally to demand a ceasefire and a free Palestine. The fact that the political establishments in the West are not listening to the voice of the people on the streets is an indication that the struggle of Palestine and the Global South is not a sprint but a marathon. The Palestinian people have proved to be resilient and refuse to surrender. Together with the Global South, which also experienced settler colonialism, Palestinians continue to fight for the day when walls will fall, reparations are made, and nations will wage war no more. There is no option other than to continue working toward this utopian vision despite the understanding that it may not be achieved in our lifetime.

---

[23] International Court of Justice, "Application of the Convention on the Prevention and Punishment of the Crime of Genocide in the Gaza Strip (South Africa v Israel)," The Hague, January 26, 2024.

7

South Africa and Apartheid

Brian Joseph Brown

In 1948, a senior pastor of the White Dutch Reformed Church (DRC) and leader of the pro-apartheid National Party, D. F. Malan, was elected prime minister of South Africa. His cabinet's architect of the implementation of the apartheid ideology, with a portfolio of "native affairs," was Hendrik Verwoerd. Verwoerd was a believer in building walls of division, albeit of the metaphorical kind, to secure what he called a policy of "good neighbourliness."[1] His disenfranchised Black neighbors had little cause to share this estimation.

I was ten years old at the time. My father had inculcated in me ideas of "gentlemanly" behavior, which today might be viewed by some as sexist; for example, a gentleman was to offer his seat to a woman who was having to stand. So, when on a crowded tram in Cape Town I observed a Coloured (mixed-race) woman standing, complete with baby and baggage, I instinctively offered my seat. A bellowing tram conductor ensured that no gallantry transpired: "Sit down! Coloured girls must stand." That night my father explained why, under new state laws, I was to be diminished

---

[1] Tim Crowe, "Verwoerd Should Not Be Remembered Fondly," *Politicsweb*, September 19, 2016.

in acts of consideration, as even the woman had been diminished by her humiliation and dehumanization. For the next decade or so, I lived with the tension of whether to passively accept a racist system that bestowed constant privilege and benefits to Whites, or to resist and bite the hand that fed me. While this was a daily dilemma for all the minority White population, it seemed to bother few.

The South African policy of apartheid—pronounced "apart-hate"— was often lazily equated with segregation, understood as the enforced separation of different racial groups and invariably associated with inequality between them. Segregation is not unique to South Africa. What made the apartheid policy distinctive was much more than state-enforced separation of facilities along racial lines, with Black people deemed second-class citizens deserving of inferior facilities and White people as first-class citizens deserving of superior facilities. Although this situation did prevail, what Blacks called their struggle had little to do with some widely felt need to sit on a Whites-only park bench.

Important Distinctions: Grand and Petty Apartheid

Segregation in South Africa, albeit viciously implemented, was known as "petty apartheid." The struggle of the Black oppressed was to end "grand apartheid." It was about obtaining freedom from ethnic domination, ending institutionalized state violence in South Africa and an illegal occupation in Namibia, and the realization of a democratic society that would promote racial equality for all. Grand apartheid was understood as the primary racist evil, the ending of which would inevitably mean the ending of petty apartheid. Grand apartheid's distinctiveness was its dispossession, disenfranchisement, and domination of the Black majority by the White Nationalist regime and its security forces.

The importance of this distinction occurred to me when writing a book in 2021 that compared the policies of apartheid

South Africa regarding its racist oppression of Blacks with those of the State of Israel regarding its racist oppression of Palestinians. The book argues that, in regard to the implementation of the determining policies of grand apartheid, Israel's current replication of them is sufficiently intense to call it an apartheid regime.[2] This argument would have been flawed had it suggested Israel's replication of the policies of petty apartheid. The park benches of Tel Aviv do not bear "Jews only" signs debarring Israeli Arabs (Palestinians) from comfortably observing the passing show.

Legislating for Racism

South Africa's White dominance was achieved through the passing of legislation enacted by a racist parliament and implemented by the overt and covert violence embedded in the structures of apartheid society. Laws demanded that the entire population be registered, contributing to the demarcation into prescribed ethnic groups; Whites and non-White Black Africans, Coloureds, and Indians. (As the term "non-White" is likely unacceptable and offensive to many, the word "Black" is instead used in this analysis when describing these communities, except when a distinctive ethnic community is being discussed.) The growth of Black Consciousness in the 1970s facilitated this growing identification by Coloured and Indian people as Black. Blackness was seen as not solely descriptive of pigmentation but rather a state of shared racial oppression. From the inception of apartheid in 1948, a geographic separation was implemented in the Black communities by way of house demolitions, forced removals, ethnic cleansing, and land theft. The establishment of these segregated "group areas" along ethnic lines was complemented by the creation of so-called tribal homelands or Bantustans[3] for Black Africans.

---

[2] Brian Joseph Brown, *Apartheid South Africa! Apartheid Israel!: Ticking the Boxes of Occupation and Dispossession* (Church in the Market Place, 2021), 33.

[3] A Bantustan—also called a Bantu homeland, Black homeland,

Also greatly resented and the cause of constant acts of protest were laws requiring Black Africans to carry permits or passes. The massacre of Blacks by police fire in 1960 in the township of Sharpeville, during a nonviolent protest by the Pan Africanist Congress of Robert Sobukwe, reverberated around the world. It was an ugly demonstration of the violence of the apartheid system. The pass document[4] determined whether permission was granted to a Black person to leave the Bantustan and find work in an area designated as White. South Africa's White area was about 80 percent of the land mass of the country, while the African population was also about 80 percent of the total. Such inequalities in South Africa were stark and brutal. Black Africans were required to inhabit the generally valueless 13 percent of land allocated for the Bantustans. A publication in 1970 by Roman Catholic Father Cosmas Desmond described that land as "the dumping grounds" for labor that was surplus to White needs, which had an obscenely high mortality rate within their borders, notably for babies and children.[5] Complete White control of a migrant labor market was thus assured, and its destruction of Black family life was a rarely acknowledged tragedy.

To Be a South African Was to Be White

The total denationalization of the Black population meant that Whites alone were nationals of a state that was defined by its Whiteness. As in Israel today, where any Jew may "return" who has

---

Black state, or homeland—was a territory set aside by the National Party for Black inhabitants of South Africa and South West Africa (now Namibia) as part of the apartheid policy.

[4] The official document that Black people had to carry with them to prove their identity and where they could live or work, derogatorily referred to as the *dompas* (Afrikaans for "stupid pass").

[5] Cosmas Desmond, *The Discarded People: An Account of African Resettlement* (Penguin, 1971).

never before seen the country, although no displaced indigenous Palestinian may return, so under South African apartheid only White immigrants could settle permanently. A labor system, increasingly drawing on the populations of neighboring Black states, met the thriving mining and industrial interests of the time. These migrant workers had to return to their countries on ending employment. The apartheid regime had the effrontery to claim to be the only democracy in the region. It was an arrogance bewildering to the people of neighboring Botswana, whose democratic state had prevailed since independence in 1966. Apartheid ensured that national rights attributable solely to Whites were always to be superior to citizen rights, which conferred on Blacks an inferior status and identity.

Democracy Devoid of Equality?

Rather than being a democracy, South Africa was a White ethnocracy in which one ethnic group dominated the other: a democratic state for White citizens and an apartheid state for Black citizens. Similarly, Israel's claim to be a democracy is of this pattern. Jonathan Cook, author and commentator on Israel-Palestine affairs, points out that, rather than being a legitimate democracy as Israel would self-define, it is a democratic state for Jewish citizens and a Jewish state for its Israeli Arab citizens.[6] Its Jewish Nation-State Law of 2018 guarantees precisely this. Devoid of the essential principles of equality, the democracy claim for South Africa was oxymoronic. In the territory between the Limpopo River and the confluence of the Indian and Atlantic Oceans, apartheid ensured that no Black could vote as the national of an internationally recognized state. Likewise, in the territory between the Jordan

---

[6] Jonathan Cook, "Why Israel Is an Apartheid State," *Jonathan Cook* (blog), March 18, 2018.

River and the Mediterranean Sea today, Israel ensures that no Palestinian can vote as the national of an internationally recognized state. Israel is an apartheid state masquerading as "the only democracy in the Middle East."

Immunity That Encourages Impunity

In addition to South Africa's lengthy and illegal military occupation of Namibia on its northwest border, its periodic cross-border raids against nations in the region declared its political and military domination. Punitive measures would follow in blatant disregard of principles of territorial integrity, if harboring of members of the South African liberation movements was claimed. Apartheid destabilized the region by intent, and Western nations allowed its perpetrators to get away with it for decades. This was the era of the Cold War, and South Africa was seen both as a strategic ally and a bulwark against communist incursions in the region.

Kith and kin factors were also determinative of much international response, or more particularly nonresponse. Few dared to suggest the obvious factor of racial prejudice as a major influence in this pattern. Dispossession of Blacks took place with impunity because immunity from detrimental consequences was assured. It was with the forthright reemergence in the 1980s of the call for boycott, divestment, and sanctions (BDS)—led by Anglican archbishops Desmond Tutu and Trevor Huddleston—that cracks in the apartheid edifice began to appear. BDS became the primary international pressure on the regime and strengthened the growing internal and near-universal resistance of the Black oppressed under the unifying banner of the United Democratic Front. This people's movement, essentially nonviolent of choice and necessity, became the major factor in securing liberation.

In the late 1980s, the apartheid regime had serious reasons—mainly financial—to consider the need for fundamental change.

Spokespersons started to inform the party faithful that moving away from apartheid was an imperative—not for ethical reasons, but rather self-interest. Ending the effects of BDS would slow the impending economic collapse of the state, occasioned by minimal investment, capital flight, shrinking exports, curtailed supply lines, and unmanageable demands to meet loan repayments. The promotion of this understanding was assisted by the relative pragmatism of President F. W. de Klerk, who had succeeded the hard-right ideologue P. W. Botha as party leader.

Report after report by human rights bodies over the forty-plus years of apartheid revealed the increasing violation of rights. Calls for apartheid to end in South Africa and Namibia, and the observance of international law by bodies such as the UN General Assembly, UN Security Council, and the International Court of Justice had been treated with the same contemptuous disregard by the regime as were accusations of human rights atrocities. Only with the escalating violence of the military-state and the sacrificial resistance of the oppressed did the West come to belatedly acknowledge that grand apartheid denied to Blacks nationality, land, enfranchisement, human rights, equality, and justice. Rather than "good neighborliness," the South Africa system relied on discrimination, domination, dispossession, and dehumanization of the "other."

Why Blame Afrikanerdom Alone?

While the reasons for the predominantly Afrikaner population's endorsement of apartheid were essentially racist, some contributory factors can be understood without condoning the evils of apartheid. Afrikaners had suffered under the British Empire's settler colonial project and economic pursuits in South Africa that led to the Anglo-Boer Wars at the end of the nineteenth century. Britain's military forces imposed a scorched-earth policy whereby Boer farms were burned and women and children were placed in a new innovation called "concentration camps." From 1899 to 1901, at least 20,000 of the imprisoned Blacks (essentially employees of Boers and their families) and more than 26,000 Boers died in the camps, most of them children. Death through illness was compounded by near-starvation rations and malnutrition. Thomas Pakenham's *The Boer War* recounts how the camps left a gigantic scar on the psyche of Afrikaners—enduring reminders of an understandably feared genocide of their small community.[7]

Ironically, it was an Afrikaner who arguably became South Africa's leading White figure in revealing the evils of apartheid and in contributing to its demise. C. F. Beyers Naudé was a moderator of the White DRC and a leader in the Broederbond (Band of Brothers) secret society, which certified apartheid's major decisions, when he came to the conviction that the ideology was both racist and heretical.[8] His Damascus road moment (as when Saul the great persecutor of Christ became Paul the passionate apostle of Christ) ensured that he was defrocked by his peers. Far from being thus silenced, Beyers established a multiracial body, the Christian Institute of Southern Africa (CI), that proved a major force in declaring truth to political and ecclesiastical power. In particular, he energized the worldwide church to promote nonviolent actions that encouraged not a tinkering with apartheid's policies but a radical and total transformation of South Africa. Beyers invited me to join his team, and during the 1970s, he was my mentor as we traveled together to and from the offices of the CI in Johannesburg.

---

[7] Thomas Pakenham, *The Boer War* (Abacus, 1991).

[8] The Afrikaner Broederbond (AB) was an exclusive, secret Afrikaner nationalist organization that played a determining role in the political development of South Africa, promoting Afrikaner political, cultural, and economic interests.

CI Insights of Dealing with Injustice that Might Be of Relevance Today

To understand oppression, it is more reliable to listen to the oppressed than to the oppressors, who have reason to hide truth.

If this appears a self-evident statement, it is remarkable how frequently it is ignored. The CI engaged with the Black Consciousness Movement (BCM) and its charismatic leader Steve Biko as the primary source in understanding apartheid's consequences for the oppressed. Significantly, after the state's murder of Biko and the banning of eighteen BCM bodies that followed in 1977, the multiracial CI was the only non-Black body to be banned. Declaring oppression is often a dangerous pursuit.

Discovering the truth in regard to violence and terrorism is helped by asking, "Who perpetrates the primary or instigating violence, and who the secondary or counter violence?" The violence of the apartheid state and the terror it imposed were instances of primary violence.

In court proceedings that culminated in his twenty-seven years of imprisonment,[9] and again when offered conditional freedom if willing to renounce violence,[10] Nelson Mandela, as head of the African National Congress (ANC), called on the regime to cease its institutionalized violence that caused the conflict. This approach of determining the instigator was helpful when, in the 1980s, with the support of Anglican archbishop Robert Runcie as president of the British Council of Churches (BCC), I organized a meeting of church leaders with Oliver Tambo, president in exile of the ANC and a devout Christian. I had also asked Prime Minister Margaret Thatcher to meet with him. Her letter of refusal stated that the UK government did not do business with terrorists.

---

[9] Nelson Mandela, "On Freedom: 'Black Man in a White Court.' Nelson Mandela's First Court Statement—1962," United Nations.

[10] "President P. W. Botha offers Nelson Mandela Conditional Release from Prison," South African History Online, March 16, 2011.

For more than an hour, Tambo described to the leaders of the BCC the reality of Black suffering and persecution under the overt and covert violence of apartheid. I undertook to see Tambo out of the building. On returning, the room was still enveloped in silence. Runcie broke it, saying, "Thank you, Brian, for allowing us to meet a remarkable terrorist." The room exploded in laughter. Runcie would come to say, "If South African Christians cry out we cannot shut our ears; if they need support we cannot turn our backs; if they are being hurt we must be ready to share their suffering." Within a year, the BCC's Assembly and then its member bodies voted for the implementation of targeted sanctions against the apartheid regime.[11]

Acutely aware of the historic suffering imposed by forces of imperialism on his Afrikaner *volk*, Beyers Naudé sympathized with their cry: "Never again!" But he insisted it be: "Never again to any people!"

Beyers balanced the tension of condemning Britain's violence and its consequences for his people with the need to understand but not condone the angst that caused Afrikanerdom to impose a similar violence on the Black population.

Religious beliefs that confer a tribal identity of unique election, entitlement, exceptionalism, exclusivity, and ethnicity need to be redeemed by beliefs in a global identity that is inclusive—as even God's love is inclusive and without favor.

In a secular world impatient with theological niceties, such issues may appear trivial. But too many wars abetted by too many religions arise from this sense of exceptionalism for it to go unchallenged. The South African "war" was won in part when an ecumenical conference in 1990 brought representatives of some eighty denominations together, significantly of diverse races

---

[11] Brian Joseph Brown, *Born to Be Free: The Indivisibility of Freedom—A Methodist Minister's Quest for Justice and Freedom on Two Continents* (Church in the Market Place, 2015), 244.

and theological traditions. The then leader of the White DRC addressed the gathering:

> I declare before you and before the Lord, not only my own sin and guilt, and my personal responsibility for the political, social, economic and structural wrongs that have been done to many of you, and the results of which you and our whole country are still suffering from, but vicariously I dare also to do that in the name of the DRC of which I am a member, and for the Afrikaner people as a whole.[12]

This astonishing mea culpa sounded the death knell of any religious undergirding of apartheid and aided the ending of apartheid itself.

The Rainbow Nation

In 1994, after four years of negotiations, the government of President Mandela and a cabinet dominated by former political prisoners was ushered in. The "Rainbow Nation" was born. However belated its arrival and however costly its pursuit, democracy dawned. Namibia, where South Africa's occupation had long revealed a commitment to annex the mandated territory, saw its democracy dawn in 1990. This event was assisted by twin factors: a concerted commitment from the UN General Assembly and Security Council to address the issue after decades of inertia and the challenge posed to the occupier by the introduction of military forces from communist Cuba. The country offered crucial support to the armed wing of the South West Africa People's Organisation

---

[12] Ferdinand Kruger and Hennie Pieterse, "Reasons Why Government Leaders, Officials and Church Leaders Have to Act against Corruption," in *Corruption in South Africa's Liberal Democratic Context. Equipping Christian Leaders and Communities for Their Role in Countering Corruption*, ed. Ferdinand Kruger and Ben de Klerk (AOSIS, 2016).

(SWAPO), whose movement would govern come independence. No longer could the regime's propaganda protest that it was fighting a "defensive war" on South Africa's national borders. Its armed forces had been stretched by a war within the borders of Namibia that spilled over into Angola and violated the territorial integrity of both countries.

New Global Alliances

While the imperialist powers no longer dominate Southern Africa, emerging transnationalism ensures that the region has become even more connected and interdependent regarding trade and technology. Cultural globalization remains Western orientated, as do historic economic dependencies and the relationship of the ANC with its corporate powers. However, new political and economic alliances allow South Africa's reliance on the Global North—and the interests of Western Europe and the United States in particular—to be reduced.

Being a member of BRICS—an intergovernmental organization that initially comprised Brazil, Russia, India, and China—is an instance of these new developments. With further countries having become open to membership of the BRICS bloc in 2024—Egypt, Ethiopia, Iran, Saudi Arabia, and the United Arab Emirates—old alliances are threatened. In 2020, the BRICS countries overtook the Global North's Group of Seven (G7) countries in the share of the world's total gross domestic product (GDP) in terms of purchasing power parity (PPP); by 2023, BRICS held a total of 32 percent of the world's GDP compared to the 30 percent of the G7 bloc.[13] At a time when some analysts inquire if South Africa is becoming a failed state,

---

[13] Statista Research Department, "BRICS and G7 Countries' Share of the World's Total Gross Domestic Product (GDP) in Purchasing Power Parity (PPP) from 2000 to 2023," *Statista*, February 13, 2024.

the prestige bestowed by participation in BRICS is seen by its leaders as invaluable.

Former South African Foreign Minister Naledi Pandor was an avid supporter of BRICS. The nation's new alliances are reflected in its foreign policy pronouncements regarding the conflicts in Russia-Ukraine and Israel-Palestine. Whereas South Africa's democracy of 1994 looked more to the G7 for its political identity and sought to emulate its dominant capitalist ethos, much has changed. BRICS loyalties encourage the ANC to recall the historic contributions of solidarity with their liberation by communist China, Cuba, and Russia, as well as India, Sweden, Norway, and smaller nonaligned nations such as Libya and Palestine. An outcome is the emergence of new ways of engaging in transnationalism and a desire to strengthen relationships forged in the struggle era.

The Indivisibility of Freedom

Mandela was fiercely loyal in expressing his people's gratitude to those who had sided with them. When Minister Pandor defended the action of her government in calling on the International Court of Justice (ICJ) in late 2023 to declare Israel's genocidal pursuits in Gaza, she invoked the declaration of Mandela in 1999: "But we know too well that our freedom is incomplete without the freedom of the Palestinians."[14] Visiting blockaded Gaza, he stated how he felt "at home amongst compatriots" and endorsed their right to long-deferred self-determination.[15] Globalization will continue to grow the international institutions in which marginalized and disempowered nations from the Global South play significant roles.

---

[14] "Pandor Says Israel Is 'Ignoring' the ICJ Order to Stop Killing in Gaza," *South African Government News Agency*, January 31, 2024.

[15] Huthifa Fayyad, "Nelson Mandela and Palestine: In His Own Words," *Middle East Eye*, February 11, 2020.

UN Special Rapporteur on the Occupied Palestinian Territories Francesca Albanese suggests that, in bringing its case to the ICJ, South Africa opened a new era between the Global North and South.[16] It resulted in the court's declaration of preliminary measures whereby Israel was instructed to prevent genocidal acts in Gaza.

The Disappearance of Rainbows

The term "de-development" has been used to describe how South Africa's pursuit of economic growth, improved living standards, and better infrastructure is in reverse.[17] GDP per capita has declined over the last decade and no longer is South Africa's status that of an upper-middle-income developing country. De-development also manifests itself in the degradation of public life. It acts to reverse the forces that gave birth to democracy and weakens the achievement of social and structural equality. These negative forces have been enhanced by a single-mindedness of ending apartheid that allowed an indifference to environmental degradation that is still little addressed.

Anticipated postapartheid benefits of improved transport infrastructure, enhanced health care, rising educational standards, and a national power grid serving the entire community have not transpired. Often these standards have regressed, as the following instances suggest.

Transport

The Zondo Commission into state malpractices, named after its chairperson Chief Justice Ray Zondo, includes over five thousand pages about how state resources were plundered. Transnet, the state

---

[16] Benjamin Fogel, "South Africa: 30 Years Later," *New Internationalist* 50, no. 548 (March–April 2024): 24–25.

[17] Fogel, "South Africa," 24–25.

rail operator, was a primary site of looting and provided irregular contracts valued at $2.7 billion.[18] An average of 43 million rail passenger trips per month by the end of the 2000s was reduced to a monthly average of 1.7 million by 2021–2022 due to insufficient trains and associated problems.[19]

Health

As with access to most services in South Africa, the disparity between the provision of private and state health services is vast. While the patient divide is no longer exclusively along racial lines, access to medical excellence is invariably determined by factors of wealth.

Education

The number of Black children in education increased after 1994, but thirty years later, 80 percent of government schools are rated as dysfunctional, and approximately 50 percent of the learners drop out of school before completing matriculation.[20]

Energy

Eskom, the state's failed electricity agency, imposes euphemistically called "load shedding" (a total cessation of electricity supply) for extensive periods, leaving business, industry, and households without power. The South African Reserve Bank reported in 2023

---

[18] David Hindley, "How Three Brothers 'Captured' a Country," *Financial Times*, July 7, 2022.

[19] James Stent, "These Graphs Show PRASA's Disastrous State. No Trains, No Hope? We Show Just How Bad Things Are at PRASA," *GroundUp*, September 21, 2022.

[20] Londiwe Buthelezi, "SA Lost R1.5 Trillion to Corruption in Five Years and Continues to Bleed—Report," *News24*, June 23, 2021.

that power cuts cost South Africa around $47 million a day.[21]

Questions remain unanswered as to why the ANC in government moved away from its commitment to prioritize redistributive economic policies and embraced policies more affirmed by Western markets, with their focus on privatization and the removal of exchange controls. The preferred policy of growth, employment, and redistribution (GEAR) failed to address the legacy of widespread inequality, particularly that of public service delivery. Only the relatively wealthy are likely to access the alternative facilities offered by privatization, and the emerging Black middle class is insufficient to make inroads into either the gross inequality or rampant unemployment.

South Africa has the highest income inequality in the world, with the top 10 percent owning 86 percent of the country's wealth and the top 0.1 percent almost one-third of the wealth.[22] Six out of ten young South Africans are jobless, and more than half of the country's inhabitants live in poverty.[23] The Black unemployment percentage of 36.8 contrasts starkly with the White percentage of 7.4.[24]

Consequences, Crime, and Corruption

Such disproportionate figures inevitably have consequences, encouraging crime and corruption to flourish even more. The violence of crime is extraordinary, with figures for murder over

---

[21] Bartholomäus Grill and Fritz Schaap, "Gangs, Corruption and Collapse: The Slow and Steady Demise of South Africa," *Spiegel International*, September 8, 2023.

[22] Victor Sulla, Precious Zikhali, and Pablo Facundo Cuevas, "Inequality in Southern Africa: An Assessment of the Southern African Customs Union," World Bank, March 13, 2024.

[23] Grill and Schaap, "Gangs, Corruption and Collapse."

[24] Natalie Cowling, "Unemployment Rate in South Africa from Q1 2019 to Q2 2023, by Population Group," *Statista*, October 6, 2023.

a period of three months in 2023 averaging sixty-eight per day, making the murder rate one of the world's highest.[25] A report published in 2021 states that, over a period of five years, $80 billion of South Africa's public purse was lost to corruption.[26] Transparency International reports that 18 percent of public service users paid a bribe.[27]

Confidence in looking to national, regional, and local government to address maladies is weakened by "state capture," in which systemic political corruption allows private interests to significantly influence governmental decision-making processes. Something similar occurred during the death throes of the Soviet Union, with the rise of the oligarchs. A prescient warning as to the corporate capture of government was made at the dawn of democracy in 1995 by Kgalema Motlanthe, a future South African president: "Big business will shower those comrades who are now in office with all sorts of gifts. That's the first line of attack. The trick is whether they will have the ability to deal with it."[28]

President Jacob Zuma and his comrades in power from 2009 to 2018 fell over one another in the scramble for gifts. A culture of entitlement, nepotism, and patronage—allied to a ready compliance with nontransparency and nonaccountability—became embedded in governance. Civil society monitors committed to good governance continue to produce their condemnatory reports, but the ANC-led political structures (all of the nine provinces, bar the Western Cape, remain under its jurisdiction) invariably act without fear of prosecution. As an instance of how endemic corruption

---

[25] Staff Writer, "The Latest Crime Stats for South Africa—Everything You Need to Know," *BUSINESSTECH*, August 18, 2023.

[26] Buthelezi, "SA Lost R1.5 Trillion to Corruption."

[27] Transparency International, *Global Corruption Barometer: Africa*, 10th ed., 2019.

[28] Conrad Landin, "Editorial," *New Internationalist* 50, no. 548 (2024): 3.

has become, the auditor general found that, for the fiscal year 2021–2022, of the country's 257 municipalities, 219 did not have clean audits.[29]

Draining the Swamp?

The experience of neighboring Zimbabwe suggests that electoral support—albeit much manipulated—for the political party foremost in securing national liberation has an enduring quality. Deviating from this support, particularly for a generation with memories of suffering and sacrifice, is viewed as a lack of gratitude or even a betrayal. A sense that the legacy of iconic ANC leaders Chief Albert Luthuli, Oliver Tambo, and Nelson Mandela should be protected prevents any challenging of political realities. However, new generations are less compromised by history, and present realities demand fresh appraisals, even of those activists who avidly supported the ANC and its liberation cause. A friend from the days when we were colleagues in the CI, Horst Kleinschmidt, offers his disturbing appraisal, arising out of sorrow, not pleasure: "The party is rotten to the core and no longer reformable. We need to start again from scratch otherwise the country will sink into the swamp."[30] These sentiments reflect something of the CI's understanding of the National Party when in power, seeing it and its political ethos as "beyond reformable."

Even the secretary-general of the ANC, Fikile Mbalula, is on record lamenting, "If certain things are not resolved, we will become a failed state."[31] The maladies of state capture and endemic corruption are replicated in party capture, whereby the needs of the party outweigh those of the nation and its people. Many hoped that, with the appointment of Cyril Ramaphosa to succeed

---

[29] Grill and Schaap, "Gangs, Corruption and Collapse."
[30] Grill and Schaap, "Gangs, Corruption and Collapse."
[31] Grill and Schaap, "Gangs, Corruption and Collapse."

Zuma in 2018, a significant addressing of corruption would occur. Be it from a lack of political will or human resources, this has not transpired with anything like the required intensity.

In earlier times, South Africans revealed the vision, the will, and the resilience to drain the swamp and redeem the capture of the state by apartheid's forces. Partially in response to a feared hard-right White insurrection with the dawn of Black majority rule, Mandela established a Truth and Reconciliation Commission (TRC) under the leadership of Tutu. Apartheid's victims were enabled to confront perpetrators who expressed penitence or truth or both, tell their own oft harrowing stories, and discover new self-respect, no longer as victims but "survivors." Perpetrators were granted amnesty if rising above a state of amnesia in regard to their past. Justice was essentially restorative. Complaints that the needs of reconciliation and national healing trumped those of punitive justice were understood but not determinative. Whatever the reservations, the TRC's contribution to a swamp-cleaning and a peaceful postapartheid era was enormous.

Demographics

The state census of 2022 shows South Africa's predominantly young population to be 62 million, a growth of almost 10 million in a decade. Black Africans comprise 81.4 percent of the population, Coloureds 8.2, Whites 7.7, and Indians/Asians 2.7.[32] The declining White percentage is explained in part by an estimated 611,500 Whites having left over the past thirty-five years.[33] This figure contrasts with the 2.4 million international

---

[32] "Media Release: Census 2022 Population Count Results 10 October 2023," *Statistics South Africa*, October 13, 2023.

[33] Staff Writer, "White South Africans Are Leaving the Country in Their Thousands: Stats SA," *BUSINESSTECH*, July 19, 2021.

migrants—mainly from other parts of Africa—who have settled to make it the top immigration destination on the continent.[34] Despite divisions in the ANC and a majority vote that has decreased progressively over the past thirty years, come elections, it presents a united front that is beyond the capacity of a fractious political opposition to threaten.

If radical change through the parliamentary party system appears unlikely in the short term at least, might civil society summon up the energy and unity to address the nation's needs, as it did so dramatically when breaking down the walls of apartheid? Its strength as a change-maker has decreased since 1994, as has the receipt of international solidarity. The much-applauded constitution of democratic South Africa does allow access to the courts for civil society groups that seek to hold the government to account, but this can prove a lengthy and expensive process. The other side of the coin is that the constitution can constrain economic rights and wealth redistribution with its strong commitment to the safeguarding of private property.

South Africans of all colors and persuasions have much to recall and indeed replicate by way of their heroic history of the pursuit of justice, of altruistic leadership couched in integrity, and of a disciplined people-power. These factors contributed to the day when the Rainbow Nation was born and the renowned broadcaster John Simpson was able to declare of the event: "It's a miracle!" Neither the necessity nor the attainment of fresh miracles should be discounted.

---

[34] Khangelani Moyo, "South Africa Reckons with Its Status as a Top Immigration Destination, Apartheid History, and Economic Challenges," Migration Policy Institute, November 18, 2021.

8

Denationalized, Decolonizing, and Transborder Hermeneutic in an Age of Border-Wall Politics

GREGORY L. CUÉLLAR

Long before the post-9/11 era, the southern US border was given a policing function against people deemed by dominant white society to be racially inferior and socially prone to banditry. Here, border security is the violent materiality of an entrenched political conviction about who is worthy of social belonging and future well-being. In subduing the geography for border security, the United States relies on military-trained personnel, surveillance equipment, and intermittent border fencing that stretches nearly fifteen hundred miles, from the Gulf of Mexico to the Pacific Ocean. Although not natural to the landscape, these border-walls are natural to the US nation-state, so much so that both Republican and Democratic presidents have legislated their construction and maintenance.[1]

Made to appear as a necessary protective measure, these border-walls perform violence, first on the earth itself, then to wildlife, plant life, and human lives. While the result of political rhetoric,

---

[1] Eileen Sullivan and Colbi Edmonds, "Biden, the Border, and Why a New Wall Is Going Up," *New York Times*, October 6, 2023.

their permanency provides an emblem for white supremacist violence against the very people they are designed to exclude.[2] And, by extension, these border-walls are the templates for the carceral walls of the mega US immigration detention industrial complex.[3] To complete this repertoire of state violence, the border-walls mark in the end the place of removal for the deported, or more precisely, the graveyard of the nameless Other. For racialized people migrating across these border-walls, the US detention-deportation nexus is just one facet of a larger aggregate of trauma-inducing experiences, from economic scarcity to transnational cartel exploitation to state-sanctioned violence.

With the rampant political currency of Trump's "build the wall" mantra, it is imperative that a radical vision of the US-Mexico borderlands contravene the normativity of this violent approach to difference or, more precisely, the negation of our interconnectedness. For a racialized Chicano, born and living in the Texas-Mexico borderlands, this task is especially pressing given that much of the current border-wall politics has targeted ethnic Mexicans as a premier public enemy of the US nation-state. As revealed in the 2020 US Immigrations and Customs Enforcement (ICE) enforcement and removal operations report, the top four nationalities detained and deported from the United States for fiscal years 2018, 2019, and 2020 were Mexican (six digits), Guatemalan, Honduran, and El Salvadoran.[4] Rather than concede to the notion of borderlands as the death zone of homeland security, can borderlands serve as a denationalized, decolonizing, transborder activist hermeneutic of interconnectedness and interdependence that sacralizes our unique differences?

---

[2] Angela Kocherga, "El Paso Remembered," *Texas Observer*, August 3, 2020.
[3] "United States," Global Detention Project, online report accessed December 16, 2023.
[4] US Immigrations and Customs Enforcement, *U.S. Immigration and Customs Enforcement Fiscal Year 2020 Enforcement and Removal Operations Report* (Immigrations and Customs Enforcement, 2020).

Indeed, any attempt to theorize on the US-Mexico borderlands, especially in ways that subvert the reigning border-wall paradigm, cannot avoid the writings of Gloria Anzaldúa and her borderlands spirituality, which is either undervalued or dehistoricized in the broader border studies literature.[5] Latent within her spiritual vision is a decolonizing project that registers in her reframing of borderlands as *nepantla*—a Nahuatl word meaning *tierra entre medio* (the in-between space).[6] For Anzaldúa, the *nepantla*-borderland serves as a liminal zone of interconnectedness and transformation that lies between the mind, the body, and the spirit.[7] Here, the borderlands are reconstituted as an awakening experience that she calls *conocimiento*. Like the human imagination, this conceptual term refers to an integrative perception that functions as a type of consciousness for recognizing connections and commonalities while clearly acknowledging the value of differences.[8] Thus, contrary to a border-wall paradigm, which has in view the state's removal of brown and black bodies, there is a denationalized borderlands dynamic that connects different social bodies together in ways that are mutually life-giving. In essence, Anzaldúa's recourse to contextualization and intersubjectivity as a counterframework for understanding borderlands models for us a denationalized activist hermeneutic that approaches difference in inclusive ways and renders people, the earth, and things as interconnected primarily because of their unique differences.

---

[5] Gloria E. Anzaldúa, *Interviews/Entrevistas*, ed. AnaLouise Keating (Routledge, 2000), 7.

[6] Gloria E. Anzaldúa and AnaLouise Keating, eds., *This Bridge We Call Home: Radical Vision for Transformation* (Routledge, 2002), 1.

[7] Anzaldúa, *Interviews/Entrevistas*, 7–8.

[8] AnaLouise Keating, ed., *Entre Mundos / Among Worlds: New Perspectives on Gloria Anzaldúa* (Palgrave, 2005), 182.

The Border-Walls in Western Biblical Interpretation

As a Chicano biblical scholar from the Texas-Mexico borderlands, I inhabit a context in which brownness is bifurcated as subject and object. In the US context, border-walls are not simply done discretely on the natural landscape but are continually imposed upon brown- and black-bodied people. For migrants crossing into the United States from Mexico, brown bodies are legally understood to carry what Aviva Chomsky observes as "the border with them," which renders their brown bodies as criminal objects—and hence exploitable, incarcerable, and finally, disposable.[9] Another way in which the brown body constitutes a border site in the US-Mexico borderlands can be described by the following post-1848 Texas-Mexican saying: "We didn't cross the border; the border crossed us."[10] In thinking about what it means to be "border-crossed," there is first the notion of an imposed racial branding that has violently seized upon my Chicano-Mexican self. Racialized inscriptions of brownness as criminal, semisavage, and diseased were concurrent with the invasion of an Anglo-American social order. The monumentalized history of Anglo-Texas has served to perpetuate this racial stigma of ethnic Mexicans, thereby ensuring that both the border-crosser and the border-crossed remain stateless and dispossessed.

Another way I think about my border-crossed condition is to use it as an activist hermeneutic of embodiment that privileges the racialized bodies of ethnic Mexicans—specifically those long settled in the Nueces–Rio Grande strip of South Texas.[11] Such a

---

[9] Aviva Chomsky, *Undocumented: How Immigrant Became Illegal* (Beacon, 2014), 54.

[10] Matthew C. Gutmann et al., eds., *Perspectives on Las Americas: A Reader in Culture, History, & Representation* (Wiley-Blackwell, 2003), 10.

[11] Alex Lubin, *Geographies of Liberation: The Making of an Afro-Arab Political Imaginary* (University of North Carolina Press, 2014), 4.

hermeneutic is less concerned with the "original" biblical text than with redressing the generational wounds that the state has inflicted on brown-bodied people in the US-Mexico borderlands. By designating my embodied state as border-crossed, my intellectual loyalties shift to a decolonizing value system in which master narratives are interrogated and the postcolonial trauma of border people is honored. At the nexus of my border-crossed condition and biblical scholarship, Western scientific objectivity registers as a master-narrative that aims to disincarnate me so that I become an ally of border-wall thinking. As a border-crossed reader, I seek to dismantle this master-narrative effect, using the very research instincts and close reading techniques ("master's tools") that are hailed within the field's dominant discourse. My intention here is a liberative mode of truth-making that attends more fervently to the postcolonial wounds of border-crossed and border-crossing people. It does so first by mapping the empire's violent operations on Black and Brown bodies. This means interrogating the ways in which scientific objectivity employs Western border-wall thinking to construct a master-narrative about the biblical world that in turn legitimates the current world of anti-immigrant violence.

When applying an Anzaldúan-informed hermeneutic to the reading of Scripture, there is first the reader's self-awareness as an Other to the biblical text's otherness, particularly in terms of its cultural production and accumulated iconic currency, yet the reader also acknowledges a resonance with the human traces inscribed in the text. As such, the violence of empire imagined in the text is not disconnected from the realities of elite power working either through or against the reader. The same can be said for the theme of migration in the biblical text in that this theme serves as a lived social reality that is playing out on a mass scale in the US-Mexico borderlands.[12] Empire and migration function as viable nodes for

---

[12] US Customs and Border Protection, "Southwest Land Border Encounters," report last modified November 14, 2023.

reader-to-text interchange because of the recrudescence of these lived realities. Again, conceptualizing the reading of Scripture through Anzaldúa's vision of borderlands not only lays claim to the interchange of otherness occurring between the text's humanness and the living reader, but also the felt resonance that moves the reader toward a consciousness or *conocimiento* of how elite power operates and the ways it is resisted by people.

Under the dominant discourse of Western biblical interpretation, the operative mode of reading Scripture reflects more of a border-wall dynamic whereby readers are severed from their social location in an effort to foreclose on all sense of their subjective selves. By conforming to a self-policing reflex—which is a form of violence[13]—the producers of this discourse ensure the results of untainted truth about what the Bible means. Similarly, biblical texts undergo a bordering process in that their "true" meaning is constricted to objects exhumed and deciphered by Western experts and preferably within exclusive Western research spaces like museums, special collections libraries, and university reading rooms. This guarding of knowledge production is then transferred into the dominant discourse of Western biblical interpretation, thereby creating a fixed discourse governed by a specific language, people, and argumentation.

In his critique of dominant methods of criticism in the humanities, Edward Said alluded to this bordering dynamic with this question: "Is it the inevitable conclusion to the formation of an interpretive community that its constituency, its specialized language, and its own self-confirming authority acquires more power, the solid status of orthodoxy, and a stable constituency?"[14] Here, self-policing and citational politics point to a preserving and concealment of "the hierarchy of powers that occupy the center,

---

[13] Étienne Balibar, *Citizenship* (Polity, 2015), 72–73.
[14] Edward W. Said, "Opponents, Audiences, Constituencies, and Community," *Critical Inquiry* 9, no. 1 (1982): 9.

define the social terrain, and fix the limits of use functions, fields, marginality, and so on."[15] In biblical studies, those occupying the center of the dominant discourse constitute a cadre of white male citizen scholars, who are responsible for maintaining its purity by pushing out dissenters. Here, the dominant discourse is less concerned with "original meaning" than a border-wall politics that assimilates readers and Scripture into a Western economy of truth-making that privileges white male citizens.

An Activist Hermeneutic of the Borderlands

The borderlands theory that informs my proposed denationalized activist hermeneutic involves more than acknowledging the interactivity of otherness occurring between the reader and the biblical text. For Anzaldúa, the borderlands are rooted in US-Mexico geopolitics in which the border-wall is both a colonizing project as well as an everyday policing structure that performs violence on brown bodies. Although Anzaldúa's activist hermeneutic of the borderlands has in view a state of transcendence, it remains politically grounded given that her experience with borderlands is inextricably tied to a US-inflicted social wound on the people and the landscape or in her words, *una herida abierta*, where the Third World "grates against the first and bleeds."[16] Here, political activism functions as a spiritual exercise, which, for Anzaldúa, is achieved through the power of the pen.[17]

Her recourse to discourse production as a political act stems from her understanding of the power that archives have in defining identities and shaping social realities. In this sense, the border-wall functions as an archive of US imperialism, racism, and anti-immigrant

---

[15] Said, "Opponents, Audiences, Constituencies, and Community," 22.

[16] Gloria E. Anzaldúa, *Borderlands / La Frontera: The New Mestiza* (Aunt Lute, 2012 [1999]), 53.

[17] Anzaldúa, *Interviews / Entrevistas*, 252.

sentiments. Through her knowledge production, therefore, Anzaldúa aims to trespass on this archive or, more specifically, cross the border-wall by offering a counterreading of the history, culture, beauty, resilience, and creativity of ethnic Mexicans. The notion of border-wall as both a politic and an archive speaks to how borders and walls in general are the result of a cultural value system and shared social beliefs about the Other. As Anzaldúa indicated in a 1994 interview with Debbie Blake and Carmen Abrego,

> Myths and fictions create reality, and these myths and fictions are used against women and against certain races to control, regulate, and manipulate us. I'm writing the myths, using the myths back against the oppressors. An example of how a myth has created reality is the stereotype that Mexicans are dumb. For decades people have said that Mexicans are dumb and after a while it becomes part of the cultural perspective itself. There was the myth and the fiction that blacks were less intelligent than whites and therefore should not be given education, not be sent to school.[18]

The southern border-walls separating the United States from Mexico are a reality rooted in the widespread belief that ethnic Mexicans are entirely inferior and hence more prone to criminality. The genealogy of such myths can be traced to the mid-nineteenth century and the expansionist ideology of Anglo-American Manifest Destiny. This ideology relied heavily on a theology of providence, which, in turn, made the Anglo-Protestant church its most ideal ambassador. Thus, trespassing on the archives that legitimate the current southern US border-walls must be attentive to the North American church and its scientific and literal uses of Scripture. With the church as a state agent, crossing the border-wall is construed not only as a crime against the nation-state but rather a sin against God.

---

[18] Anzaldúa, *Interviews / Entrevistas*, 219.

This conflation of state agenda and divine will is also operative in chaplaincy services provided in US immigration detention facilities to the extent that convicted border crossers are led to accept detention and deportation as part of their Christian duty.[19]

In the US-Mexico borderlands, border-crossing points to a transgressive act with criminal implications; yet for a denationalized activist hermeneutic of the borderlands, this act of transgression can be harnessed as a method of knowing, especially in relation to academic biblical criticism. Just as Anzaldúa's borderlands theory helps us to reimagine the reading of Scripture as an open interchange between a multiplicity of otherness, the US-Mexico border writings of Américo Paredes also direct us to take up this border-crossing as a deterritorializing tactic. As José David Saldívar describes,

> Because Paredes's modernist cultural work represents the complex self-fashionings brought about by the bloody US-Mexico borderland conflict, it also constitutes needed insights into the boundary disputes between and among academic disciplines as well as geographic territories. His bold deterritorializations thus serve both as tactical political strategies specifically designed to counter Anglocentric hegemony in border disputes and as transdisciplinary phantasms designed to transgress rigidly "border-patrolled" discursive boundaries.[20]

Paredes's border-crossing strategy functions as a counterresponse to the physical border-walls—which are monuments of the US empire—and to the territorialization that dominant academic

---

[19] Gregory Lee Cuéllar, "Deportation as a Sacrament of the State: The Religious Instruction of Contracted Chaplains in U.S. Detention Facilities," *Journal of Ethnic and Migration Studies* 45, no. 2 (2019): 253–72.

[20] José David Saldívar, *Border Matters: Remapping American Cultural Studies* (University of California Press, 1997), 37.

discourses practice to exclude him from knowledge production. Hence, when applied to a denationalized activist reading of Scripture, border-crossing as a method of knowing requires a transdisciplinary engagement with the human voices captured in biblical texts. Here the method of crossing over to critical theorists—particularly those concerned with radical emancipation—must also remain in conversation with the lived experiences of colonized people in the borderlands. As gleaned from Paredes's diagnosis of post-1848 border ethnic Mexicans, Anglo colonization created an identity crisis that was redressed in part by their cultural productions:

> The Mexican, on the other hand, has always been on the defensive in the border situation, afraid of being swallowed whole. He does not have to be sophisticated or an intellectual to realize the risk to his way of life the culture contact entails. The folklore [the people's commentary] shows his preoccupation about remaining Mexican even when he is becoming most Americanized.[21]

Placing this border commentary alongside the ancestral stories, poetry, and prophetic texts in the Bible, the reader's border-crossing gaze uncovers shared traumas of empire as well as mutual desires to be freed from all forms of colonizing violence.

The cultural values and rules of self-making that govern disciplinary boundaries in biblical studies have the tendency to dismiss the cultural productions of colonized people, arguing that their expressions of postcolonial traumas are crude exaggerations. This banalizing of coloniality promotes a deplorable state of self-degradation for conquered and dishonored people. They are not only "afraid of being swallowed up whole," but as Frantz Fanon describes, the colonized "native is so starved for anything, anything at all that will turn him into a human being, any bone of

---

[21] Américo Paredes, *Folklore and Culture on the Texas-Mexican Border* (CMAS, 1993), 41.

humanity flung to him, that his hunger is incoercible, and these poor scrapes of charity may, here and there, overwhelm him."[22] Thus, crossing over the borders of the dominant discourse in biblical studies—especially those that guard against believing the trauma claims of those wounded by empire—is an essential step toward a decolonized activist hermeneutic. Rather than describe colonial symptoms as benign, the reader accepts the embedded traumas within the cultural archive of colonized people—their names, laments, jokes, and songs.

Whether in the biblical text or in the lived commentary of border people, their cultural expressions of social wounds are taken just as seriously as the state-sanctioned violence that inflicted them. Here, the lived commentary of border people and the human traces in the biblical text interact in kinship-like ways, both in terms of affirming their felt wounds of empire and their mutual desire for freedom. By transgressing the boundaries of the dominant discourse in this way, readers expose the superficial nature of its scientific investments and their inability to offer remedy to the continual cycles of violence and trauma that are endemic to the empire-building impulse. At the same time, the lived commentary of border people emerges in this interfering border-crossing hermeneutical enterprise with increased value within the professional literature, which, in turn, contributes to their sacralization in the social realm.[23]

A Transborder-Wall Perspective

Thus far, the activist hermeneutic I have proposed responds to ways of knowing that make possible a world of dehumanizing and socially disconnecting border-walls. Here, the southern US

---

[22] Frantz Fanon, *The Wretched of the Earth*, trans. Richard Philcox (Grove, 2005 [1963]), 140.

[23] Said, "Opponents, Audiences, Constituencies, and Community," 24.

border-walls offer specificity of place and praxis for why this hermeneutical project is necessary, particularly within the bounded academic discipline of biblical studies. As excluding structures of the US nation-state, the southern border-walls desacralize the landscape by creating death zones for brown- and black-bodied people and, inversely, life zones for white citizenship. As Cristina Beltrán argues, "Today, the noncitizen migrant is the Other that both threatens and consolidates white citizenship."[24] This is partly justified by the border-walls' sacralization of a Western version of nation-state building in which white citizenship is privileged as the standard measurement for social, political, and economic belonging. These words by Joel Olson are especially fitting: "Whiteness was not a biological status but a political color that distinguished the free from the unfree, the equal from the inferior, the citizen from the slave."[25] For biblical critics to attend to the white supremacy undergirding the US border-wall complex requires a denationalizing strategy—or more specifically a de-Westernizing of how we conceptualize social belonging—that invites two seemingly disparate human experiences of trauma and liberation in Scripture and the borderlands to speak to each other in life-giving ways.

The post-1848 coloniality that the southern US border-walls perpetuate also necessitates a radical decolonizing intervention. At issue here is the liquidity of US border-walls in which their function as policing structures is harnessed as a method of biblical interpretation that reinforces Western nationalist thinking. Indeed, Étienne Balibar offers a more compelling description of the multifunctionality of border-walls:

---

[24] Cristina Beltrán, *Cruelty as Citizenship: How Migrant Suffering Sustains White Democracy* (University of Minnesota Press, 2020), 45.

[25] Joel Olson, *The Abolition of White Democracy* (University of Minnesota Press, 2004), 43.

The empirical, historical, phenomena of territorialization and de-territorialization (such as the displacement of populations, migrations, the fortification of borders, barriers to communication) are transformed into determinations of the universal, which is to say, into regimes of rights and access to rights.[26]

To have the US border-walls transition seamlessly into a discourse of truth-making, the users of this discourse inevitably adopt a racialized excluding reflex that targets brown- and black-bodied people. Just as this population is deemed unfit for full social inclusion (white citizenship), their claims against imperial violence and postcolonial traumas are, by extension, excluded from the reading of Scripture. What is privileged instead is a network of insiders/experts—preferably Anglo-European—who conform by performing a mode of Western scientificity that arrives at truth through what Said identifies as "noninterference in the affairs of the everyday world."[27]

Rooted in the original premise of Manifest Destiny, the physical and discursive manifestations of the US border-walls preserve a colonizing strategy of casting brown- and black-bodied people as inferior, deficient, and unworthy of social belonging. Where the sacralized US nation-state justifies the violence that border-walls perform against migrants (detain and deport), these same walls are the ensuing reality of the US empire and its Protestant ideology of white superiority. Hence their exclusion of people—whether in structural form or as a discourse—works as a colonizing mechanism to perpetuate a psychosocial condition of inferiority and self-hatred in brown- and black-bodied people. As a discourse within biblical studies, instilling a lack of self-worth in today's colonized people occurs not only by excluding their

---

[26] Balibar, *Citizenship*, 69.
[27] Said, "Opponents, Audiences, Constituencies, and Community," 22.

truth-claims from the interpretation of Scripture but also by trivializing their lived experiences with imperial violence and postcolonial traumas.

And yet when violence in the biblical text is properly diagnosed, the lived experiences of today's colonized people—migrants, asylum seekers, refugees, noncitizens, and the incarcerated, to name a few—are kept out of the interpretive analysis in efforts to achieve a fictional state of pure scientific objectivity. All the while, these excluding tactics are inflections of an original colonial project in which black- and brown-bodied people were deemed void of intellectual capacities and incapable of civilizational progress. Hence, the mode of decolonization that my activist hermeneutic aims to practice is an interpretive reflex that automatically includes the lived experiences of colonized people—their mappings of empire and visions of liberation—to elevate their human value within a discourse investing in the sacred. Moreover, this revaluation of experiences deemed inferior and hence irrelevant by the dominant discourse in biblical studies has in view a therapeutic function that undoes our colonized minds.

Lastly, my activist hermeneutic enlists a transborder-wall perspective. This conceptual move is informed by a migrant way of being in the US-Mexico borderlands that moves beyond a border-wall approach to social connectedness and earthly belonging. To follow astutely migrant life—their remittances, social media communications, religious practices, and cultural productions—border-walls emerge as but one factor in a transnational blend of interconnectedness and broader global processes.[28] In other words, for migrants to find a state of belonging that is life-sustaining requires superseding border-walls

---

[28] Nina Glick Schiller, "Beyond the Nation-State and Its Units of Analysis: Towards a New Research Agenda for Migration Studies. Essentials of Migration Theory," Center on Migration, Citizenship, and Development, Working Paper 33 (2007): 17–19.

(either by breaking through them or crossing over them) as the primary source for social meaning. Conversely, if we fix our critical gaze on border-walls as the central social field of analysis, our knowledge production is prone to perpetuate their presumed naturalness as necessary structures of the nation-state.

As migrant life reveals, navigating successfully through the world points to the fluidity and versatility of identities that scaffold an intricate set of transborder relationships at multiple junctures. Beginning with border-walls as the basis of social meaning, however, the trajectory of our analysis inevitably follows a bounded approach to identity, society, and power. Under this truncated framework, we are drawn to define people according to a racial-ethnic-nationality nexus, which for Western nation-states provides tidy ideological support for their biased system of citizenship-belonging. And yet the global economic systems that allow Western nation-states to monopolize wealth acknowledge the transborder exploits of elite power in the very places of departure and origin for migrants, from their local villages to hometowns to capital cities. To allow borders to govern all social meaning, our mapping of dominant systems of power would be an acute misdiagnosis of a broader system and in turn hinder any substantive counteractivism for today's colonized people.

For migrants, not only their bodies cross back and forth over border-walls but also their wages, networks, politics, processions, prayers, laments, and dreams. Indeed, their remittances alone are transborder transactions that convert wages received in the United States into revenue for family and friends in their places of departure and origin. Where the global economic system aims to extract wealth from their hometowns, their remittances reflect a counterconnectional process that is less about wire transfers of US dollars than about social enterprising, employment versatility, and frugal living. Thus, within this transborder process, we see what Nina Glick Schiller defines as "a network of networks without specifying a particular set of cultural practices or identities contained within them."[29] Moreover, these transborder ways of being for migrants also point to ways of becoming that are fluid, dynamic, and innovative. Where the border-walls would restrict our critical gaze to a nationalistic binary system of immigrant versus citizen, transborder migrant life offers a more nuanced interpretation of human interconnectedness and interdependence across multiple social fields. Drawing on Jacqueline Maria Hagan's research, migrant life is not one-dimensional but sustained by an array of transnational social networks that include pastors, couriers, deportees, and extended families.[30] While under a border-wall framework, such a nuanced social meaning is undiscernible, in part because of its fixation with otherness and homogeneity.

Applied to the reading of Scripture, a transborder perspective has the potential to avoid the trappings of border-wall thinking in which all social meaning begins with boundaries rather than connectedness. Combined with a racializing logic, border-wall thinking fits into Western nation-building logics—a system that, by default, divides people according to superior and inferior, in-group and out-group, civilized and uncivilized, citizen and noncitizen, white and nonwhite, to name a few. Approaching the reading of Scripture with this interpretive optic reveals how biblical people, kingdoms, and empires are construed in the commentary literature as bounded ethnic nation-states with fixed territorial and cultural borders. In the end, while such a construal appears to pertain to the ancient world, its constitutive logic ensures the preservation of the current nation-building world of bordered territoriality, white citizenship, and the negative othering of migrants.

---

[29] Schiller, "Beyond the Nation-State and Its Units of Analysis," 17–18.
[30] Jacqueline Maria Hagan, "Religion and the Process of Migration: A Case Study of a Maya Transnational Community," in *Religion across Borders: Transnational Immigrant Networks*, ed. Helen Rose Fuchs Ebaugh and Janet Saltzman Chafetz (AltaMira, 2002), 90–91.

Conclusion

To move from the southern US border-walls to the dominant discourse in biblical studies is rooted in a political awareness (*conocimiento*) of the elasticity and multifunctionality of Western nationalist thinking. Here, the borders that bar brown and black bodies from US citizenship (with whiteness as the norm) also transform into a discourse of interpretation that restricts knowledge production to solidify an exclusive power center of insider experts. Within biblical studies, its dominant discourse is also the most bounded in terms of its scholarly demographic, citational practices, terminology, and research methods. This not only benefits insider-experts at the center of this discourse, but its border-wall thinking provides support to the broader nation-building project. Both those who produce this knowledge and the discourse they generate affirm the naturalness of the US nation-state and its standards of citizenship-belonging. With the Bible as their sacralizing source, both content and critics serve as agents of the US nation-state, which, ultimately, is a role in which white citizen-scholars stand to benefit the most.

9

Extraction, Militarization, and Trump's Border Wall

The Circumstances That Led Up to the O'odham Revolt of 2020

NELLIE JO DAVID

Currently, a large portion of O'odham lands are being used as a tactical battleground for the Department of Homeland Security and the US military, causing havoc in the daily lives of O'odham families. Harassment by border patrol is a daily reality for those within the one-hundred-mile border-enforcement zone, and the closer to the border, the worse it gets. Over the years, our territory has become increasingly militarized. This has culminated in the construction of a thirty-foot steel border wall across O'odham land. The damage done is beyond words and could not have been possible without the dispossession and diaspora created by the industry of mineral extraction.

O'odham territory is carved out by international borders, reservations, national monuments, wildlife refuges, bombing ranges, military bases, and settled areas. Because of historic interagency collaboration in establishing these institutions, it is common for local police, border patrol, park service officers, and private security to carry out systematic acts of discrimination toward O'odham and other indigenous people. But how did this come to be?

Displacement of O'odham by the National Park Service

A'al Wappia, also known as Quitobaquito, was once one of many traditional homesites for Hia Ced O'odham families. Hia Ced had maintained seasonal homes in the area since time immemorial. However, as settlers were making mining claims in and around the surrounding areas, concerted efforts were made to push O'odham away from their original homes. In August 1935, F. Bonaventure Oblasser sent letters to local and Washington, DC, officials, local governor Carl Hayden, and the then-commissioner of Indian Affairs, John Collier, notifying them of certain lands excluded from the newly coined Papago reservation, which would eventually be renamed the Tohono O'odham Nation.[1] The text of the letter read as follows:

> Honorable Sir: When the Papago Indian Reservation was formed in 1917, it was the intention to include all the Papagos and their lands. Since none of the committee members had more than a few years experience in this West territory, it is not surprising that some of the Papago holdings should have been overlooked. As a member of the committee of 1917, I am writing these few lines to suggest means of rectifying our errors, by confirming to the Papagos the few parcels that have been omitted from the Reservations. I refer specifically to three tracts. First, to the Coyote Mountain and especially the land of Pablo Ligero. Second, to the village of Akchin, in the

---

[1] Father Bonaventure Oblasser, OFM, Collection, Box 4, Courtesy of University of Arizona Libraries, Special Collections.

Southwestern part of the Papago Domain, and *thirdly to the holdings of the nomadic Papagos, sometimes called Arenenos* [Hia Ced O'odham] *in the barren lands West of the Papago Reservation.* All of these tracts should have been included in the Reservations in 1917. The Indians, I know, ask that they be included now.

Bonaventure goes on to describe the land in detail, noting that the local copper mining company, Phelps Dodge Corporation in Ajo—"the party most interested in the land questions of this section of the country"—had "no objections." He then concludes by mentioning that Hia Ced O'odham were "overlooked."

Finally I am asking you to secure for the nomadic members of the Papago tribe, who formerly roamed over the rough stretches between the Western boundary of the domain of the Papago Pueblos and the lands of the Yumas, but who have now settled into small communities South of Ajo, a secure title to their lands. *These Indians, have to date, been entirely overlooked by the Government.* I would suggest that under the guidance of the Sells agency, these Indians be induced to file on their present fields and wells. Since these have been occupied for more than five years, this should form no difficulty.

However, rather than grant recognition of any type of land holdings to Hia Ced O'odham, the US government instead began to uphold a policy of removal and erasure. The Ajo area became a booming copper mining company town. The surrounding areas became subject to land grabs by various agencies under the Department of the Interior. The US intra-agency collaboration historically ensured that areas in and around Organ Pipe National Monument would no longer be hospitable to O'odham. After the park service designation in 1937, Cabeza Prieta Wildlife Refuge in 1939, and the Barry Goldwater Bombing Range in 1941, Hia Ced O'odham were effectively cut off from accessing important ceremonial sites, foraging, praying, or living on their traditional areas.[2] Park service officials became increasingly hostile toward O'odham living in the area, and families were forced to move.

National Park Service (NPS) officials often go by the mantra of conservation, yet the claim that these federally managed lands "protect" often belies the experience of the indigenous peoples who have been dispossessed of land. When Hia Ced O'odham were forced to forever abandon their homes at Quitobaquito in the late 1950s, the NPS cited conservation goals. The ultimate irony of this situation is that if O'odham had been allowed to stay in and around their homes, Trump's recent border wall would not have been possible. Ultimately, the NPS collaborates with and often serves alongside the goals of US economic interests and border policy, which are a far cry from the stated goals to protect.

Mining Connections to Militarization

Many O'odham in surrounding villages were forced to move to nearby towns to survive. For much of the twentieth century, the copper industry boomed, and Ajo was very much a company town. Like many mining communities in the Southwest, Ajo was segregated. In my grandparents' days, the local swimming pool was drained on a weekly basis before "whites only" days to swim. The mine itself is located on historic villages where brown folks lived. In my parents' day, Mexican Town and Indian Village were closest to the mine, reflecting a good portion of its labor force. Around the time I was born, all the houses in Mexican Town and Indian Village were knocked down to make way for a larger copper mine.

---

[2] Peter S. Bennett and Michael R. Kunzmann, *A History of the Quitobaquito Resource Management Area, Organ Pipe Cactus National Monument, Arizona*, Technical Report Number 26 (Cooperative National Park Resources Studies Unit, 1989), 24–31.

Then copper prices tanked and the copper mine closed forever. A mass exodus of brown families followed. My aunts, uncles, and cousins had to leave town to find work elsewhere, but they did not let us kids forget our family's history there. As a tiny toddler, my aunt and uncle had us cousins pose on the stoop of the freshly bulldozed home of my grandparents. They had stories about every rock and marker around that place—the smell of the food, the layout of the families, the games they would play. I grew up very much in envy of the community they once had.

I was lucky enough to grow up in an Ajo that still had some connections to its roots. We all grew up with links to Mexico. A lot of families had people on both sides and would travel back and forth regularly. We had a lot more freedom to cross back and forth in the 1990s. Things started to rapidly change after September 11, 2001. That is when I first remember the xenophobia, and rapid militarization followed. I remember feeling the sense of impending doom for my hometown as early as the Real ID Act of 2005, the act that allowed the "waivers of law" along the border in the first place. Soon after, internal checkpoints were installed. As every year passed, more border patrol. Before we knew it, they were an unavoidable aspect of my hometown. Ajo was no longer this lonely mining town in the middle of the desert. Border patrol had overtaken it.

Around 2012–2013, US Border Patrol put its housing in the middle of town, right next to where my mother and all her sisters and brothers went to Catholic school. Things grew progressively worse and more militarized from this point on, to where my tiny little hometown has transformed into an entirely different place.

The Border Wall Crosses Hia Ced O'odham Territory

Although the history books in public schools don't speak of it, O'odham have a long history of resistance—from mission revolts during the Spanish conquest era to current times. Our fight against the border wall brought back the spirit of that resistance. For the first time in centuries, O'odham from different communities came together to resist an occupation.

Border wall construction began in August 2019, and those of us opposed to it were desperate to do everything in our power to stop construction. It was a difficult time, full of bad and worse news as we watched hordes of construction vehicles move into Ajo, turning our quiet desert town into a loud, angry, and bustling place. Pro-wall media came and made a spectacle about detonating explosives on Monument Hill, a place where Apache warriors are buried from historical battles. They strategically chose the day the Tohono O'odham Nation chairman, Ned Norris, was in Washington pleading for protection of the area. The blatant disrespect for ancestral remains was a theme throughout this time. From August 2019 to the summer of 2020, we scrambled together to resist in any way possible. Though it was O'odham ancestral territory, conditions were inhospitable to us.

The pandemic began in March 2020. By the summer of 2020, an outbreak within Southwest Valley Constructors (SWVC) slowed construction a bit, fooling many of us into thinking we had a few more months until construction workers reached A'al Wappia. However, construction crews were determined to build the wall in record time. Saguaros and other protected desert life were toppled and discarded without a second thought. Before we knew it, the wall was closing in on our sacred site. Those of us opposed to it were incredibly distressed, as water levels at the spring had dropped down to an all-time low. We feared it would dry out completely. On top of that, damage to the desert and ecosystem was vast and permanent.

Construction workers ended up transporting the pandemic to Ajo, with their nonstop travel from their homes to the main camps that surrounded the community, bringing death and disease to my area—as if the death rate from the prevention through deterrence policy wasn't enough. Ironically, fear of disease traveling north from south of the border was one of the xenophobic outcries that had prompted a call for a wall between the United States and Mexico in the first place. Yet here it was the wall workers who brought disease. Not only that, but many were also obnoxious about the pandemic and refused to wear masks.

That summer felt somewhat apocalyptic. Wildfires ablaze in the Catalinas and along the coast in California caused the normally blue desert sky to morph into an eerie reddish-orange color. To make things even scarier, the beautiful oasis at Quitobaquito was drying up as construction came nearer and nearer the spring. As endangered turtles and fish scrambled to survive, the once flourishing ecosystem did not look good. Meanwhile, O'odham had been coming together in prayer and to account for the losses. As we prepared through ceremonial runs and prayer gatherings, things were looking grim. Meanwhile, we were inspired by actions on Kumeyaay traditional territory to resist the wall in their area.

The O'odham Revolt of 2020

After a year had passed and so much damage was done, a formidable collective resistance finally started to take shape. The first action to actively block construction took place at Stinger Bridge and Iron on August 26, 2020, on Akimel O'odham traditional territory, in Coolidge, Arizona. The company was assembling and transporting the metal bollard panels to the border. A group of O'odham blocked the entrance of the facility for two hours.[3] While this action generated press and excitement in making opposition known, we knew a greater amount of resistance was needed to achieve our goal of stopping the wall.

---

[3] Alisa Reznic, "Indigenous Activists Protest Wall Contractor in Coolidge," Arizona Public Media, August 27, 2020.

On September 9, 2020, Amber Ortega and I woke before sunrise to check on the status of A'al Wappia. We had established a routine of monitoring Quitobaquito and documenting changes whenever we had the chance to make it out there. As we went our separate ways to say our prayers for this sacred place, we both heard a loud noise and ran toward it. In the circumstance, we didn't give it much thought—we could not allow the desecration of such a sacred place. We each ran in front of a heavy piece of machinery, using our bodies to block construction from taking place. We sang songs and took turns exchanging water in the desert heat. After an hour of planting ourselves there, a camera crew arrived and our subsequent arrest was published on Indigenous Action's site.[4]

We were there for approximately two hours before we were taken away. We were arrested by cross deputized NPS agents with the help of several border patrol agents, who worked together to lift me out of the bulldozer bucket. Amber followed me, and we were loaded into a van and taken to the Lukeville Station for booking. We were then taken and imprisoned overnight in Corecivic in Eloy, Arizona—Akimal O'odham territory.[5] We were charged with violating the initial closure order, issued by the NPS to give clearance for construction.[6] While we were in prison, other O'odham and allies showed up in solidarity to further halt panels from going up in and around Quitobaquito. In some instances, land defenders were nearly detained. However, there was strength in numbers, and due to group effort, many evaded arrests. In the weeks and months that followed, several violent exchanges took place with border patrol and NPS officials protecting the interests

---

[4] Rudy, "Arrested Halting Border Wall Construction Threatening Sacred Site," Indigenous Action, September 9, 2020.

[5] Ryan Devereaux, "Indigenous Activists Arrested and Held Incommunicado after Border Wall Arrests," *The Intercept*, September 16, 2020.

[6] US Department of Interior, "Temporary Closure Order—Southeast Border Road (Roosevelt Reservation) from Lukeville Port of Entry East to Santa Rosa Mountains," August 22, 2019.

of wall workers.[7] By September 28, 2020, the NPS issued another closure order effectively sealing the area off from all O'odham.[8]

Efforts culminated on October 12, 2020, Indigenous Peoples' Day, when land protectors held a prayer action at the checkpoint near Organ Pipe National Monument headquarters. They were met with tear gas and rubber bullets. An O'odham man was shot in the heart with a rubber bullet at close range while engaged in song and prayer. Eight adults and three minors were arrested and jailed. By that point, we were overwhelmed by court cases and could no longer sustain our revolt. Sadly, our uprising had come to an end. By the end of Trump's term, the border wall in Organ Pipe National Monument and Cabeza Prieta Wildlife Refuge was completed. Under Biden's term, construction of the wall on the Barry Goldwater Bombing Range also continued. Since then, we continue to hear of the devastating impact.

Future generations of O'odham on both sides of the border face significant challenges on our traditional territory. Along with the travesty of the border wall, a "virtual wall" composed of Elbit surveillance towers has been built across the borderlands. These spy towers effectively force people crossing the border on foot into deadlier areas of the desert. These towers also monitor our communities 24/7, while the border patrol continues to violate

---

[7] "Officials with U.S. Border Patrol and the National Park Service repeatedly ordered the group to move, warning them the site was closed to the public. But when the protesters refused, armed federal agents knocked them to the ground, yanked them apart and drew stun guns in a confrontation caught on camera." Teo Armus, "Indigenous Groups Protesting Wall Construction Clash with Federal Agents," *Washington Post*, September 23, 2020.

[8] National Park Service, "Temporary Closure Order "West Border Road (Roosevelt Reservation) from Monument Hill west to Quitobaquito Springs • The entirety of South Puerto Blanco Drive from SR85 west to Quitobaquito Springs • North Puerto Blanco Drive from the intersection of North Puerto Blanco Drive and Pozo Nuevo Road, south to South Puerto Blanco Drive," September 28, 2020.

our human rights and dignity. The US Border Patrol continues to take both immigrant and O'odham lives with impunity. Injustices have been so numerous that many have lost hope. However, by standing up for our ancestral territory, we are showing future generations that the spirit of resistance is still alive and well. In the continued presence of adversity, we must maintain strong relations with our families and connections across all borders and barriers that come between us. We must remember that our roots are stronger than any walls will ever be.

10

El Bloqueo

Walling In a Nation

Miguel A. De La Torre

Attempts to economically relegate a country into submission are often sought through economic isolation, specifically preventing the country from participating in global trade and engaging in international commercial opportunities. Usually employed during times of military conflict, a blockade (*bloqueo*) seeks to prevent food, supplies, medicine, and weapons from entering or leaving a country. This military strategy of erecting an invisible wall—employed for millennia—has proven effective. For example, during the US Civil War, the Union forces successfully imposed a blockade (known as the Anaconda Plan) upon ten crucial Confederate States' ports, crippling the South's main economic engine: cotton exports. The economy of the Confederacy nearly collapsed, contributing to their eventual military defeat.

Blockades are considered a legal international tool, as per the United Nations, which verified their legal status in 1945. Probably the longest *bloqueo* in history involves the United States and its sixty-plus-year economic act of aggression against Cuba. Originally an arms embargo, it was imposed on the island by the Eisenhower administration in March 1958 to prevent the sale of weapons to the Batista dictatorship. Two years after Batista's overthrow, in October 1960, the Eisenhower administration imposed another embargo on the island, this time on all US exports to Cuba (except food and medicine) in retaliation for Cuba nationalizing three US-owned oil refineries. The Castro regime was, at the time, responding to the US refusal to export oil to the island.

Since the emergence of the US empire at the conclusion of the Spanish-American War, the United States has engaged in what came to be known as gunboat diplomacy. Basically, the United States reserved for itself the right to send Marines into any country bordering the Caribbean—or engage in covert CIA-led operations—to protect US business interests. These regime changes were pursued whenever any country on the "American Lake" chose to exercise its own sovereignty or follow its own destiny in ways perceived as unfavorable or unprofitable to US concerns. In some cases, brutal dictatorships and military juntas were installed after the United States deposed democratically elected presidents. Millions of peasants, students, church leaders, and intellectuals throughout the twentieth century were abducted, tortured, disappeared, or killed while opposing these US-backed installed governments.

In April 1961, the Kennedy administration, in keeping with the gunboat diplomacy legacy and committed to the Eisenhower administration's plan to overthrow the Castro regime, approved a military intervention that resulted in the Bay of Pigs fiasco. By February 1962, the embargo was extended to include almost all exports. The Castro regime, fearing the United States would attempt another military operation, obtained ballistic missiles from the Soviet Union to serve as a deterrent. US spy surveillance, however, discovered the installation of the missile bases, leading to the thirteen-day Cuban Missile Crisis of 1962. The Kennedy administration responded by imposing a "quarantine" on all medium-range ballistic missiles headed for Cuba capable of delivering a nuclear attack. As we know, Khrushchev blinked, and the crisis was averted. The blockade officially ended on November 20, 1962, when the missiles were removed from the island.

As far as the United States was concerned, the blockade terminated with the end of the physical naval cordon, but for the Cubans on the island, *el bloqueo* continues to this day. Attempting to soften the harshness of the term "blockade," the United States has referred to its strategy as an embargo. Some, like former senator Marco Rubio of Florida (appointed as secretary of state during the second Trump administration), go so far as to proclaim from the Senate chamber that there is not even an embargo on Cuba.[1] But such semantics are not lost on the inhabitants of the island. A blockade by any other name is still a blockade. True, naval ships no longer patrol the shores of the island, but a military presence is no longer necessary within a global economy to obtain the same suffocating results. According to a UN report, *el bloqueo*, since its inception, has cost Cuba about $130 billion in damages by 2020.[2] Ironically, the United States is also impacted negatively, to a tune of about $1.2 to $3.6 billion per year, according to the US Chamber of Commerce.[3]

Assuming the role of dictating the sovereignty of other nations, the United States threatens any nation that engages in trade with Cuba for nonfood items with the termination of financial aid. Any food imported from the United States must be paid for in cash, unlike all other nations, which can use credit. This *bloqueo*, this invisible wall, impacts every aspect of Cuban life, creating a humanitarian crisis and contributing to the devastation of the Cuban economy, especially after the fall of the Soviet Union—a time dubbed as "the Special Period." Unable to obtain

---

[1] Marco Rubio, "Press Release: Cubans Aren't Protesting Because of an Embargo—They Want Liberty," Senate Office of Marco Rubio, July 20, 2021.

[2] David Adler, "Cuba Has Been Under US Embargo for 60 Years. It's Time for That to End," *The Guardian*, February 3, 2022.

[3] Daniel Hanson, Dayne Batten, and Harrison Ealey, "It's Time for the U.S. to End Its Senseless Embargo of Cuba," *Forbes*, January 16, 2013.

machinery replacement parts has impacted their ability to provide clean water. Unable to obtain medicine and soap, hospitals are understocked, contributing to an increase in the spread of infectious diseases like COVID-19. Not surprisingly, the world community has condemned this *bloqueo*. Since 1992, the United Nations has voted each year calling to end the *bloqueo*, with only the United States and Israel voting against the resolution.[4] The question before us, ignoring the humanitarian considerations, is how effective has this *bloqueo* been?

Assessing *el Bloqueo*

When John F. Kennedy signed Proclamation 3447 (Embargo on All Trade with Cuba) on February 3, 1962—during the height of the Cold War—it was designed to stop the spread of communism by isolating Cuba. At the time, Lester D. Mallory, the assistant secretary of state, stated that because "the majority of Cubans support Castro," and that "there is no effective political opposition," then "the only foreseeable means of alienating internal support is through disenchantment and disaffection based on economic dissatisfaction and hardship." He envisioned that *el bloqueo* would make "the greatest inroads in denying money and supplies to Cuba, to decrease monetary and real wages, to bring about hunger, desperation and overthrow of government."[5] Despite the majority of the Cuban population at the time supporting the Castro regime, and because there existed no creditable opposition, the US gunboat-diplomacy attitude took it upon itself to overthrow

---

[4] UN Affairs, "UN General Assembly Calls for US to End Cuba Embargo for 29th Consecutive Year," *UN News*, June 23, 2021.

[5] Lester D. Mallory, "Memorandum #499 from the Deputy Assistant Secretary of State for Inter-American Affairs (Mallory) to the Assistant Secretary of State for Inter-American Affairs (Rubottom), April 6, 1960," in *Foreign Relations of the United States, 1958–1960, Cuba*, vol. 6 (Office of the Historian, US Department of State).

the new government simply because a people chose to pursue a sovereign destiny that did not align with US interests. The explicit purpose of *el bloqueo* was to create such economic devastation and hunger that the people would turn and revolt against the government they once supported.

After sixty-plus years, we can definitively state that *el bloqueo* has failed to achieve any of its geopolitical goals. The people did not overthrow the government, Fidel retired and died of old age on his satin sheets, his brother Raul also retired and is living a tranquil, peaceful life, while a new generation of Cubans has taken the reins of the revolution. The only things that *el bloqueo* has accomplished are denial of money and supplies, decrease of monetary and real wages, and hunger and desperation for most ordinary people. Both Republican and Democrat officials, including presidents, may fool themselves into believing their draconian measures only target the regime, but as a frequent visitor to the island, I can attest to the hardships faced by everyone due to *el bloqueo*.

Having returned to my homeland during the Special Period, shortly before and after Fidel's death, during the thawing of relationship under the Obama administration, and during the "maximum pressure" levied by the first Trump administration, it is obvious that the constant hardships faced by the people are due to the economic consequences of *el bloqueo*. US rhetoric claims these measures are necessary to stand with the people in their quest for liberty, but one is hard-pressed to understand how this is accomplished when the policies only make them poorer, hungrier, and sicker. Additionally, it provides the regime with justification to crack down on dissidents, who are portrayed as working with a foreign enemy who is determined to undermine and overthrow the government. Ironically, I noticed greater openness among the people as *el bloqueo* was loosened during the Obama administration and greater restrictions as the Trump administration tightened the screws. If the expressed goals of *el bloqueo* have not been realized—if, instead, it has strengthened the grip of an authoritarian government—then why pursue a failed strategy, especially after some six decades? This chapter argues that the invisible wall called *el bloqueo* erected around the island of Cuba is more the result of a fanatical vengeance against the first country defying US hegemony within the Western Hemisphere than it is a strategy to achieve any realpolitik goals.

A Covetous US Eye

Cuba's proximity to the United States creates a relationship where neither can ignore the other. This continues to be true despite the present-day *bloqueo*. In fact, the proximity is its cause. Since the inception of the United States, a covetous gaze has always been cast toward the island, best expressed in a letter by then–secretary of state John Quincy Adams of the Monroe administration to his minister in Madrid, Hugh Nelson. Adams wrote,

> These Islands [Cuba and Puerto Rico], . . . are natural appendage to the North American continent; and one of them, Cuba, . . . has become an object of transcendent importance to the political and commercial interest of our Union. . . . The annexation of Cuba to our federal republic will be indispensable to the continuance and integrity of the Union itself.[6]

Similarly, former president Thomas Jefferson, in a letter to then-president Monroe, wrote, "I candidly confess, that I have ever looked on Cuba as the most interesting addition which could ever be made to our system of States."[7]

---

[6] John Quincy Adams, "Letter to Hugh Nelson, Minister in Madrid: April 23, 1823," in *Writing of John Quincy Adams*, vol. 7, ed. Worthington Chauncey Ford (Macmillan, 1917 [1823]), 369–421.

[7] Thomas Jefferson, "Letter to President James Monroe: October 24,

Interest in Cuba was due to its military importance. During the Revolutionary War, British troops used ports in La Habana to attack rebel strongholds, a fact the strategic-minded new republic never forgot. US policy concerning Cuba was based on the geographical proposition that the island would be the first line of defense (offense) of the southern flank. The desire of the United States to possess Cuba was met with an equal desire by Cuba's elite to be possessed. During the Madison administration, negotiations for the island's annexation transpired with rich Cuban landowners. They failed due to fears of a British invasion if annexation occurred. Britain, at the time, represented the greatest impediment to US expansionist desires. An invasion would surely have introduced the abolition of slavery in Cuba, a consequence dreaded by powerful slaveholding groups in both the United States and Cuba.

By 1822, during Cuba's Golden Age, the idea of annexation was reintroduced. The island's elite saw union with the United States' slavocracy as the salvation of their sugar plantation economy and the prevention of a slave revolt akin to Haiti's. Additionally, sugar, which was being produced in over one thousand plantations throughout the island, would become available to US markets without paying tariffs. But concern on how Britain would react persisted. Then–secretary of state John Quincy Adams, considering negotiations, wrote in his diary, "The question was discussed what was to be done.... There are two dangers to be averted ... one that the island should fall into the hands of Great Britain; the other that it should be revolutionized by the Negroes."[8]

Spain's colonial grip on the Americas loosened during Napoleon's invasion of Spain, as wars of independence spread

---

1823," in *The Life and Selected Writings of Thomas Jefferson*, ed. Adrienne Kock and William Peden (Random House, 1944 [1823]), 708–10.

[8] Louis A. Pérez Jr., *Cuba: Between Reform and Revolution* (Oxford University Press, 1988), 100.

throughout Spanish America. The 1823 Monroe Doctrine—a British proposal made to the United States—sought to protect the Western Hemisphere from non-British European colonial powers filling any vacuum caused by the Spanish Empire's declining influence. The doctrine opened Latin America to British trade, bringing most of the hemisphere under their economic orbit. As Latin America fought for their independence from Spain (1823–1825), General José Antonio Páez (named commander of the proposed Mexican-Colombian expedition by Bolívar) planned to assist those in Cuba wishing to join the struggle. But Cuba was the richest colony within the Spanish Empire and the largest world producer of sugar, and economic booms generally are not fertile ground for revolutions.

While white *criollos* (those born on the island) in the rest of Latin America resented the power of *los peninsular* (those born in Spain), Cuba's white *criollos* were placated by Spain's assurance of providing a market for Cuban sugar and by stationing Spanish troops to alleviate fears of the "Africanization" of the island, à la Haiti. Then–secretary of state Henry Clay, concerned that a liberated Cuba might lead to an abolition of slavery, negatively impacting southern states, blocked any movement toward independence. Assuming Cuba would eventually be joined to the United States, he perceived independence as complicating future designs for annexation.[9]

In 1848, the Cuban exilic community of New York, witnessing the annexation of Texas, urged then-president Polk to purchase Cuba from Spain. Against the opposition of northern states, Polk offered to purchase Cuba for $100 million. Spain rejected Polk's offer. Unable to purchase Cuba, the United States sought to take it by force. General Narciso López—who fought against the forces of Simón Bolívar—organized an invading expedition force

---

[9] Hugh Thomas, *Cuba: The Pursuit of Freedom* (Da Capo, 1998 [1971]), 104.

from New Orleans. There he fashioned the Cuban flag, which was based on the Texas flag. Several US veterans who partook in the invasion of Mexico joined the expedition, along with others who were attracted by the offer of one thousand dollars plus 160 acres of Cuban land. The 1848 expedition did not sail, due mostly to the newly elected president and Mexican War hero Zachary Taylor, who preferred buying Cuba rather than risking the possible destruction of a slave-based system. When his efforts to purchase the island again failed, an 1850 second expedition force was developed by López, with the assistance of Mississippi governor John A. Quitman, who wanted to absorb both Cuba and the rest of Mexico. A six-hundred-man force landed near Cárdenas and succeeded in capturing a Spanish garrison and governor. However, the locals refused to join López's forces, correctly perceiving it to be a US invasion. López retreated to Key West, where, months later, he organized a third expedition and sailed with four hundred men. This time, he was captured by the Spaniards, tried for treason, and publicly garroted.

By 1854, President Pierce returned to the negotiation table and offered to purchase the island for $100 to $130 million to no avail. In retaliation for Spain's rejection of the offer, the United States signed the Ostend Manifesto, maintaining that Spain's refusal to sell justified—both by human and divine laws—the United States' seizure of Cuba. When the United States abolished slavery after a bloody civil war, the Cuban sugar elite's support for annexation abruptly shifted to opposition lest it threatened the interests of their own sugar plantations. Once Spain also ceased supporting slavery and called for its abolition, Cuba's sugar elite abandoned its loyalty to the Crown and called for independence.

On October 10, 1868, Carlos Manuel de Céspedes issued a proclamation for independence, known as *el grito de Yara*, launching the first of three wars for independence. Despite patriotic revisionism, the first war for independence, known as the

Ten Years' War (1868–1878), was motivated more by frustrated planters seeking alternatives to the impending abolition of slavery and Spain's obstinacy in dealing with the planters' concerns. The resulting war was limited to the eastern part of the island, causing havoc and millions of dollars' worth of damage. By war's end, closer investing connections between US firms and Cuban planters developed. North Americans, becoming naturalized Cubans, were soon controlling the sugar industry, and, by extension, the Cuban economy. By 1885, US engineers, technicians, machinists, and scientists (mostly Bostonians) flocked to Cuban sugar plantations to fill the need for skilled laborers. US investors underwrote many of the sugar *centrales*, leading to the transfer of sugar production from Cuban to North American hands.

Under North American leadership, the old Cuban oligarchy came to an end, as a monoculture economy, which pushed out most other crops, developed. As Ramon O. Williams, the US consul to La Habana, reported in an 1886 dispatch to the United States: "Cuba is already inside the commercial union of the United States. The whole commercial machinery of Cuba depends upon the sugar market of the United States."[10] By 1896, the American Sugar Refining Company (Sugar Trust), organized in 1887 by Henry Osborne Havemeyer, controlled 70 to 90 percent of all refined sugar eaten within the United States.[11] As Cuba was becoming economically Americanized, a third attempt for independence was made (1895–1898), originally called the Cuban War for Independence.

This final rebellion was against Spanish colonialism and those locals who remained complicit. Sugar planters became the enemies of independence, and their plantations became battlefields. *La*

---

[10] Elizabeth Abbott, *Sugar: A Bittersweet History* (Duckworth, 2009), 279.

[11] Leland Jenks, *Our Cuban Colony: A Study of Sugar* (Vanguard, 1928), 28–29.

tea, the torch, became the revolutionary strategy where cane fields were set ablaze, and the means of sugar production destroyed. This scorched-earth policy ground sugar production to a halt. Of the 1,100 sugar mills in operation in 1894 prior to the war, only 207 survived; those that did were hopelessly in debt and at the brink of financial ruin.[12] More tragic was how the "war for independence" from the Spanish colonial power was transformed into the "Spanish-American War." War with Spain launched the United States' first venture into world imperialism. Less interested in settler colonialism (via Manifest Destiny), the United States became more concerned with controlling peripheral economies to obtain financial benefits for the center.

US military participation converted the independence war into a war between two colonial powers—one declining and one rising. The prize was possession of Cuba, along with Puerto Rico, the Philippines, and Guam. Prior to declaring war, President William McKinley offered Spain $300 million for the island with an additional $6 million going directly to the Spaniard mediators. When those negotiations failed, the yellow journalists at Pulitzer's *New York World* and Hearst's *New York Journal*—along with a mysterious internal explosion aboard the warship USS *Maine* on April 25, 1898—provided the necessary justification for the United States to enter the conflict. When the war ended, the Cuban army requested to be present during the ceremony, witnessing Spain's departure from the island, but the United States rejected the request. Thus, on January 1, 1899, at noon, the Spanish flag was lowered in Santiago and the US flag—not the Cuban flag—was raised. It was the new empire who was present during the symbolic "transfer of power," bidding Spain farewell as the United States took its first imperialist steps.

---

[12] Pérez, *Cuba*, 193.

The Rise of the US Empire

Prior to the United States entering the conflict, Cubans were on the threshold of winning their long-fought thirty-year struggle for independence. A year after the start of the third war, the insurgents were operating virtually unchecked across the entire island, fighting demoralized Spanish troops.[13] But a covetous United States acted on their jealously as they witnessed European powers carving up Africa and Asia for colonial exploit through the Berlin Conference of 1884, believing that they, too, must enter the race of conquering foreign lands in order to be great. General Leonard Wood, commander of the Rough Riders and later colonial governor of Cuba (1899–1902) understood and conveyed this sentiment in a letter to his wife: "the first great expedition our country has ever sent oversea and marks the commencement of a new era in our relations with the world."[14]

Upon Cuban soil, the United States launched its first venture into world imperialism. The earlier conquests of Texas and northern Mexico represented the expansionist Manifest Destiny settler-colonial ideology of extending the US boundaries and physically possessing and repopulating lands occupied by Others. But with the 1890 Wounded Knee massacre, the Wild West was won. No more Indian land existed to conquer. Cuba and Puerto Rico represented a new shift, where conquest was tied to a US economic structure that was transitioning from competitive capitalism to monopoly capitalism. This ideological shift within capitalism merged with imperialism and found its first expression within the Caribbean. The United States became less interested in acquiring territory. Instead, they strived to control and benefit from peripheral economies. Then-senator John Mellen Thurston,

---

[13] Louis A. Pérez Jr., *Cuba between Empires: 1878–1902* (University of Pittsburgh Press, 1983), 68.

[14] Hermann Hagedorn, *Leonard Wood: A Biography*, vol. 1 (Harper & Brothers, 1932), 160.

former chief counsel for Union Pacific Railroad, while mindful that the United States was amid the deepest economic depression up to that date, bluntly expressed these sentiments:

> War with Spain would increase the business and earnings of every American railroad, it would increase the output of every American factory, it would stimulate every branch of industry and domestic commerce, it would greatly increase the demand for American labor and in the end every certificate that represented a share in any American business enterprise would be worth more money than it is today.[15]

On the verge of Cuban military victory, the United States entered the conflict without an invitation, declaring war on Spain to ensure that the States did not lose the island to the Cubans. President McKinley made this point clear in a private correspondence: "While we are conducting war and until its conclusion, we must keep all we get; when the war is over we must keep what we want."[16]

As the Spanish-American War ended, the idea of annexation was in the air. In 1887, newspaper articles called for Canada's annexation—a proposition the Democratic Party attempted to add to its 1888 presidential platform. By 1898, the United States annexed Hawaii and Guam, followed by parts of the Samoa Islands in 1899. The annexation of Cuba was also expected, especially as a substantial contingency of Cubans favored union with the States. These Cubans, mainly wealthy planters who feared possible political instability caused by the expulsion of the colonial power, questioned the ability of the rebels to engage in self-government. They believed the United States could fill the vacuum left by a departing Spain.

---

[15] Abbott, *Sugar*, 371.
[16] James A. Henretta, Rebecca Edwards, and Robert O. Self, *America: A Concise History*, vol. 2, *Since 1865*, 5th ed. (Bedford / St. Martin's, 2012), 633.

The original goal of US military occupation was to Americanize the island to facilitate annexation by reorganizing their social and political systems along US mores and traditions.[17] The end results were neither annexation nor protectorate, but neocolonialism. The United States wanted little to do with annexing what they perceived to be an inferior and ungrateful people. In a letter to diplomat Henry White, President Theodore Roosevelt seethed, "I am so angry with that infernal little Cuban republic that I would like to wipe its people off the face of the earth."[18] Senator Henry Cabot Lodge, in a September 16, 1906, letter to the president, best captured the mood of his fellow congressional colleagues:

> Disgust with the Cubans is very general. Nobody wants to annex them, but the general feeling is that they ought to be taken by the neck and shaken until they behave themselves. It is a great disappointment to me and I had hoped better things from them.... I think that this Cuban performance would make the anti-imperialists think that some people were less capable of self-government than others.[19]

In another letter written on September 29, just two weeks later, Lodge goes on to express that

> the conduct of the Cubans is disheartening. After all we did for them and the way in which we started them without debt and the Island all in perfect order, to find

---

[17] Louis A. Pérez Jr., *Essays on Cuban History: Historiography and Research* (University Press of Florida, 1995), 38, 41.

[18] Theodore Roosevelt, "Letter to Henry White," in *The Works of Theodore Roosevelt*, vol. 14, memorial ed. (Charles Scribner's Sons, 1923), September 13, 1906.

[19] Henry Cabot Lodge, *Selections from the Correspondence of Theodore Roosevelt and Henry Cabot Lodge, 1884–1918*, vol. 2 (Charles Scribner's Sons, 1925), 233.

them fighting and brawling at the end of four years furnishes a miserable picture of folly and incompetency.[20]

Although annexation was off the table, the neocolonial project that economically doomed Cuba was not. As racial classifications were becoming more rigid within the US milieu, as the so-called science of eugenics was becoming more acceptable, as Jim and Jane Crow was becoming more established, the United States entered the race for colonial possessions and tightly tied their colonial ventures with racism. This economic colonial spirit made its first appearance in Cuba. Within twenty years of US occupation of the island, almost every other nation along the Caribbean, perceived as being occupied by inferior people, was invaded by the US Marines to establish what is now euphemistically called "regime change."[21]

The Spanish-American War reduced Cuba to a wasteland. Nonetheless, a new generation of North American carpetbaggers arose, seeing Cuba as virgin territory. The war created large indebtedness for Cubans. North Americans easily acquired bankrupt properties by simply paying back taxes. The now-defunct hegemonic Cuban sugar ruling class was replaced by US companies thanks to the 1903 United States–Cuba Reciprocity Treaty and the 1903 Permanent Treaty, which shifted the profitability of sugar production and marketing toward the United States while

---

[20] Lodge, *Selections from the Correspondence of Theodore Roosevelt and Henry Cabot Lodge*, 2:237.

[21] During the twentieth century, either US military incursions (*italicized*) or covert/indirect operations (**bold**) occurred in the following countries to bring about regime change or protect the status quo: Cuba, *1906*, *1912*, *1917*, *1933*, **1960**, **1961**; Costa Rica, **1948**; Dominican Republic, **1904**, *1916–24*, **1930**, **1963**, *1965*; El Salvador, **1932**, **1944**, **1960**, **1980**, **1984**; Granada, *1983*; Guatemala, **1921**, **1954**, *1960*, **1963**, **1966**; Haiti, **1915**, *1994*; Honduras, *1905*, *1907*, **1911**, **1943**, **1980**; Mexico, *1905*, *1914*, *1917*; Nicaragua, **1909**, *1910*, *1912*, *1926*, **1934**, **1981**, **1983**, **1984**; Panama, *1908*, *1918*, *1925*, **1941**, **1981**, *1989*.

increasing the island's dependency on manufactured finished goods. In 1903, there were thirty-seven American-land-owned companies operating in Cuba.[22] By 1905, North Americans acquired title to 60 percent of all rural Cuban property, while another 15 percent of rural land remained in the hands of the Spaniards.[23] US military occupation of the island denied Cuba its independence, transforming the island into a vassal state. The Cuban army was disbanded, an American-style education system was imposed, the Stars and Stripes flew from public buildings, and the economy was restructured under US hegemony.

The US takeover of the sugar industry is best demonstrated when we consider that, in 1905, twenty-nine mills were in North American hands, representing 21 percent of production; by 1916, there was an increase to sixty-four mills, representing 53 percent of the harvest. A decade later, 1926, the number of mills owned by US interests rose to seventy-five mills, accounting for 63 percent of the harvest. US companies that depended on sugar (e.g., Coca-Cola, Charles Hires Company [soft-drink manufacturer], and Hershey's) attempted to buy sugar directly from Cuba or acquire their own mills on the island.[24] The political leaders who arose after the Spanish-American War developed close relationships with the largely US-controlled sugar companies because they generated most of the state and nonstate revenues. *Caudillos*, profiting from this arrangement, were able to maintain power through their ability to distribute wealth, land, market access, jobs, and political office based on the loyalty and support received.[25] While Cuban land and labor became a source of wealth

---

[22] Robert Whitney, *State and Revolution in Cuba: Mass Mobilization and Political Change, 1920–1940* (University of North Carolina Press), 23.
[23] Pérez, *Cuba*, 195–96.
[24] Thomas, *Cuba*, 541.
[25] Whitney, *State and Revolution in Cuba*, 8.

for large US sugar companies, the country's political structures became a source of wealth for an emerging Cuban elite that was aligned with foreign sugar interests. Subjugating Cuba's economy to the US economy aggravated several major socioeconomic problems throughout the first half of the twentieth century as Cuba became a dependent vassal. These problems included development at a slower rate of economic growth; the cultivation of one crop—sugar—creating an excessive dependency on exports; political dependency on the United States (during the 1920s, Cuban delegations to international conferences were led by North Americans with Cuba voting with the United States on all issues); high rates of unemployment and underemployment; large inequalities in living standards, particularly between the urban and rural populations; and passive monetary policy, which allowed US dollars to circulate freely.

Between 1909 and 1929, US capital investment in Cuba increased by 700 percent. Approximately 80 percent of Cuba's imports came from and 60 percent of her exports went to US markets. During the 1920s, 95 percent of Cuba's main crop, sugar, was United States bound. Forty percent of all raw sugar production was owned by North Americans, two-thirds of the entire output of sugar was processed in US-owned mills (mostly located in Baltimore), and the product left the island through the Havana Dock Company, also in US hands. Additionally, 23 percent of nonsugar industry, 50 percent of public service railways, and 90 percent of telephone and electric services were owned by US firms. Investments in Cuba ranged from $700 million to $1 billion, controlling Cuba's most profitable sectors. Nickel deposits were mined and processed by Nicaro, a US-built plant. This capture of the Cuban economy was possible because, during US military occupation, Military Governor Wood granted 218 tax-exempt mining concessions mostly to US firms. Of the four oil refineries, two were owned by US companies, the other two by Royal Dutch Shell and British Petroleum. All banks were in US and British hands, with one-quarter of all deposits located in foreign branches. Approximately 90 percent of the export trade of Havana cigars went through North America, which controlled half of the entire manufactory process.[26]

Punishing Cuba's Defiance

Denied independence, Cuba existed to enrich its northern neighbor. So, when the 1958 Castro Revolution occurred, it was first and foremost an anti-US colonial rebellion within the Western Hemisphere. Rather than a Marxist-Leninist revolution (even though Raul Castro did have ties to Soviet-based movements), the revolution was a third-world rebellion against the subjugation of Cuba to the region's hegemonic power. This became obvious when, a few days after the revolution's triumph, Fidel Castro went to the town square of Santiago during the sixty-year anniversary of when the Cuban rebels were not allowed to enter the city to accept Spain's defeat in 1899. To mark the occasion, Castro said, "It will not be like 1895 when the Americans came and took over, intervening at the last moment, and afterwards did not even allow Calixto Garcia to assume leadership, although he had fought at Santiago de Cuba for thirty years."[27] Castro's move toward communism, occurring after the Bay of Pigs fiasco, was more about finding allies to circumvent another invasion than any ideological commitment. The 1959 revolution served to demonstrate that nations in Latin

---

[26] Robin Blackburn, "Themes of the Cuban Revolution," in *The Cuba Reader: The Making of a Revolutionary Society*, ed. Philip Brenner et al. (Grove, 1989), 5–7, 45; Franklin W. Knight, *The Caribbean: The Genesis of a Fragmented Nationalism*, 2nd ed. (Oxford University Press, 1990), 237; Philip C. Newman, *Cuba before Castro: An Economic Appraisal* (Prentice Hall, 1965); Thomas, *Cuba*, 466.

[27] Fidel Castro, *Speech to Citizens of Santiago*, Town Main Plaza, January 3, 1959.

American could break free from US hegemony and dependency, demonstrating how Latin American nations did not have to be organized along a pro-US capitalist paradigm.

Cuba's success in breaking free from the United States spurred rural guerrilla movements throughout Latin America, notably in Venezuela, Bolivia, Guatemala, and Peru. For Cuba to be both a model to emulate and a sponsor of other nations breaking free from US hegemonic control was simply, in the US view, beyond the pale. The current *bloqueo* makes more sense if it is understood as a vindictive US attitude toward Cuba for successfully leaving an abusive relationship and encouraging others to do likewise. Think of the jilted and forlorn lover. After centuries of pursuit, the United States finally captured and ravished their conquest. But the relationship that was established was economically abusive and appalling. Finally, the battered partner breaks away and changes the locks to the bedroom. With a hurt pride, the former lover sets out to stalk, to intimidate, to harm, and to punish the former partner for the audacity of leaving them. Viewing Cuba as the battered partner who left might best explain why *el bloqueo*, which achieved none of its geopolitical goals, remains in place—simply to spite and discipline Cuba for wanting to set its own independent path.

A Literary Conclusion

I end this chapter with a popular short story about the fictious Liborio (a recognizable caricature that personifies the Cuban people) that is retold in John Sayles's 1991 novel *Los Gusanos*. Through humor, this anecdote helps explain why the existing invisible wall, *el bloqueo*—despite its irrationality—continues:

> One afternoon [in the days just after the War for Independence, Liborio] is alone in the field, still cutting as the others ate their meager lunch, and he chops through a

row of cane to discover God, sitting in an expensive white suit on a little stool, the type *colonos*[28] used when they stopped to survey their property.

"Buenos días, Liborio," said God. "I have come to see how my Cubanos are doing."

Liborio stands with his cloths soaked with sweat, his hands cracked and bleeding, his feet bare and filthy. He sticks his machete into the ground, spits out the piece of cane he had been chewing on, and thinks for a long time about what he should say to God.

"First of all, *Señor*," he said, "we are no longer subjects of the King of Spain. We are free men."

"I can see that," said God, looking at Liborio from head to foot. "The difference is astounding."

"But I wonder something," Liborio continued, "why life is still so hard."

God smiled at him. "My son, nothing on this earth can be perfect, or nobody would want to go to Heaven. Sugar is sweet, but man has to labor to take it from the ground. The ocean is wide and bountiful, but it has sudden storms and dangerous currents to pull you under and drown you. This Cuba is so beautiful, the pearl of all my creation, so I had to make the pests, los mosquitos, the sea urchin, the thorn of the marabú, all so life here would be less than Paradise. Nothing can be perfect in this world."

Liborio pondered this, trying to fathom the wisdom of God's ways. "But nothing can mar the beauty of freedom," he said finally. "Surely freedom is perfect?"

God smiled again. "For that," he says, "I created *los yanquis*."[29]

---

[28] Sugar planters.
[29] John Sayles, *Los Gusanos: A Novel* (HarperCollins, 1991), 258–59.

11

This Is US

Borderline Citizens, Borderscape Colonialism, and the Borderlands of Black Folk in America

STACEY FLOYD-THOMAS

How do we actively and honestly "think" about borders and how they not just configure but undeniably control our sense of being in the world? Whether we are talking about physical barriers erected to separate two sovereign nation-states, dark lines drawn by a cartographer to demarcate different mapped sections of the globe, or the conceptual designation of such boundaries in accordance with how we understand our genetic, geopolitical, and generative realities, the true power of any border is how it is imagined by an individual, institutional, or international determination of difference between us and them.

As a Black woman who is also a womanist Christian social ethicist born and raised in Texas (arguably the loudest and most "borderline" state in the Union), when I think about borders, I cannot help but think about how I was taught to color within the lines. While I was taught to see the world in living color, to behold any beauty within it was to color inside the lines figuratively and literally. Just as borders moved over Mexico and became Texas, likewise coloring within the lines became how to follow rules or act within borders generally. Just as hues marked people's humanity, red and blue marked our party politics and the world differently. These color lines marked the borderlines of our existence, and the borderscape was the dynamic, ever-changing negotiation of living in color in ways that our citizenship and belongingness gave us space and place that were constantly being made and remade by how actions kept us within the lines and never beyond the border.

The US versus Them Border

By definition, borders are designed to establish a sense of being and belonging for those people caught on either side of them. According to British social psychologist Henri Tajfel, our human predilection for a positive self-image motivates us to boost the reputation of our own group, often at the expense of devaluing and the investment of debasing others. This dynamic of "us" versus "them" is at the core of intergroup dynamics.[1] Even before we can intervene in actions to decolonize occupied lands and oppressed peoples, we must first interrogate our own sites of torment and torture—our occupied minds and oppressed spirits. In order to mount up the crucial modes of resistance leading to our liberation, we must begin that process by recognizing that, no matter the state when, where, and how we find ourselves in this world, *this is US*.

Best known for his concept of "imagined communities," political theorist Benedict Anderson argues that nations are not natural entities but rather are constructed through shared narratives and symbols. With this perspective in mind, in Anderson's estimation, borders are not merely geographical lines but also symbolic boundaries that define and maintain national identities. Taking this concern a step further, psychiatrist and revolutionary thinker Frantz Fanon exposed the psychological

---

[1] Henri Tajfel, "Social Identity and Intergroup Behaviour," *Social Sciences Information* 13 (1947): 65–93.

effects of colonialism as a system of subjugation. Fanon viewed borders as instruments of domination designed and implemented to control colonized peoples, especially those indigenous inhabitants of what we call the Global South, through geopolitical division and subsequent dispersal.[2] Fanon argued for the necessity of decolonization vis-à-vis the dismantling of colonial borders and the active pursuit of liberation both physically and psychologically. Paying special attention to the palpable tensions in the transition from colonial and postcolonial experiences of Africa, philosopher Achille Mbembe critiques the way borders were drawn and enforced during colonialism, often disregarding cultural and historical realities. Mbembe argues that these borders continue to shape the lives of people in postcolonial Africa and elsewhere around the globe (such as Palestine), leading to brutal conflict and inequalities.[3] Black feminist geographer Katherine McKittrick, who emphasizes the racialization and engendering of space, argues that borders are not just physical boundaries but also social and cultural constructs that reinforce racist and sexist hierarchies.[4] McKittrick's work highlights the ways in which borders are used to exclude and marginalize certain groups.

To be certain, while scholars such as Anderson, Mbembe, Fanon, and McKittrick all impart different perspectives on the premise of borders and their significance on human interactions with distinct nuances and emphases, they all share a critical understanding of borders and boundaries altogether. They recognize that borders are not neutral entities but are shaped by power dynamics, historical processes, geopolitical contexts, and

---

[2] See Frantz Fanon, *The Wretched of the Earth*, trans. Richard Philcox (Grove, 2004 [1963]).

[3] Achille Mbembe, "The Idea of a Borderless World," *Chimurenga Chronic*, republished by *Africa's Country*, November 11, 2018.

[4] See Katherine McKittrick, *Demonic Grounds: Black Women and the Cartographies of Struggle* (University of Minnesota Press, 2006).

cultural ideologies. Their work challenges the idea of borders as natural or inevitable and highlights the ways in which they can be used to create and maintain inequalities.

From Color Line to Borderline

Centuries went into constructing the geopolitical architecture of the United States as a bastion of whiteness in order to become a first world power. To make such a grandiose claim, the greatly whitewashed fiction about this place called "America" not only erased the borders of Canada to its north as well as Mexico and Latin America to its south, but it also entirely hijacked the lifeworld of Indigenous Peoples of the Western Hemisphere. Moreover, it kidnapped and hauled African bodies by the millions across the Atlantic Ocean and left decimated and dis-membered African civilizations in its wake. As the dreadful Middle Passage served to create a debased, dehumanized blackness that casts a vast and wide shadow upon the global map, it simultaneously marked its imaginary contingent borders and built its immense colonial power vis-à-vis variegated hues of white supremacy while entrapping all nonwhite, non-Western humanity in its conceptual cave as illustrated in Plato's *Republic*.[5]

In his 1903 masterpiece *The Souls of Black Folk*, W. E. B. Du Bois advances two separate yet related concerns that are germane and critical to consider. On the one hand, DuBois describes the psychological traumatized state of Black humanity under the unbearable weight of white supremacy as "double consciousness." He famously defines it in the following fashion:

> It is a peculiar sensation, this double-consciousness, this sense of always looking at one's self through the eyes of others, of measuring one's soul by the tape of a world that

---

[5] Plato, "Allegory of the Cave," in *The Republic*, trans. Thomas Sheehan, 514–17.

> looks on in amused contempt and pity. One ever feels [one's] two-ness—an American, a Negro; two souls, two thoughts, two unreconciled strivings; two warring ideals in one dark body, whose dogged strength alone keeps it from being torn asunder. The history of the American Negro is the history of this strife—this longing to attain self-conscious [personhood].[6]

Arguably, Du Bois's observation asserts that, in many ways, the entirety of Black existence—mind, body, and soul—is a veritable battleground in which tyrannical whiteness has run roughshod over the contested terrain that renders our national identity defined by borderline citizenship rather than birthright citizenship, reveals the borderscapes of colonialism, and marks the borderlands of Black folks' existential being in America.

On the other hand, Du Bois traces the traumatic and prophetic demarcation of the twentieth century as the salient era that defined the terror of the "color line" as the imperialistic, hegemonic global divide that was effectively configured in Manichaean terms of honorable whiteness versus dishonorable Blackness with *all* other racial-ethnic identities caught negotiating their fate and waging their best and bets between these extremes. Du Bois famously described the concept of the color line: "The problem of the twentieth century is the problem of the color-line—the relation of the darker races to the lighter races of men in Asia and Africa, in America and the islands of the sea."[7] More than one hundred years after Du Bois advanced the color line, we now acknowledge that the United States has situated itself as the center of this racist moral geography. To escape the defiled trappings of the manifold oppression and indignities that confront the rest of the planet is not just what it means to be a part of the so-called first world but also what it means to be

---

[6] W. E. B. Du Bois, *The Souls of Black Folk* (Penguin, 1989 [1903]), 5.
[7] Du Bois, *The Souls of Black Folk*, 1.

American. Yet, when Black people in general and Black women in particular find themselves within a nation that claims to be the paragon of democracy that purportedly grants the gifts of life, liberty, and the pursuit of happiness to everyone within its borders and shores, their experiences actually give proof to the contrary. The productive and reproductive labor of Black women increased the territorial and material expansion of whiteness even as it exponentially increased the marginalization and thingification of Black people. DuBois's color line was enfleshed, not just theorized, most poignantly onto Black women's bodies.

When one thinks about what it means to be "borderline," it invokes the following issues: being in an intermediate position or state; not fully classifiable as one thing or its opposite; not quite up to, typical of, or as severe as what is usual, standard, or expected; characterized by psychological instability in several areas (such as interpersonal relations, behavior, and identity) but only with brief or no psychotic episodes. In weighing those various definitions, the lattermost one presents the greatest cause for alarm. Unfortunately, the border induces a perception that is only intensified by physical jeopardy and reinforced by a dreaded space of liminality for far too many people. For people whose existential reality depends on how they navigate and negotiate a mental and emotional crisis of being, the permanence of place does more than merely objectify the person and persecution of Black women in a process called "thingification,"[8] wherein one's agency is not self-determining

---

[8] Anthony Pinn argues that "thingification" in this instance, "Black religion" represents "a capacious term that … plays a key role in African Americans' struggle" for what he calls "complex subjectivity, a mode of being defined by ambiguity and multidimensionality, which is an experience mediated by and through the Black body [and] constitutes an important site of resistance against oppression. It contains an aesthetic, both in performance and style, that must be more prominently considered" in our reflection on Black life, agency and being. See Anthony B. Pinn, "Black Bodies in Pain and Ecstasy: Terror,

but only an instrument that marks utility for someone other than oneself. The border, thus, develops them as property and underdevelops them as human—form and function but divided in its purposes and never whole. The process of thingification makes the human a tertium quid—an unidentified third element made up of two elements that are known but whose formation becomes another entity.[9] When Plato introduced the *tertium quid* in 360 BC as the "third something"—literally defined in Latin as the "third what"—we got a glimpse of how bodies become borderlines of geopolitics but also borderscapes that signify how others must understand their formation as citizen, civilized, or communal within the divided state of America. This subtle alchemy when enfleshed by Black women is implicitly clear and explicitly exercised in the Black feminist sentiment that if "all the women are white and all the Blacks are men," then the remnant of those who remain as Black women necessitates that "some of us [must be] brave" or break under the weight of such in(visible)dignity.

This third something is akin to the third rail on a train track. While appearing similar to the other two tracks that run alongside it, it is the most necessary and more powerful track, just as its agency is the hardest to discern. Better known as the "live rail" that borders the rail system and provides the electric power to the train, it keeps the conductor of the train literally on track and carries such an inordinate amount of voltage, easily enough to guide the train and carry all the cargo, but it is so charged that it alone is untouchable and deadly. Black women's agency represents the third rail of US geopolitics; when and where race and gender enter the public sphere, their presence marks the spatiotemporal configuration of American existence itself. This phenomenon not

---

Subjectivity, and the Nature of Black Religion," *Nova Religio: The Journal of Alternative and Emergent Religions* 7, no. 1 (2003): 76–89.

[9] George Grate, *Plato, and the Other Companions of Sokrates*, vol. 2 (Adegi Graphics, 1999 [1865]), 418.

only holds gravitas thematically but it analogously bears terrible weight: if the "Black woman" can be seen as a particular figuration of the split subject that DuBoisian sociodemography or Fanonian psychoanalytic theory posits, then this century marks the site of "its" profoundest revelation. The violation and violence visited upon Black women's wombs has made it so that, for centuries, Black women's progeny have been held captive as property and prisoners while being perennially profiled as predators and parasites—regarded thusly as any and everything except persons. In one fell swoop, the project, the process, and the progeny of modernity have, in many ways, cited Black women's bodies as the bounty for colonialism, capitalism, and citizenship for whiteness and made their Black women's persona the herstory of white horror, seemingly belying Black hope.

Whiteness as Contested Territory

Key scholars of race and racism, such as American studies professor and sociologist George Lipsitz and critical race theorist Cheryl Harris, have argued that whiteness has been deemed a form of property in a world defined by white supremacy. I would like to extend and expand that metaphor to envision whiteness as territory that, for those clinging to that identity, has to be protected and preserved. Without question, Cheryl Harris's "Whiteness as Property" and George Lipsitz's *The Possessive Investment of Whiteness* both argue that whiteness is a form of sociopolitical and economic capital. However, they approach this concept from different though related angles.[10]

When considering whiteness as investment, Lipsitz argues that whiteness yields marked dividends for white people in a tripartite

---

[10] See Cheryl I. Harris, "Whiteness as Property," *Harvard Law Review* 106, no. 8 (June 1993): 1707; George Lipsitz, *The Possessive Investment in Whiteness: How White People Profit from Identity Politics* (Temple University Press, 1998).

fashion in terms of economic benefits (access to greater economic opportunities, education, and social networks), social privileges (advantages such as being less likely to be subject to discrimination or stereotyping), and psychological benefits (a sense of moral superiority and personal entitlement). Lipsitz emphasizes the active and ongoing nature of this investment by arguing that white people often maintain and reproduce systems of white supremacy to protect their privileges either consciously or unconsciously as a means of safeguarding the status quo. Meanwhile, as a legal scholar and critical race theorist, Harris's perspective on whiteness as property was a groundbreaking argument wherein she explicitly argued that whiteness is a form of property that has material significance in regards to the ways it can be bought, sold, and inherited. This property confers certain rights and privileges, such as the right to exclude others and to benefit from the labor of nonwhite people. Harris's perspective highlights the structural and institutional aspects of whiteness, emphasizing how it is embedded in laws, policies, and social practices. While both Lipsitz and Harris approach the concept of whiteness as property from somewhat different perspectival angles, their arguments are fundamentally interconnected. Both scholars argue that whiteness is a form of social and economic capital that is unequally distributed and maintained through systems of power, privilege, and positionality.

Yet my argument departs from their viewpoints in my contention that the literal and figurative boundaries imposed both by and on behalf of whiteness are an intrinsic effort to preserve whiteness as a precious territory wherein nonwhite beings are both unwanted and unwelcome in any capacity approaching equality. According to antiracist scholar Robert Jensen, "White is not, by definition, the norm, the standard, the best. White is just white."[11] Nevertheless, Jensen asserts the cold, harsh reality that

---

[11] Robert Jensen, *The Heart of Whiteness: Confronting Race, Racism, and White Privilege* (City Lights, 2005), 2.

> Politically, white is not just white, of course. White is power. And using the terms white/non-white reminds us of that. What do people of color have in common? That is, what makes the category "people of color" make sense? The only commonality is that the people in that category are on the subordinated side of white supremacy. Nothing intrinsically links people of indigenous, African, Latino, and Asian descent in the United States except their common experience of being targeted, abused, and victimized—albeit in different ways at different times—by a white-supremacist society. Take that experience away, and the category of "people of color" vanishes. The people, of course, don't vanish, nor does their color change. But nothing links them except the experience of oppression. And the group perpetuating that oppression is white, another socially created category defined by power.[12]

In his 1902 novel *Heart of Darkness*, Joseph Conrad wrote, "The conquest of the earth, which mostly means the taking it away from those who have a different complexion or slightly flatter noses than ourselves, is not a pretty thing when you look into it too much."[13] Ironically, although Conrad's masterwork was a fiercely anti-imperialist project, it also is fervently racist in its perspective. Several decades later, James Baldwin used the moral authority of his experience in a debate with William F. Buckley that unmasks the American phase of this white supremacist settler colonialism by contending, "What one begs the American people to do, for all our sakes, is simply to accept our history."[14]

---

[12] Jensen, *The Heart of Whiteness*, 2–3.
[13] Joseph Conrad, *Heart of Darkness* (Bantam, 1981 [1902]), 65.
[14] "James Baldwin vs. William F. Buckley: A Legendary Debate from 1965," February 18, 1965. Baldwin's moral authority made a fool of the disingenuous Buckley's patrician racism. Video and transcript available at the American Archive of Public Broadcasting website.

According to Pulitzer- and Nobel Prize–winning novelist Toni Morrison, in her classic *Time* interview titled "The Pain of Being Black," the border that will never be bridged nor crossed in America is inscribed into the very fabric of American life and seared in the brains of all its residents and immigrants as imaged and marked on Black flesh. In explaining this as part of the impetus in her writing, Morrison states,

> I feel personally sorrowful about black-white relations a lot of the time because black people have always been used as a buffer in this country between powers to prevent class war, to prevent other kinds of real conflagrations.... If there were no black people here in this country, it would have been Balkanized. The immigrants would have torn each other's throats out, as they have done everywhere else. But in becoming an American, from Europe, what one has in common with that other immigrant is contempt for me—it's nothing else but color. Wherever they were from, they would stand together. They could all say, "I am not that." So in that sense, becoming an American is based on an attitude: an exclusion of me. It wasn't negative to them—it was unifying. When they got off the boat, the second word they learned was "nigger." Ask them.[15]

Herein, human migration is not merely about relocation but also aspiration. The capacity of one's ability to assimilate to whiteness not only gives passage and proximity to whiteness. It also determines who can im/migrate and who can claim citizenship; where and under what conditions one can find belonging is at the core of moving from borders to a brave new world. As such, border crossing is the praxis and performance of being adept at leaving one's familiar terrain—be it land or frame of reference

---

[15] Toni Morrison, "The Pain of Being Black," *Time*, May 22, 1989.

(home)—with the prospect of finding a better territory (hope) so that one can enjoy the rights of a better life, liberty, and pursuit of happiness (humanity).

Overcoming the Boundaries of a Colonized Mind

Drawing quite heavily on British colonial explorer Henry Morton Stanley's favorite phrase to refer to Africa, Sigmund Freud infamously described the purported challenges for psychoanalysis to explore women's sexuality as being comparable to exploring the "dark continent." While providing a long-overdue postcolonial critique of psychoanalysis, theorist Ranjana Khanna illustrates how the convergence of psychoanalysis, colonialism, and femininity together serves as the ideological engine for Western imperialism. Moreover, Khanna argues how nation-statehood for Europe's former colonies institutes the violence and domination of European imperialist history as a normative feature.[16]

In *Dark Continent of Our Bodies: Black Feminism and Politics of Respectability*, Black feminist scholar E. Frances White takes on one institution after another as she recenters the role of Black women within the broader intellectual heritage of the United States.[17] Confronting the ignominious and much-maligned politics of respectability in what it means to be honorable as white/citizen, White moves the reader from simplistic views of race and gender in the nineteenth century through Black nationalism and the radical movements of the 1960s and their latter-day relationship to Black feminist thought, to the linkages between race, gender, and sexuality made evident by the likes of Toni Morrison and James Baldwin. White provides a rigorous critique of Freudian

---

[16] Ranjana Khanna, *Dark Continents: Psychoanalysis and Colonialism* (Duke University Press, 2003).

[17] E. Frances White, *Dark Continent of Our Bodies: Black Feminism and Politics of Respectability* (Temple University Press, 2001).

psychoanalysis for its white supremacist and patriarchal biases as well as its tendency to pathologize all female sexuality. She argues that Freud's theories are rooted in a patriarchal worldview that privileges male experiences and constructs female sexuality as deficient or deviant. White contends that the foundation of Freud's psychoanalytic theories is deeply rooted in a thoroughly racist and sexist worldview that assumes white cisgender male dominance and against the assumed inferiority of female and racial-ethnic Others, most evident in classic Freudian concepts such as the Oedipal complex, penis envy, and the Electra complex, among others. Next, White argues that Freud's wholesale pathologization of female sexuality often renders female sexuality to be abnormal and aberrant in nature, portraying it as problematic or deviant. By way of illustration, his concept of hysteria is often linked to women's repressed sexual desires. Moreover, Freud's essentialization of gender, in White's view, marks his tendency to argue that gender roles are naturally prescribed, assuming an inherent difference between men and women that are primarily and indelibly biological. Ultimately, White believes that Freud's overemphasis on biological factors in shaping gender identity, human behavior, and sexual traits abnegates the significantly detrimental impact of sociocultural factors. In sum, White's critique of Freudian psychoanalysis highlights its limitations in understanding negative impressions of racial subordination, female sexuality, and gender dynamics in a global imperial-colonial regime.

Taking seriously bell hooks's rallying of all feminists of color—especially Black ones—to move "from margin to center," White presents identity politics as a complex activity with entangled branches of race, gender, and sexuality bound up in alternate waves of invisibility and hypervisibility, as well as of defiance and passivity and conformism.[18] White highlights the specific elements of psychoanalysis's conceptual framework that drew

---

[18] bell hooks, *Feminist Theory: From Margin to Center* (South End Press, 1984).

upon, and advanced, the conjoined racist and sexist ideology at the heart of colonial conquest. White augments Sander L. Gilman's arguments that Freudian psychoanalysis reflects how Freud dealt with his anxiety about himself as a Jew by projecting it onto other cultural "inferiors"—such as women and people of color. Remarking on Freud's own struggles to reconcile his feelings and fears about his own Jewish identity in racial and gendered terms, the internalization of these ideas and images of racial difference shaped the questions of psychoanalysis.[19] Freud's fixation on the "primitive" or "savage" mind, which infects psychoanalytic thinking to this very day, is a prime example. On the other hand, psychoanalysis's assertion that all human subjects are inhabited by such "primitivity" continues to not just obscure but undermine developmental assumptions.[20]

While dissecting and dismantling the preternatural misogynoir at the core of Freudian psychoanalysis, in the compelling opening of her book White employs oral stories from her family's past to shed light on the essence of storytelling, focusing not only on what is expressed but also on what remains unspoken. From within those silent liminal zones and interstitial spaces—the border spaces of Black womanhood—she embeds the phenomenological framework to construct a helpful history of the inception and development of Black feminism and a critique of major Black feminist writings. In the three chapters that follow, she addresses the obstacles Black feminism has already surmounted and must continue to traverse.

Written during the fin de siècle in this landscape of horror and hope, Black female educator and activist Anna Julia Cooper famously declared in her 1892 book *A Voice from the South* that

---

[19] Sander L. Gilman, *Freud, Race, and Gender* (Princeton University Press, 1993).

[20] Stephen Frosh, "Psychoanalysis, Colonialism, Racism," *Journal of Theoretical and Philosophical Psychology* 33, no. 3 (2013): 141–54.

"only the BLACK WOMAN can say when and where I enter, in the quiet, undisputed dignity of my womanhood, without violence and without suing or special patronage, then and there the whole Negro race enters with me."[21] As an exemplar of Black women's agency, authority, and autonomy, Cooper spent much of her more than a century of life striving to redefine the limitations and opportunities for women of color in a white supremacist heteropatriarchal society set up for their disregard and ultimate downfall. Cooper was a distinguished scholar, educated in the United States and beyond. She demonstrated the elevated status of Black womanhood in direct opposition to the subjugation and disempowerment of Black humanity in a regime dominated by the ascendancy of Jim and Jane Crow within the United States and eurocentric imperialism that held much of the globe. Cooper boldly pronounced that Black womanhood must attain the full equality and guaranteed progress promised by the nation—even as it was still eluding many of her Black male and white female counterparts. Central to her call was the vital belief that, in order to assert one's sense of being, one also needs to make claims on the sacred primacy of space and time in this world. To wit, as Lipsitz notes in his dissection of race, place, and power, "We learn that race is produced by space, that it takes places for racism to take place."[22] Expanding and extending this observation to include other intersectional facets of human identity—gender, sexuality, class, age, ability, religion, and education, to name only a few—it could be reasonably noted that a Black woman finds herself every time and everywhere in contested terrain in a world that is desperately trying to exclude her. Cooper fought tirelessly throughout her life to recenter the visions and uplift the voices of Black women in pursuit of a freer, fuller, and more just society for everyone.

---

[21] Anna Julia Cooper, *A Voice from the South* (Aldine, 1892), 31.
[22] George Lipsitz, *How Racism Takes Place* (Temple University Press, 2011), 5.

Unfortunately, little has changed since Cooper's declaration. Sojourner Truth changed her name to be synonymous with the real lived journey that Black women have had to chart for themselves and their community, but to be a border crosser, intersectional intercessor, and cultural conveyor of the race has meant that Black women have had to "sell the shadow to support the substance"[23] of what it meant to be chattel and citizen while in what Maya Angelou termed these "yet to be United States":[24]

> "Let's face it," says literary critic Hortense Spillers, as a Black woman, "I am a marked woman, but not everybody knows my name. 'Peaches' and 'Brown Sugar,' 'Sapphire' and 'Earth Mother,' 'Aunty,' 'Granny,' God's 'Holy Fool,' a 'Miss Ebony First,' or 'Black Woman at the Podium': I describe a locus of confounded identities, a meeting ground of investments and privations in the national treasury of rhetorical wealth. My country needs me, and if I were not here, I would have to be invented."[25]

Since their ancestors' arrival via enslavement, African Americans continue to be perceived, profiled, policed, and pathologized by the manipulation of national borders. The physical and virtual borders that force out and fortify oppressive structures have always been marked by the parameters of dishonorable blackness and honorary whiteness by determining who is stereotyped, shunned, and segregated within society. Likewise, the moral activity, spiritual aspirations, and sociopolitical intervention that take place while resisting these forces give way to the formation of borderlands as a subaltern counterpublic.

---

[23] "I sell the shadow to support the substance." See Sojourner Truth, The Library Company of Philadelphia holdings, 1864, available online.

[24] Maya Angelou, "These Yet to Be United States," in *Maya Angelou: The Complete Poetry* (Random House, 2015), 234.

[25] Hortense Spillers, "Mama's Baby, Papa's Maybe: An American Grammar Book," *Diacritics* 17, no. 2 (Summer 1987): 65.

The borderlines of the borderlands pertaining to Black life and culture marked by American settler colonialism are informed and designed with the colonization of the mind and racial profiling of Blackness as the veritable cartography of colonized consciousness. American settler colonialism has ensured that captive-based capitalism has been alongside the creative genius and social critique of those who would not allow color to cast them out of their consciousness or collective resolve for freedom and flourishing. Thus, the very concept of Blackness is the true border that traces the power of whiteness in the United States. Whether in analog or digital, no matter what format the map I depict, the borderlines are always drawn in the blackest tones possible. Similarly, the borderscape illustrates how colonialism has been played out in living color wherein the geopolitics of race, space, and place of power occupy the materiality and mentality of many Americans in persistent efforts to chart a variety of borders—geographic, racial, cultural, economic—for the dehumanization of those perennially trapped on the wrong side of the borderline.

The Strange Case against Kamala Harris

When thinking of the Black women ensnared by the literal and liminal nature of the US border, let's take notice of the strange case of Kamala Harris. Witnessing the influx of tens of thousands of migrants from Central America reaching the US-Mexico border during the early months of his administration, President Joe Biden tapped Vice President Harris as his second-in-command to help address the influx. Seeking a decidedly long-term approach to the burgeoning humanitarian crisis, this emergency at the US-Mexico border afforded Republicans an opportunity to exploit what they felt was one of her biggest political liabilities: a perceived weakness on immigration. As the 2024 Republican presidential nominee, Donald Trump took aim at Harris, his 2024 election rival, with the adamant belief that her biggest policy weakness was immigration. Trump, as well as countless conservative operatives, inveighed against Harris by calling her "America's border czar." The Trump campaign blasted Harris for her role in dealing with the border crisis. Yet ever since the Trump campaign's first attack ad, "border czar" has been a loaded, contested term used as a dog whistle among conservatives who believe it is utterly appalling for any Black woman to be given the authority for policing the border and responsibility for safeguarding national sovereignty. Although Harris was preeminently well suited for her role, thanks in large part to her decades of public service as both a lawyer and a lawmaker, this castigation of Harris was emblematic of the deep-rooted history of misogynoir embedded in the nation's culture wars as well as its cartography.

When confronting accusations from her conservative critics that the roughly 10 million illegal border crossings and alleged 250,000 fentanyl-related overdose deaths were the vice president's fault, the Harris campaign quickly responded that former president Trump was relying on "his trademark lies" as usual. While her foes and critics on the right were attacking her for the failure of an immigration bill that they had orchestrated, immigration reform advocates insisted that Harris should be providing more legal pathways to citizenship. Only a few years after her first failed US presidential bid in 2019 and now written into history based on her 2024 bid as the first Black woman to have run a formidable national campaign, Harris as a biracial child of immigrant parents was now challenged on the national stage about her record on border security during her vice presidency in the Biden White House. In turn, she promised to resurrect the failed bipartisan border legislation, crafted by a Republican US senator, that would increase funding for much-needed border patrol agents, ICE detention beds, and immigration judges—all as fulfillment of the GOP's wildest dreams. Further, she was caught in the crossfire of the right's twin attack on both immigration policies and identity politics of whether she was really Black enough due her racial heritage or woman enough due to the fact that she bore no children of her own.[26]

Conclusion

In Kamala Harris, like Barack Obama before her, W. E. B. Du Bois before him, and Sojourner Truth and Anna Julia Cooper before him, we see blackness become the horrific conjured marker and hope-filled character mark of these yet-to-be-united-states. Blackness becomes a bold border not only for North Americans but for the two-thirds world (as their first world power), for civilization (marked by a color line), and for hope (amid the horrors of colonization). From its perception to reception, the past pillage, the perennial profiling, and this present political predicament lay a broad, universal truth in stark relief: What we *say* bonds us is not necessarily what we *see* bond us. In fact, the difference between what we believe (*theos*), what we value (*ethos*), what we feel (pathos), and what we understand (*logos*) often contradicts what we see and behold as bonds when they border us.

The best rendition of "America the Beautiful" is Ray Charles's. Though he couldn't see the beauty of America in living color, neither across its socioeconomic, racial, or political landscape nor its "purple mountains majesty," in reality his profound musical imagination—fueled by his faith, artistry, and hope as a blind Black man in segregated America—helps us envision what we never would have been able to imagine on our own. This sort of

---

[26] Will Grant, "Is Kamala Harris a 'Failed Border Czar' as Trump Says?" BBC News, August 14, 2024; Dan Gooding and Billal Rahman, "As DNC Looms, Kamala Harris Faces Attacks from Both Sides on Immigration," *Newsweek*, August 16, 2024; Dan Merica, Nicholas Riccardi, and Chris Megerian, "Kamala Harris Chose a Long-Term Approach When Tasked to Tackle Rise in Border Crossings," PBS, August 14, 2024.

insight from someone who could actually see other realities or was freer to dream new, better possibilities empowers all of us. What is the meaning of holding on to something (be it home, hope, or humanity) that seems elusive amid existential evil in the face of terror and territory? Our border crossings today suggest that the measure of BIPOC inner conviction and inward character toward liberation and promised lands emerges against the walls of whiteness that have been built upon the bodies of blackened people. Blackness is the gravitational pull and the cultural memory that has every resident of these yet-to-be-united-states wagering whether they will be honorary whites or dishonorable Blacks. But there are those who are skinfolk and kinfolk who seek a brave new world, who keep their hands on the plow with hope, who pull off the vote, and who pray in hope of forging on to increase the promise of freedom rather than the territories that have designated plantations, prisons, and other parcels of pain, poverty, and powerlessness. In the face of such a problematic and perplexing history of the border, inducing such grievous physical and psychological menace to far too many people for far too long, we must declare that this is us no longer, for some of us are brave.

Conclusion

Miguel A. De La Torre

In late June 1960, when I was but a toddler, a very official looking letter from the government arrived at the run-down tenement housing where my parents lived. This rat- and roach-infested slum building in Hell's Kitchen, New York—one bathroom per tenement floor—was where my parents, who were refugees, found sanctuary after just one month of living in the United States. The government's affidavit, citing Section 242 of the US Immigration and Nationality Act, placed me on notice that I was in violation of US immigration laws and that my deportation was imminent. My crime? I overstayed my tourist visa. The letter ordered that I voluntarily self-deport in lieu of forced expatriation. Even before I could comprehend concepts like selfhood, nationhood, borders, or immigration, I already was being relegated to the shadows of empire, finding myself living and depending on the very country responsible for the expatriation from the nation that witnessed my birth—as elucidated in chapter ten.

For the undocumented, which is what I was, to be labeled "an illegal alien" reconstructs the identity as some*thing* that is "alien"—a thing that is strange and foreign, literally out of this world, usually reserved to describe Martians; and some*thing* that is "illegal"—a thing that is dangerous, literally a trespasser of laws, usually reserved to describe criminals. In the minds of those with proper and correct documentation on the right (white) side of the border, those of us from the wrong side are, by our very being, if not nature, a threat to the safety and security of the dominant culture. Ironically, the safety and security of those for whom the wall is designed to protect exists by shredding asunder the safety and security of those who have been disenfranchised, dispossessed, and disinherited for the wall's sake. To mask those abused, the term "illegal" is intentionally used as a terror-inflicting semantic technology that, with each utterance, reinforces repression and submission.

"Illegal alien" is not some neutral word when it is employed. Consider why I am called an "alien," a word that has come to signify "not belonging," but those of the dominant culture who chose to also traverse walls and live in the Global South—at a profit—are called "expats," a term that signifies adventure. To be labeled "illegal" connotes malfeasance. Those of us who have been called "illegal" are perceived as inherently bad, if not evil. Do we call a driver who forgot their driver's license at home an illegal driver? Or do we call a taxpayer who failed to file their income tax documents on time an illegal citizen? Of course not. Not having proper documentations, either as a driver or taxes filed on time, does not make the person a criminal. Their status can be corrected by obtaining proper documentation, either by retrieving their driver's license or filing their taxes. While it is not too difficult to obtain proper documentation in these cases, when it comes to the undocumented, their demonization has given rise to bureaucratic red tape designed to make it almost impossible to migrate and obtain any proper documentation.

The reason migrants without proper documentation are labeled "illegal" has nothing to do with their character. They are constructed as "illegal" because those in power have the legislative authority to impose their definitions upon members of society. This, of course, is nothing new. Those from dominant cultures have used language to separate *them* from *us* for generations and in various contexts. Let us not forget that there was a time when it was illegal for the colonized and/or enslaved to experience the same freedom as those representing the Global North. Even within nations of the Global North, there was a time when it was illegal for women to vote. What is legal for the colonizer is usually illegal for the colonized. When laws restrict those crossing walls (physical or invisible) to participate in their full humanity, it is not the individual who is illegal; rather it is the prevailing laws that are depriving a certain group of people of their dignity that are illegal. In short, the walls themselves are illegal.

This sentiment of "illegality" was best captured by President Donald Trump who when announcing his first presidential campaigned stated, "When Mexico sends its people, they're not sending their best. They're not sending you. They're not sending you. They're sending people that have lots of problems, and they're bringing those problems with us. They're bringing drugs. They're bringing crime. They're rapists."[1] Not only did Trump undergird his political aspirations on his, and the nation's xenophobia, but he mainstreamed fear and hatred of those of us from the other side of the wall. His success in becoming the 45th and 47th president of the United States bears testimony to the fact that his message resonated with a substantial portion of the populace.

In 1969, I became a naturalized citizen of the United States. Even though I received "proper" documentation, I nevertheless spent most of my life being seen and treated as not belonging, as an outsider supposedly sucking up the social services of a generous nation. As discussed throughout this book, walls are more than just a geographical reality constructed on international lines separating the First World from the Two-thirds World. Walls signify the existential reality faced by those, like the contributors to this book, who encounter barriers that have been erected within the dominate culture's imagination to mark who is and is

---

[1] Michelle Ye Hee Lee, "Donald Trump's False Comments Connecting Mexican Immigration and Crime," *Washington Post*, July 8, 2015.

not "illegal." Regardless as to where we live, how long we have lived there, the status of our documentation, or how we or our ancestors came to find ourselves on the side of the wall designed to protect power, privilege, and profit, we live under the long darkening shadow of the wall. To trespass this erected structure of separation is to constantly live on the border between power and disenfranchisement, between privilege and dispossession, between profit and disinheritance.

As we discovered from the different chapters appearing in this book, walls are more than brick and mortar designed to delineate between two nations, two political entities. Walls can be invisible. Yes, living on the border can literally mean living in a principality adjacent to some physical barrier demarcating an artificial line. Borderlands, however, are more than just a geographical reality—they symbolize the existential reality of those being exploited by more politically powerful entities. Invisible borders separating white from Black, wealthy from impoverished, Global North from Global South exists in every nation, every city, every community, and every street within the terrain of colonizers, regardless as to how far away they may be from the physical wall. As a Latino in the United States, living 1,400 miles from the physical border erected due south from where I reside, my community has invisible walls erected separating me from the fruits of society that my labor cultivates. As rapper and revolutionary social critic Residente articulately explains:

> *Por tierra o por agua,*
> *identidad falsa,*
> *brincamos muros o flotamos en balsas,*
> *la peleamos como sandino en nicaragua,*
> *somos como las plantas que crecen sin agua.*
> *sin pasaporte americano,*
> *porque la mitad de gringolandia es terreno mexicano,*
> *hay que ser bien hijo de puta,*

Conclusion

nosotros le sembramos el árbol y ellos se comen la fruta
somos lo que cruzando,
aquí venimos a buscar el oro que nos robaron,
tenemos más trucos que la policía secreta,
metimos la case completa en una maleta,
con un pico, una pala y un rastrillo
le construimos un castillo
cómo es que dice el coro cabrón
'Immigrants we get the job done'.[2]

Walls may be impenetrable when it comes to the movement of bodies, but they remain porous to neoliberalism as the finished goods of industrial nations flow southwards while cheap labor and raw materials flow unabated in the opposite direction. Walls exists to protect what was stolen, to protect—at all costs and by any means necessary—the wealth built at the expense of those labeled "illegal" who might seek reclamation and/or restitution. Hence, borderlands under the shadow of a physical or invisible wall become a killing field.

For example, the US-Mexico wall is the locale where, every four days, five preventable deaths occur:[3] deaths of predominantly brown bodies that remain invisible within the public consciousness. And for those "lucky" not to perish in a desert, they still face

---

[2] "By land or water, false identity, we jump over walls or float on rafts, we fight like Sandino in Nicaragua, we are like the plants that grow without water, without an American passport, because half of gringolandia is Mexican terrain, one has to be a real son of a bitch, we plant the tree and they eat the fruit, we are the ones who crossed, here we come to look for the gold that was stolen from us, we have more tricks than the secret police, we packed our entire house in one suitcase, with a pick, a shovel and a rake, we built them a castle, how does the chorus go you bastard: 'Immigrants we get the job done.'" See K'naan, featuring Residente, Riz MC & Snow Tha Product, "The Hamilton Mixtape: Immigrants (We Get the Job Done)," 2018.

[3] Santos and Zemansky, "Arizona Desert Swallows Migrants on Riskier Trails," May 20, 2013.

death-dealing consequences for crossing into privileged spaces. One in ten migrants have reported some sort of physical abuse while in Border Patrol custody, and one in four reported verbal abuse.[4] My own research conducted at the border has brought me face-to-face with many who have shared similar stories of abuse. Patrol agents have been known to kidnap and rape the undocumented, brown girls some as young as fourteen years old.[5] Agents have beaten individuals to death, like Jose Gutierrez Guzman, whose assault was captured on an iPhone.[6] Border Patrol has been involved in fatal shootings, like any other United States law enforcement agency, and yet, they have less oversight. We who attempt to cross over walls, whether they be the physical one in Gaza or the invisible racial one in every US city, are the acceptable "collateral damage" that might hopefully deter others from straying from their assigned spaces in society.

For many, like me, who find themselves in the belly of the beast, living under the shadow of walls entails our disjointedness from the culture of our heritage and the culture in which we now reside, outsiders and foreigners to both. In this in-between space of borderlands, we confront economic exploitation and political marginalization. Seesawing on the wall means vacillating between the indigenous customs and traditions of our colonized heritage and the eurocentric worldview of the colonizers, brought together by the vicissitudes of conflicting cultures. Even if I sought assimilation, in the popular imagination of the Global North, I remain "illegal" and "alien," whose buffoon attempt to mimic civilization is dismissed as clownish, a task they suspect I am incapable of ever mastering. The irony, of course, is that,

---

[4] The Center for Latin American Studies, *In the Shadow of the Wall: Family Separation, Immigration Enforcement and Security* (University of Arizona, 2013), 24.

[5] Ildefonso Ortiz, "Agent Sexually Assaults Family, Kidnaps Girl, Commits Suicide," *Brownsville Herald*, March 13, 2014.

[6] Southern Border Communities Coalition, "Bring Justice Home for Jose Gutierrez," SBCC Media, YouTube, 2012.

as a refugee, I live in the country responsible for my exile. The country of my residency is a country within the Global North that constantly spews a hyperindividualist, hypermaterialist worldview while lacking the communal and the spiritual, a worldview believed inferior by those on the other side of the walls that the Global North has erected.

Walls are traversed to escape the violence and terror that eurocentric colonial ventures historically unleashed to protect their right to steal land, resources, and labor while enforcing their economic right to trade and commerce; they became crucial for multinational corporations to flourish. Walls throughout the world have been built since the so-called age of exploration (starting in the 15th century), when European powers began exploiting their neighbors to the Global South, an exploitation that continues today. The undocumented migrants attempt the hazardous traversing of these walls because foreign and trade policies over the past five centuries have created economic situations in most countries where they are unable to feed their families.

In the Western Hemisphere alone, roads were built into the Global South early in the nineteenth century. President Theodore Roosevelt's (1858–1919) "gunboat diplomacy" resulted in almost every country bordering the Caribbean and several countries in South America being invaded by US forces or covertly subverted by the CIA throughout the twentieth century. No country could determine its own destiny without the permission of that countries' US ambassador. When these countries tried to establish their own sovereignty to pursue their own destinies, regime change was imposed by the United States whenever they viewed the internal political changes as detrimental to the profitability of US corporate interests. Usually, brutal dictatorships and/or military juntas were installed to ensure enough security for corporations to prosper. At times, they were installed after deposing democratically elected presidents, as was the case of Guatemala in 1954. Millions of peasants, students, church leaders, and intellectuals were abducted, tortured, or killed while opposing the US-backed installed governments. Advanced weapons technology employed to impose the will of colonizers has often been confused with proof of advanced civilization.

Global empires from Europe and North America have employed their overwhelming military to protect the freedom of multinational corporations to build roads into economically developing countries to extract, by brute force, if necessary, their natural resources for centuries. Deprived of a livelihood; or threatened by puppet governments that arose with the supposed departure of the colonizer; or simply seeking to survive in the ecological devastation caused by the Global North hunger for resources; migrants took those same roads to escape the consequences caused by those who benefitted by the lack of walls. When one country builds roads into another country to steal their resources and/or cheap labor, why should we be surprised when people traverse those same roads after having everything stolen from them? As they come, following what has been stolen from them, escaping the violence and terrorism unleashed upon them, "build that wall" becomes the global cry to prevent dealing with what is due because of colonization.

All too often, when we discuss walls, it is conducted from the social location and privilege of residency or citizenship, from the security of living on the "right" side of the border. Because these walls—even when physical—are nonetheless social constructions, we need to rethink how they are approached. More conservative members of society demonize those on the other side of the wall or those who cross over in pursuit of their stolen resources and/or labor. Those who lean liberal may repudiate conservative's cold hearts, but their response is just as damning. They often call for a religiosity of generosity; they call for hospitality. And yet, hospitality masks who actually owns the house—who retains the power to offer "hospitality." Such liberal concepts remain nonetheless rooted within the eurocentric ideology of homeownership, ignoring that this imperial house built was cheaply constructed thanks to the low wage (or free labor) and the raw material stolen from the Global South.

Hospitality is an ancient, as well as a biblical concept that connotes more than simply making one's home available to the stranger and inviting them to a meal. The Hebrew biblical text constantly reminds the reader that all the patriarchs were foreigners and sojourners, as were the Jews during their time in Egypt when enslaved, their forty years wandering through the desert, and their time as refugees in Babylonian exile. Thus, hospitality and offering justice becomes a foundational concept to be offered the stranger, for as holy writ reminds us, you were once strangers in Egypt. The New Testament tells us that some, while showing hospitality to strangers, found themselves, without realizing, entertained angels (Heb. 13:2). Hospitality is a desirable virtue to have and practice; however, when applied as a moral imperative by which to treat those on the other side of the wall, it can mask oppression and become a damning distraction from the real justice work of tearing down the walls altogether.

Often, the so-called virtue of hospitality is invoked by good liberals as the proper response when dealing with the stranger in our midst—made a stranger due to finding themselves on the "wrong" side of the wall. This hospitality is balanced with a call for law and order, specifically the law and order that protects the privileges of those on the "right" side of the wall. Maybe the correct ethical response is not hospitality but restitution—what is due to those who were made disenfranchised by wall building? We don't want your hospitality; we want our damn house back. To make it so, we can begin by crying out in unison—"tear down these walls!"

Contributors

Brian Joseph Brown served as a minister of the Methodist Church for more than sixty years. In the 1970s he became deputy-director of the Christian Institute (CI), an ecumenical body committed to prophetic activism against racial injustice. He wrote for its theological journal, *Pro Veritate*, until the publication together with the CI and its executive staff were banned by the apartheid regime in 1977. In the 1980s he worked for the British Council of Churches. Appointments in the 1990s were as lecturer at the Federation of Selly Oak Colleges and Africa Secretary within the Methodist Missionary Society. His autobiography, *Born to Be Free: The Indivisibility of Freedom*, recounts the rise and fall of apartheid. Most recently, his book entitled *Apartheid South Africa! Apartheid Israel?* details how policies of Israel toward Palestinians today replicate the violent dispossession of land, nationality, and human rights of Black people under apartheid.

Gregory L. Cuéllar is an educator, activist, transnational scholar, blogger, and borderlands theorist. He presently serves as professor of Hebrew Bible at Austin Presbyterian Theological Seminary. Much of his research represents a commitment to disciplinary interference, focusing on topics like migration and the Bible, national museums and orientalism, immigration detention and religion, and the postcolonial trauma in biblical poetry. Two of his most recent books are *Archival Criticism* and *A Borderland Hermeneutic*. He has been a visiting scholar at the Centre on Migration, Policy, and Society (COMPAS) and the Centre for

Criminology at the University of Oxford. He is the cofounder of a refugee artwork project called Arte de Lágrimas (Art of Tears): Refugee Artwork Project.

Nellie Jo David works to strengthen indigenous rights and autonomy on the imposed US/Mexico borderlands intersecting the Tohono O'odham Nation. Nellie is from Ajo, Arizona, traditionally Hia-Ced O'odham territory, just west of the Tohono O'odham reservation, north of Mexico. Nellie obtained her juris doctorate with a certificate in Indigenous law and policy from Michigan State University in 2014 and her LL.M. from the University of Arizona in 2023. She is currently the director of academic and community engagement with the Border Studies Program at Earlham College in Richmond, Indiana.

Miguel A. De La Torre is an international scholar, documentarian, novelist, academic author, and scholar activist. Since obtaining his doctorate in 1999, he has authored over a hundred articles and published fifty books (six of which won national awards). He presently serves as Professor of Social Ethics and Latinx Studies at the Iliff School of Theology in Denver. A Fulbright scholar, he has served as the 2012 president of the Society of Christian Ethics, and the 2024 president of the Society of Race, Ethnicity, and Religion. He is the recipient of the 2020 AAR Excellence in Teaching Award and the 2021 Martin E. Marty Public Understanding of Religion Award, the only scholar to receive both prestigious awards. Recently, he wrote the screenplay to a documentary on immigration that has won over seven awards. Additionally, he has written an autofiction magical realism novel.

Johanna Erzberger is a biblical scholar with a specific interest in contextuality, both regarding the original context of biblical texts and the contexts of their interpretation and reception, and author of academic articles on a wide range of topics within the field of biblical studies. After obtaining her PhD addressing the reception of biblical texts in Rabbinic Midrashim in 2009, her academic biography has included stops in France (Institute Catholique de Paris), South Africa (as a Humboldt fellow at the University of Pretoria), Wales (GB; Cardiff University), Italy (Sant'Anselmo, Rome), Israel, and Palestine. She has been a research fellow at the University of Pretoria (South Africa) since 2010, and she currently holds the Laurentius Klein Chair for Biblical and Ecumenical Theology at and serves as dean of the Theologische Studienjahr Jerusalem / Jerusalem School of Theology.

Stacey Floyd-Thomas is the E. Rhodes and Leona B. Carpenter Chair and Professor of Ethics and Society at Vanderbilt University Divinity School and College of Arts and Sciences, the founder of the nationally acclaimed Black Religious Scholars Group (BRSG), cofounder and past president of the Society for the Study of Race, Ethnicity and Religion (SRER); past executive director of the Society of Christian Ethics; and the youngest recipient of the AAR Teaching Excellence Award. Her research and teaching interests lie at the intersection of ethics, feminist/womanist studies, moral philosophy, Black Church studies, critical pedagogy, critical race theory, and postcolonial studies with an overall approach to the study of Christian social ethics that engages broad questions of moral agency, cultural memory, ethical responsibility, and social justice. Floyd-Thomas's research trajectory envisions the challenge for constructive ethics in making liberationist discourse and theologies more viable. This is exemplified in her numerous publications, which include numerous articles, book chapters, and ten books. Her notable books include *Deeper Shades of Purple: Womanism in Religion and Society*, *The Altars Where We Worship: The Religious Significance of Black Popular Culture*, and the award-winning *Religion, Race, and COVID-19: Confronting White Supremacy in the Pandemic*.

Lap Yan Kung lives and serves in Hong Kong as a teacher, public theologian, newspaper columnist, and activist. He is director of the Centre for Quality-Life Education and dean of the Institute for Advanced Study in Asian Cultures and Theologies at the Divinity School of Chung Chi College, Chinese University of Hong Kong. His current research focuses on ritual-spatial-theological hermeneutics.

Boyung Lee, a Korean diaspora and Asian/American feminist scholar-activist and an ordained United Methodist clergy, is professor of practical theology at Iliff School of Theology in Denver, Colorado, where she previously served as the senior vice president for academic affairs and dean of the faculty (2017–2022). Lee was the president of the Religious Education Association (2021–2022) and the president of the Pacific, Asian, and North American Asian Women in Theology and Ministry (2023–2025). She recently concluded her cochairship of the Women and Religion Unit of the American Academy of Religion (2025). Lee is the author of *Transforming Congregations through Community* and a coeditor of *Embodying Antiracist Christianity: Asian American Theological Resources for Just Racial Relations*, among other works.

Mitri Raheb, an international scholar, public theologian, and social entrepreneur, is the founder and president of Dar al-Kalima University in Bethlehem, Palestine. Raheb is the most widely published Palestinian theologian to date, with over fifty books to his credit, including *Faith in the Face of Empire*, *The Politics of Persecution*, and *Decolonizing Palestine*. He received the 2017 Tolerance Award from the European Academy of Arts and Sciences, the 2015 Olof Palme Prize, the 2012 German Media Prize, the 2006 International Mohammad Nafi Tschelebi Award, and the 2007 German Peace Award of Aachen. Dr. Raheb's work has received wide media attention from major international media outlets and networks including CNN, ABC, CBS, *60 Minutes*, BBC, ARD, ZDF, DW, BR, *Premiere, Raiuno, Stern, The Economist, Newsweek*, al Jazeera, al-Mayadin, RT, LBC, *Vanity Fair*, and others.

Bibliography

Abbott, Elizabeth. *Sugar: A Bittersweet History*. Duckworth, 2009.
Adams, John Quincy. "Letter to Hugh Nelson, Minister in Madrid: April 23, 1823." In *Writing of John Quincy Adams*. Vol. 7. Edited by Worthington Chauncey Ford. Macmillan, 1917 [1823].
Angelou, Maya. "These Yet to Be United States." In *Maya Angelou: The Complete Poetry*. Random House, 2015.
Anzaldúa, Gloria E. *Borderlands / La Frontera: The New Mestiza*. Aunt Lute, 1999.
———. *Interviews/Entrevistas*. Edited by AnaLouise Keating. Routledge, 2000.
Anzaldúa, Gloria E., and AnaLouise Keating, eds. *This Bridge We Call Home: Radical Vision for Transformation*. Routledge, 2002.
Balibar, Étienne. *Citizenship*. Polity, 2015.
Behar, Ruth. "Introduction." In *Bridges to Cuba—Puentes a Cuba*. Edited by Ruth Behar. University of Michigan Press, 1995.
Bellah, Robert N., Richard Madsen, Ann Swidler, William M. Sullivan, and Steven M. Tipton. *Habits of the Heart: Individualism and Commitment in American Life*. University of California Press, 1985.
Beltrán, Cristina. *Cruelty as Citizenship: How Migrant Suffering Sustains White Democracy*. University of Minnesota Press, 2020.
Benjamin, Walter. *The Arcades Project*. Translated by Howard Eiland and Kevin McLaughlin [based on German volume edited by Rolf Tiedemann]. Belknap, 1999. [Unfinished volume written between 1927 and 1940.]
———. "Thesis on the Philosophy of History." In *Illuminations*. Translated by Harry Zohn and edited by Hannah Arendt. Schocken, 1968 [1940].

Bennett, Peter S., and Michael R. Kunzmann. *A History of the Quitobaquito Resource Management Area, Organ Pipe Cactus National Monument, Arizona*. Technical Report Number 26. Cooperative National Park Resources Studies Unit, 1989.

Blackburn, Robin. "Themes of the Cuban Revolution." In *The Cuba Reader: The Making of a Revolutionary Society*. Edited by Philip Brenner et al. Grove, 1989.

Boff, Leonardo. *Cry of the Earth, Cry of the Poor*. Translated by Phillip Berryman. Orbis, 1997.

Brown, Brian Joseph. *Apartheid South Africa! Apartheid Israel! Ticking the Boxes of Occupation and Dispossession*. Church in the Market Place, 2021.

———. *Born to Be Free: The Indivisibility of Freedom—A Methodist Minister's Quest for Justice and Freedom on Two Continents*. Church in the Market Place, 2015.

"Cairo Declaration, The." In *Foreign Relations of the United States, Diplomatic Papers. The Conferences at Cairo and Tehran. November 26, 1943*. Wilson Center Digital Archive. US Government Printing Office, 1961.

Callahan, William A. "National Insecurities: Humiliation, Salvation, and Chinese Nationalism." *Alternatives* 29, no. 2 (2004): 199–218.

———. "The Politics of Walls: Barriers, Flows and the Sublime." *Review of International Studies* 44 (2018): 456–81.

Castro, Fidel. *Speech to Citizens of Santiago*. Town Main Plaza, January 3, 1959.

Chomsky, Aviva. *Undocumented: How Immigrant Became Illegal*. Beacon, 2014.

Cooper, Anna Julia. *A Voice from the South*. Aldine, 1892.

Cuéllar, Gregory Lee. "Deportation as a Sacrament of the State: The Religious Instruction of Contracted Chaplains in U.S. Detention Facilities." *Journal of Ethnic and Migration Studies* 45, no. 2 (2019): 253–72.

Cumings, Bruce. *The Korean War: A History*. Modern Library, 2010.

Dawson, Britt. "Interview with Gabriel Schivone: U.S. Borderlands, Israel's Latest Surveillance Technology Laboratory." *Journal of Palestine Studies* 47, no. 4 (2018): 57–68.

De La Torre, Miguel A. *Doing Christian Ethics from the Margins*. 2nd ed. Orbis, 2014.
Desmond, Cosmas. *The Discarded People: Account of African Resettlement in South Africa*. Penguin, 1971.
Ding, Arthur S., and Jagannath P. Panda, editors. *Chinese Politics and Foreign Policy under Xi Jinping*. Routledge, 2021.
Du Bois, W. E. B. *The Souls of Black Folk*. Penguin, 1989 [1903].
Dussel, Enrique. *Ethics and the Theology of Liberation*. Translated by Bernard F. McWilliams. Orbis, 1978.
Ellithorpe, Anne-Marie. *Towards Friendship-Shaped Communities: A Practical Theology of Friendship*. Wiley Blackwell, 2022.
Enloe, Cynthia. "Foreword." In *The Bases of Empire: The Global Struggle against U.S. Military Posts*. Edited by Catherine Lutz. New York University Press, 2009.
Fanon, Frantz. "Algeria Unveiled." In *A Dying Colonialism*. Translated by Haakon Chevalier. Grove, 1965.
———. *The Wretched of the Earth*. Translated by Constance Farrington. Grove, 1963.
Fogel, Benjamin. "South Africa: 30 Years Later." *New Internationalist* 50, no. 548 (March–April 2024): 24–25.
Frosh, Stephen. "Psychoanalysis, Colonialism, Racism." *Journal of Theoretical and Philosophical Psychology* 33, no. 3 (2013): 141–54.
Fu, Hualing, and Michael Hor, editors. *The National Security Law of Hong Kong*. University of Hong Kong Press, 2022.
Gerzon, Mark. *A Choice of Heroes*. Houghton Mifflin, 1982.
Giddens, Anthony. *Modernity and Self-Identity: Self and Society in the Late Modern Age*. Polity, 1991.
Gilman, Sander L. *Freud, Race, and Gender*. Princeton University Press, 1993.
Glick Schiller, Nina. "Beyond the Nation-State and Its Units of Analysis: Towards a New Research Agenda for Migration Studies. Essentials of Migration Theory." Center on Migration, Citizenship, and Development Working Paper 33 (2007): 1–42.
Global Jewish Advocacy. *The Working Definition of Anti-Semitism: What Does It Mean, Why Is It Important, and What Should We Do with It?* American Jewish Committee, n.d.

Grate, George. *Plato, and the Other Companions of Sokrates*. Vol. 2. Adegi Graphics, 1999 [1865].

Grey, Arthur L. "The Thirty-Eighth Parallel." *Foreign Affairs* 29, no. 3 (1951): 482–87.

Gutmann, Matthew C., Felix V. Matos-Rodriquez, Lynn Stephen, and Patricia Zavella, eds. *Perspectives on Las Americas: A Reader in Culture, History, & Representation*. Wiley-Blackwell, 2003.

Hagan, Jacqueline Maria. "Religion and the Process of Migration: A Case Study of a Maya Transnational Community." in *Religion across Borders: Transnational Immigrant Networks*. Edited by Helen Rose Fuchs Ebaugh and Janet Saltzman Chafetz. AltaMira, 2002.

Hagedorn, Hermann. *Leonard Wood: A Biography*. Vol. 1. Harper & Brothers, 1932.

Harris, Cheryl I. "Whiteness as Property." *Harvard Law Review* 106, no. 8 (June 1993): 1707–91.

Heidenreich, Ronny. "Eine Mauer für die Welt. Inszenierungen außerhalb Deutschlands nach 1989." In *Die Mauer: Errichtung, Überwindung, Erinnerung*. Edited by Klaus-Dietmar Henke. DTV, 2011.

Heinemann, Winfried. "Die Sicherung der Grenze." In *Die Mauer: Errichtung, Überwindung, Erinnerung*. Edited by Klaus-Dietmar Henke. DTV, 2011.

Henke, Klaus-Dietmar. "Die Berliner Mauer." In *Die Mauer: Errichtung, Überwindung, Erinnerung*. Edited by Klaus-Dietmar Henke. DTV, 2011.

Henke, Lutz "'Mauerkunst.'" In *Die Mauer: Errichtung, Überwindung, Erinnerung*. Edited by Klaus-Dietmar Henke. DTV, 2011.

Henretta, James A., Rebecca Edwards, and Robert O. Self. *America: A Concise History*. Vol. 2: *Since 1865*. 5th ed. Bedford / St. Martin's, 2012.

Hildebrandt, Alexandra. *Die Mauer. Zahlen. Daten*. Verlag Haus am Checkpoint Charlie, 2001.

Hinkelammert, Franz J. *The Ideological Weapons of Death: A Theological Critique*. Translated by Phillip Berryman. Orbis, 1986.

Hong, Christine. "The Unending Korean War." *Positions: Asia Critique* 23, no. 4 (2015): 597–617.

hooks, bell. *Feminist Theory: From Margin to Center.* South End, 1984.

Hu, Weixing. "Xi Jinping's Major Country Diplomacy: The Role of Leadership in Foreign Policy Transformation." *Journal of Contemporary China* 28, no. 115 (2019): 1–14.

"James Baldwin vs. William F. Buckley: A Legendary Debate from 1965," February 18, 1965. Baldwin's moral authority made a fool of the disingenuous Buckley's patrician racism. Video and transcript available at the American Archive of Public Broadcasting website.

Jefferson, Thomas. "Letter to President James Monroe: October 24, 1823." In *The Life and Selected Writings of Thomas Jefferson.* Edited by Adrienne Kock and William Peden. Random House, 1944 [1823].

Jenks, Leland. *Our Cuban Colony: A Study of Sugar.* Vanguard, 1928.

Jensen, Robert. *The Heart of Whiteness: Confronting Race, Racism, and White Privilege.* City Lights, 2005.

Keating, AnaLouise, ed. *Entre Mundos / Among Worlds: New Perspectives on Gloria Anzaldúa.* Palgrave, 2005.

Khanna, Ranjana. *Dark Continents: Psychoanalysis and Colonialism.* Duke University Press, 2003.

Keum, Jooseop. "Korean War: The Origin of the Axis of Evil in the Korean Peninsula." In *Peace and Reconciliation: In Search of Shared Identity.* Edited by Sebastian Kim and Pauline Kollontai. Ashgate, 2008.

Kim, Joo Ok. *Untelling the Tales of Empire: Intimate Epistemologies of the Korean War.* PhD dissertation. University of California, San Diego, 2013.

Kim, Nadia. *The Gendered Politics of the Korean Protestant Right: Hegemonic Masculinity.* Springer International, 2016.

———. "What Americans Need to Know about the Korean War." Scholars Strategy Network, April 1, 2019.

Kim, Nami, and Wonhee Anne Joh. "Introduction." In *Critical Theology against US Militarism in* Asia. Edited by Nami Kim and Wonhee Anne Joh. Palgrave Macmillan, 2016.

Kim, Suk-Young. *DMZ Crossing: Performing Emotional Citizenship along the Korean Border.* Columbia University Press, 2014.

Knight, Franklin W. *The Caribbean: The Genesis of a Fragmented Nationalism*. 2nd ed. Oxford University Press, 1990.
Kruger, Ferdinand, and Hennie Pieterse. "Reasons Why Government Leaders, Officials and Church Leaders Have to Act against Corruption." In *Corruption in South Africa's Liberal Democratic Context: Equipping Christian Leaders and Communities for Their Role in Countering Corruption*. Edited by Ferdinand Kruger and Ben de Klerk. AOSIS, 2016.
Kuhrmann, Anke. "Die Mauer in Malerei und Graphik." In *Die Mauer: Errichtung, Überwindung, Erinnerung*. Edited by Klaus-Dietmar Henke. DTV, 2011.
Kung, Lap Yan. "Crucified People, Messianic Time and Youth in Protest." In *Hong Kong Protests and Political Theology*. Edited by Kwok Pui-lan and Francis Ching Wah Yip. Rowman and Littlefield, 2021.
———. "Is God Our *Sau² Zuk¹*, Comrade or Friend, with Reference to the 2019 Hong Kong Anti-Extradition Law Amendment Movement and *Fratelli Tutti*?" *Lumen: A Journal of Catholic Studies* 10 (2022): 33–57.
Kwon, Heonik. *After the Korean War: An Intimate History*. Cambridge University Press, 2020.
Landin, Conrad. "Editorial." *New Internationalist* 50, no. 548 (2024): 3.
Lefebvre, Henri. *La production de l'espace*. Éditions Anthropos, 1974. [English translation: *The Production of Space* (Blackwell, 1991).]
Lee, Hyun Kyung, and Dacia Viejo-Rose. "The Eclectic Heritage-Scape of a Tense Border in the Paju DMZ, South Korea." *Korea Journal* 63, no. 2 (2023): 46–93.
Lee, Namhee. "The Korean War, Anticommunism, and the Korean American Community." *Presbyterian Mission*. (Louisville, KY: Presbyterian Church U.S.A, April 30, 2018).
Lee, Sook Jong. "Generational Divides and the Future of South Korean Democracy." In *Demographics and Future of South Korea*. Edited by Chung Min Lee and Kathryn Botto. Carnegie Endowment for International Peace, June 29, 2021.
Lein, Yehezkel. "The Separation Barrier: Position Paper September 2002." 2002.

Liebermann, Doris. "Die Mauer in der Literatur." In *Die Mauer: Errichtung, Überwindung, Erinnerung*. Edited by Klaus-Dietmar Henke. DTV, 2011.

Lipsitz, George. *How Racism Takes Place*. Temple University Press, 2011.

———. *The Possessive Investment in Whiteness: How White People Profit from Identity Politics*. Temple University Press, 1998.

Locke, John. *The Second Treatise of Government*. Edited by Thomas P. Peardon. Bobbs-Merrill Educational, 1952 [1689].

Lodge, Henry Cabot. *Selections from the Correspondence of Theodore Roosevelt and Henry Cabot Lodge, 1884–1918*. Vol. 2. Charles Scribner's Sons, 1925.

Loewenstein, Antony. *The Palestine Laboratory: How Israel Exports the Technology of Occupation around the World*. Verso, 2023.

Lovelock, James. *Gaia: A New Look at Life on Earth*. Oxford University Press, 1979.

Lubin, Alex. *Geographies of Liberation: The Making of an Afro-Arab Political Imaginary*. University of North Carolina Press, 2014.

Mbembe, Achille. "The Idea of a Borderless World." *Chimurenga Chronic*, 2018. Available at africasacountry.com.

———. "Necropolitics." *Public Culture* 15, no. 1 (2003): 11–40.

McAdam, Doug, John D. McCarthy, and Mayer N. Zald. "Introduction: Opportunities, Mobilizing Structures, and Framing Processes: Toward a Synthetic, Comparative Perspective on Social Movements." In *Comparative Perspectives on Social Movements*. Edited by Doug McAdam, John D. McCarthy, and Mayer N. Zald. Cambridge University Press, 1995.

McClintock, Anne. *Imperial Leather: Race, Gender and Sexuality in the Colonial Contest*. Routledge, 1995.

McKittrick, Katherine. *Demonic Grounds Black Women and the Cartographies of Struggle*. University of Minnesota Press, 2006.

Mitzen, Jennifer. "Ontological Security in World Politics: State Identity and the Security Dilemma." *European Journal of International Relations* 12, no. 3 (2006): 341–70.

Moltmann, Jürgen. *The Church in the Power of the Spirit*. SCM, 1977.

———. *The Passion for Life: A Messianic Lifestyle*. SCM, 1978.

———. *The Spirit of Life: A Universal Affirmation*. SCM, 1992.

———. *Theology of Hope: On the Ground and the Implications of a Christian Eschatology.* SCM, 1967.

———. *The Way of Jesus Christ.* SCM, 1990.

Mooney, James. "The Ghost-Dance Religion and the Sioux Outbreak of 1890." In *Fourteenth Annual Report of the Bureau of Ethnology to the Secretary of the Smithsonian Institution 1892–93, Part 2.* J. W. Powell, Director. US Government Printing Office, 1896.

Mörner, Magnus. *Race Mixture in the History of Latin America.* Little, Brown, 1967.

Muhareb, Rania, Elizabeth Rghebi, Pearce Clancy, Joseph Schechia, Nada Awad, and Maha Abdallah. *Israeli Apartheid: Tool of Zionist Settler Colonialism.* Al-Haq, 2002.

Murakami, Haruki. *Acceptance Address for the Jerusalem Prize.* February 2009.

National Committee for the Investigation of the Truth about the Jeju April 3 Incident, The. *The Jeju April 3 Incident Investigation Report.* December 15, 2003.

Neureiter, Michael. "Sources of Media Bias in Coverage of the Israeli-Palestinian Conflict: The 2010 Gaza Flotilla Raid in German, British, and US Newspapers." *Israel Affairs* 23, no. 1 (2017): 66–86.

Newman, Philip C. *Cuba before Castro: An Economic Appraisal.* Prentice Hall, 1965.

Ni, Michael Y., et al. "Depression and Post-Traumatic Stress during Major Social Unrest in Hong Kong: A 10-Year Prospective Cohort Study." *Lancet* 395, no. 1020 (2020): 273–84.

Olson, Joel. *The Abolition of White Democracy.* University of Minnesota Press, 2004.

Pakenham, Thomas. *The Boer War.* Abacus, 1991.

Paredes, Américo. *Folklore and Culture on the Texas-Mexican Border.* CMAS, 1993.

Pérez, Louis A., Jr. *Cuba: Between Empires, 1878–1902.* University of Pittsburgh Press, 1983.

———. *Cuba: Between Reform and Revolution.* Oxford University Press, 1988.

———. *Essays on Cuban History: Historiography and Research.* University Press of Florida, 1995.

Pinn, Anthony B. "Black Bodies in Pain and Ecstasy: Terror, Subjectivity, and the Nature of Black Religion." *Nova Religio: The Journal of Alternative and Emergent Religions* (2003). jstor.org.

Plato. "Allegory of the Cave." In *Republic*. Translated by Thomas Sheehan. n.d.

Politische Hauptverwaltung der Nationalen Volksarmee Deutschen Demokratischen Republik. *Vom Sinn des Soldatseins: Ein Ratgeber für den Grenzsoldaten*. VEB, 1987.

Poon, Hannah, and Tommy Tse. "Enacting Cross-Platform (Buy/Boy) Cott: Yellow Economic Circle and the New Citizen-Consumer Politics in Hong Kong." *New Media and Society*, June 7, 2022.

Raheb, Mitri. *Decolonizing Palestine: The Land, the People, the Bible*. Orbis, 2023.

Richter, Sebastian. "Die Mauer in der deutschen Erinnerungskultur." In *Die Mauer: Errichtung, Überwindung, Erinnerung*. Edited by Klaus-Dietmar Henke. DTV, 2011.

Rojas, Carlos. *The Great Wall: A Cultural History*. Harvard University Press, 2010.

Rousseau, Jean-Jacques. "A Discourse upon the Origin and the Foundation of the Inequality among Mankind." In *The Discourses and Other Early Political Writings*. Edited and translated by Victor Gourevitch. Cambridge University Press, 1997 [1755].

Said, Edward W. "Opponents, Audiences, Constituencies, and Community." *Critical Inquiry* 9, no. 1 (1982): 1–26.

Saldívar, José David. *Border Matters: Remapping American Cultural Studies*. University of California Press, 1997.

Sälter, Gerhard. "Die Sperranlagen, oder: Der unendliche Mauerbau." In *Die Mauer: Errichtung, Überwindung, Erinnerung*. Edited by Klaus-Detmar Henke. DTV, 2011.

Sayles, John. *Los Gusanos: A Novel*. HarperCollins, 1991.

Schlusche, Günther. "Stadtentwicklung im geteilten Berlin." In *Die Mauer: Errichtung, Überwindung, Erinnerung*. Edited by Klaus-Dietmar Henke. DTV, 2011.

Schmid, Christian. *Stadt, Raum und Gesellschaft: Henri Lefebvre und die Theorie der Produktion des Raumes*. Steiner, 2005.

Shepard, Benjamin. "Play, Creativity, and the New Community Organizing." *Journal of Progressive Human Services* 16, no. 2 (2005): 47–69.
Smith, Adam. *An Inquiry into the Nature and Causes of the Wealth of Nations.* Vol. 1. Edited by R. H. Campbell, A. S. Skinner, and W. B. Todd. Clarendon, 1976 [1776].
Soja, Edward W. *Postmodern Geographies: The Reassertion of Space in Critical Social Theory.* Verso, 1989.
Spillers, Hortense. "Mama's Baby, Papa's Maybe: An American Grammar Book." *Diacritics* 17, no. 2 (1987): 64–81.
Steele, Brent J. *Ontological Security in International Relations: Self-Identity and the IR State.* Routledge, 2008.
Suzuki, Shunryu. *Zen Mind, Beginner's Mind.* Shambhala, 2011.
Tajfel, Henri. "Social Identity and Intergroup Behaviour." *Social Sciences Information* 13 (1947): 65–93.
Roosevelt, Theodore. "Letter to Henry White," September 13, 1906. In *The Works of Theodore Roosevelt.* Vol. 14. Memorial ed. Charles Scribner's Sons, 1923.
Thomas, Hugh. *Cuba: The Pursuit of Freedom.* Da Capo, 1998 [1971].
Tinker, Tink. "How the Eurochristian Invasion of Turtle Island Created Our Environmental Crises." In *Shifting Climate, Shifting People.* Edited by Miguel A. De La Torre. Pilgrim, 2022.
———. "Spirituality, Native American Personhood, Sovereignty and Solidarity." In *Spirituality of the Third World: A Cry for Life.* Edited by K. C. Abraham and B. Mbuy-Beya. Orbis, 1994.
Truth, Sojourner [graphic]. Library Company of Philadelphia holdings, 1864. https://digital.librarycompany.org/islandora/object/Islandora%3A3252.
Tsang, Michael. "Who's the Egg? Who's the Wall?—Appropriating Haruki Murakami's 'Always on the Side of the Egg's Speech in Hong Kong." In *Modern Japanese Political Thought and International Relations.* Edited by Felix Roesch and Atsuko Watanabe. Rowman and Littlefield, 2018.
US Immigrations and Customs Enforcement. *U.S. Immigration and Customs Enforcement Fiscal Year 2020 Enforcement and Removal Operations Report.* Washington, DC, 2020.

Valverde, Kieu Linh Caroline, and Wei Ming Dariotis. "Introduction." In *Fight the Tower: Asian American Women Scholars' Resistance and Renewal in the Academy*. Edited by Kieu Linh Caroline Valverde and Wei Ming Dariotis. Rutgers University Press, 2019.

Waldron, Arthur. *The Great Wall of China: From History to Myth*. Cambridge University Press, 1990.

Wang, Zheng. *Never Forget National Humiliation: Historical Memory in Chinese Politics and Foreign Relations*. Columbia University Press, 2014.

White, E. Frances. *Dark Continent of Our Bodies: Black Feminism and Politics of Respectability*. Temple University Press, 2001.

Whitney, Robert. *State and Revolution in Cuba: Mass Mobilization and Political Change, 1920–1940*. University of North Carolina Press.

Wind, Maya. *Towers of Ivory and Steel: How Israeli Universities Deny Palestinian Freedom*. Verso, 2024.

Wong, Matthew Y. H., Ying-ho Kwong, and Edward K. F. Chan. "Political Consumerism in Hong Kong: China's Economic Intervention, Identity Politics, or Political Participation?" *China Perspectives* 3 (2021): 61–71.

Wygralak, Pawel. "'Blessed Are the Pure in Heart, for They Shall See God' (Matt 5:8) as Interpreted by the Church Fathers (4th–5th Cent.)." *Verbum Vitae* 38, no. 2 (2020): 579–91.

Yoo, Theodore Jun. *The Koreas*. University of California Press, 2022.

Yuh, Ji-Yeon. "Beyond Numbers: The Brutality of the Korean War." *Presbyterian Mission*. Louisville, KY: Presbyterian Church U.S.A, April 19, 2018.

Zhang, Feng. "The Rise of Chinese Exceptionalism in International Relations." *European Journal of International Relations* 19, no. 2 (2011): 305–28.

Index

Adams, John Quincy, 168-69
Africa
  Angola, 127
  Bantustan, 118-19
  Botswana, 120
  Christianity, 124-25
  continent, 118-19, 135, 174, 185-87, 192, 194
  Egypt, 12, 79, 101, 106, 127, 211
  Ethiopia, 127
  Libya, 128
  Namibia, 117, 119n3, 121-22, 126-27
  Rainbow Nation, 126-27, 135
  slavery of its people, 3, 22, 147, 169-72, 198, 204-5
  South Africa, xiii, 23, 114, 116-35, 124-25, 213, 215
  Yoruba, 12
  Zimbabwe, 133
African Americans, 15, 22, 32, 138-40, 143, 147-49, 152, 183-202, 206, 213, 215
African National Congress (ANC), 124, 127-28, 131-33, 135
American Academy of Religion (AAR), ix, 33, 37, 216
Amnesty International, 104
Anderson, Benedict, 184-85
Angelou, Maya, 198
Anglo-Boer War, 122-23
Anti-Defamation League, 30
Anzaldúa, Gloria, 16-17, 138, 140-44
apartheid,
  definition, 104, 117
  Israel, ix, xiii, 21, 23-24, 27, 29, 34, 100, 102-5, 108, 111, 113-14, 118, 121
  South Africa, 116-26, 129, 134-35, 213
  U.S., xiii-xiv, 15-16, 18, 152, 187, 189, 192-94, 197-99, 201-2, 205-8
Arafat, Yasser, 101

Asia,
　China, 12, 15, 56–80, 83–84, 86, 93–94, 216, 127–28
　continent, 78, 81, 85–87, 91, 93–94, 174, 187, 216
　Hong Kong, xiii, 15, 56–57, 62–76, 85–88, 216
　India, 118, 127–28, 134
　Japan, 79–82, 88, 92, 94
　Korea, xiii, 15–16, 76–99, 216
　Macau, 63
　North Korea, 76–77, 79, 81–84, 88n27, 89–96, 98–99
　Philippines, 86, 173
　South Korea, 76–77, 79, 81–86, 88–96, 98
　Taiwan, 15, 62, 94
　Tibet, 62
　Vietnam, 84, 90

Baik, Crystal Mun-hye, 97
Baldwin, James, 192, 194
Balfour Declaration, 38, 100, 102
Balibar, Étienne, 147–48
Banksy, 113–14
Bannon, Stephen K., 19
Barak, Ehud, 103
Batista, Fulgencio, 164
Behar, Ruth, 19
Beltrán, Cristina, 147
Benjamin, Walter, 17–18
Berlin Conference of 1884, 174
Berlin Wall, xiii, 21, 39–55, 104, 111, 113
Biden, Joe, 94, 161, 199–200
Biko, Steve, 124

Bloqueo, el, xiv, 15, 163–182
Boff, Leonardo, 13–14
Bolívar, Simon, 170
Bonaventure Oblasser, Father, 154–55
Botha, Pieter Willem, 122
Brandeis Center, 30
Breyers Naudé, C. F., 123, 125
Buckley, William F., 192
Buddhism, 69–70
Bush, George W., 111

Canada, 28, 115, 175, 186
capitalism, 4–6, 43, 62, 86–89, 122, 128, 174, 179–81, 190–91, 199
Castro, Fidel, 164, 166–67, 180
Castro, Raul, 167, 180
Charles, Ray, 201–2
Chomsky, Aviva, 139
Christianity
　African, 116, 119, 121, 124–25
　Anglican, 121, 124
　Bible, 14, 20, 33, 35, 69–70, 72–75, 123, 139–49, 151–52, 211, 213–15
　British Council of Churches, 124–25, 213
　conservative, 88, 90–91, 144
　Dutch Reform, 116
　euro-, 6–8, 11, 13, 65, 70, 72, 88, 98, 100, 116, 119, 121, 124–25, 144–44, 148, 213
　God of, 6, 13, 70, 74, 99, 110, 143–44, 182
　Jesus Christ, 69–70, 72–74, 123

Korean, 88–91, 98–99
Paul, St., 75, 115, 123
persecution of, 88n27, 108
   Protestant, ix, 98, 116, 143, 148
   Reformation, the 70
   Roman Catholic, 119, 157
   rituals, 68
   Sinicization of, 65
   womanist, 183, 215
Clay, Henry, 170
Cold War, 77–83, 87, 94, 99, 121, 155
colonial
   conquest, 3–4, 8–11, 37, 78, 145, 157, 174, 177, 181, 192, 195–96, 209
   de-, ix, xiii, 38, 76, 79, 87, 89, 92–99, 136–40, 146–9, 184–85
   neo-, 102, 176–77
   post-, 9, 87n23, 90, 140, 145, 148–49, 175, 180, 185, 194, 213, 215
   project, xiii, 1–7, 21–23, 32, 35, 38, 78, 86–87, 93–94, 99–108, 113–15, 122, 145–47, 149, 169–74, 177, 184–88, 190, 192–95, 199, 209
   as sexual, 8–10, 20, 102, 114, 177
   See also *settler colonialism*
communism, 21, 61–62, 78, 82–92, 95, 98, 111, 121, 126, 128, 166, 180, see also *Marxism*
Conrad, Joseph, 192
Cook, Jonathan, 120

Cooper, Anna Julia, 196–98, 201
Co¹ Sam¹, 57, 66, 68–70, 73–74
COVID-19, ix, 158–59, 166, 215
Crow, Jim and Jane, 177, 197
Cuban Missile Crises, 164
Cuban Wars for Independence, 171–75, 180
Cumings, Bruce, 87

Darwin, Charles, 4
de Céspedes, Carlos Manuel, 171
de Klerk, Willen Fredrik, 122
De La Torre, Miguel A., ix–x, xii– xiii
Demilitarized Zone (DMZ), xiii, 77–79, 83–85, 88–93, 96, 99
Deng Xiaoping, 58
DeSantis, Ron, 30
Desmond, Cosmas, 119
detentions, x, 137, 144, 200, 213
DuBois, W. E. B., 186, 188, 190
Dussel, Enrique, 7

Eisenhower, Dwight, 163–64
empire
   biblical, 151
   British, 61, 86, 100–1, 122, 124, 169–70, 179–80, 184, 194, 213
   China, 60
   French, 169–70
   Japanese, 79–81, 88, 92
   Ottoman, 100
   Spanish, 86, 157, 164, 170–75, 177–78, 188
   Soviet Union, 87

empire *(continued)*
  United States, 78, 81, 83–88,
    92–93, 140–41, 144–46,
    148–49, 164, 167–81, 210
  Western, 3, 20, 23, 38, 61,
    79–80, 81, 83–87, 92–93,
    100–1, 113, 115, 122,
    140–41, 144–49, 157, 164,
    169–80, 188, 197, 209–10
Enloe, Cynthia, 87
enslavement,
  of Africans, 3, 22, 147, 169–72,
    186, 198, 204–5
  of Jews, 211
  of Koreans, 80
  of land, 11, 13
environmentalism, x–xi, 4, 10–11,
  58–59, 129
Europe
  as barbaric, 17–18
  Christianity, 6–8, 11, 13,
    72, 88, 100, 144
  colonialism, 3, 79–80, 113, 115,
    122, 157, 169–172, 197, 209
  continent, 11, 21–23, 27–28,
    38, 86, 100, 127, 148, 170,
    174, 193–94, 209–10, 216
  Denmark, 113
  Federal Republic of Germany
    (West), 42–45, 47–52, 110
  France, 40, 169, 215
  German Democratic
    Republic (East), 42–53
  Germany, xiii, 17, 21, 28,
    39–55, 104, 110–11,
    113, 115, 174, 216

Great Britian, 3–4, 27, 61–62,
  79–80, 86, 100–1, 113, 115,
  122, 169
Hague, the, 103, 107
NATO and Warsaw Pact, 46
Netherlands, 113
Norway, 128
settler colonial, 4, 22, 38, 100,
  115, 209
Spain, 86, 113, 157, 164,
  169–75, 177–78, 180, 182,
  188
Sweden, 113, 128
Ukraine, 23, 128
worldview, 1–15, 17, 19–20,
  148, 150, 208–11

Fanon, Frantz, 5, 8, 145, 184–85,
  190
Freud, Sigmund, 194–96
Fuk⁶ Seong⁴, 67

Geneva Convention, 104, 107–8
genocide,
  of Black Africans, 123
  of Afrikaner, 123
  cultural, x
  definition of, 15, 27
  of indigenous, 102
  of Jews, 31
  of Koreans, 82
  of Palestinians, xiv, 21–32, 38,
    114, 128
Gerzon, Mark, 9
Giddens, Anthony, 58–59
Gilman, Sander L., 196

Global South, 9, 22, 38, 115, 128–29, 185, 204, 206, 209, 211
Goodman, Amy, 29
Gorbachev, Mikhail, 111
Great Wall of China, 21, 57–58, 61, 66
gunboat diplomacy, 164, 166–67, 209

Hagan, Maria Jacqueline, 151
Harris, Cheryl, 190–91
Harris, Kamala, 199–201
Havemeyer, Henry Osborne, 172
Hegel, Georg Wilheim Friedrich, 18
Hindu, 12
Hinkelammert, Franz, 7
Hodge, John R., 81
Hong, Christine, 85–86, 88
hook, bell, 195
Huddleston, Trevor, 121
Human Rights Watch, 104

Indigenous People,
  Apache, 158
  Aztec, 12
  Chicano/a, 137, 139
  genocide of, 102
  of Global South, 9, 185
  Incas, 12
  Kumeyaay, 159
  Nahuatl, 138
  of North America, xiii, 3, 8–12, 113, 137, 139, 153–62, 185–86, 192, 214

O'odham, xiii, 153–62, 214
Osage, 11
Palestinians, 24, 38, 101–3, 114, 120, 186
Papago, 154–55
stereotyped as primitive, 4–5, 10–12, 17–20, 24, 102, 114, 139, 145, 196
U.S., xiii, 3, 11–12, 113, 153–56, 160–61, 185, 192, 214
Wanapum, 12
worldview, 2, 5, 11–14, 208
Yumas, 155
International Court of Justice, 23, 103, 106–8, 114, 122, 128–20
invisible wall, xiii–xiv, 15–16, 18, 21, 46, 48, 92, 116, 161, 163–182, 186–89, 192–94, 197–99, 201–2, 205–8
Islam
  Muslims, 27, 89, 108
  phobia of, 27
Israel,
  apartheid, ix, xiii, 21, 23–24, 27, 29, 34, 100, 102–5, 108, 111, 113–14, 118, 121
  Jerusalem, xii, 25, 56, 74, 101, 103, 108–10, 215
  military, 23–25, 34–35, 54, 101–4, 106, 108–9, 112, 114–15
  and settler colonialism, xiii, 21, 23, 32, 35, 38, 100–02, 105, 107, 113–15

Israel *(continued)*
  State of, ix–x, xii–xiv, 15,
    21–39, 53–56, 74–77,
    100–15, 118–21, 128–29,
    166, 213, 215
  Tel Aviv, 118
  See also *Israel-Gaza War, Israeli Apartheid wall,* and *Jews*
Israel-Gaza War, 21–38, 54,
  76–77, 114, 128
Israeli Apartheid Wall, ix–x,
  xii–xiv, 15, 21, 24, 27,
  39, 53–54, 100–15

Jefferson, Thomas, 168
Jensen, Robert, 191–92
Jewish Voices for Peace, 30
Jews,
  and antisemitism, 30–31, 33,
    100–1
  British, 100
  enslavement of, 211
  European, 100
  genocide of, 31
  God of, 70
  faith of, 70, 211
  of Israel, 36, 100–1, 118–20
  people, 29, 36, 196, 211
  protesting Israel, 30–31
  Russian, 100
Jiang Zemin, 63
Joh, Anne, 99

Kaisen, Jan Jin, 97
Kennedy, John F., 164, 166
Khanna, Ranjana, 194

Khrushchev, Nikita, 163
Kim, Nadia, 86, 87n23
Kim, Suk-Young, 77
Kim, Suzy, 96
Kishida, Fumio, 94
Korean War, 76n2, 77–79, 83–90,
  92–94, 96, 98

land
  agency of, 2, 5, 11–15, 19–20
  as alive, 10–15, 138
  border-, 16–17, 79, 85,
    137–49, 153, 161, 183,
    198–99, 206–8, 214
  commodification of, 1, 3–5,
    7, 9–15, 18–20, 178, 202
  exploitation of, 3–8, 13
  farm-, 105–6, 108, 123
  indigenous, 6, 102, 113,
    153–56, 160–61, 174
  mines, 76, 85
  North America, 3
  as original sin, 7–8
  Palestinian, 21, 32, 39, 101–6,
    111, 113
  as private property, 1–8, 10–15,
    18–20, 102, 107, 115, 169,
    178
  rights of, 2–3, 7, 15, 18–20, 28,
    136, 148, 191
  slavery of, 11, 13
  South African, 118–19, 122
  spirituality of, 11–14, 19–20,
    138
  sustainer if life, 2, 5–6, 11, 13,
    19

thief of, 3–8, 18–19, 102, 118, 155, 174, 184, 187, 209, 213
as virgin, 8–10, 20, 102, 114, 177
laissez-faire, 3–4, 6
Latin America
  continent, 169–70, 177m21, 180–81
  Cuba, xiv, 15, 86, 126, 128, 163–82, 177m21
  Bolivia, 181
  Brazil, 13, 127
  El Salvador, 137, 177n21
  Guatemala, 137, 177n21, 181, 209–10
  Haiti, 169–70, 177m21
  Honduras, 137, 177m21
  indigenous people, xiii, 12, 153–56, 160–61, 214
  Peru, 181
  Venezuela, 181
  See also *Spanish-American War* and *U.S.-Mexican border wall*
Lefebvre, Henri, 39–43
LGBTQ+, 16, 89
Lipsitz, George, 190–91, 197
Locke, John, 3, 5–6, 159
Lodge, Henry Cabot, 176–77
López, Narciso, 170–71
Luthuli, Albert, 133

Madison, James, 169
MacArthur, Douglas, 84–85
Malan, Daniël François, 116
Mallory, Lester D., 166
Mandela, Nelson, 124, 126, 128, 133–34

Manifest Destiny, 143, 148, 173–74
Mao Zedong, 58
Marxism, 40, 180, see also *communism*
Mbembe, Achille, 99, 185
McClintock, Anne, 9
McKinley, William, 173, 175
McKittrick, Katherine, 185
media
  Al Jazeera, 24, 30, 76n1, 217
  alternative, 29, 32–33, 149
  British, 27
  CNN, 25–26, 76n1, 217
  Democracy Now!, 29
  educational, 33, 159
  Fox News, 26
  German, 28, 216
  Guardian, The, 25–26
  impunity of, 24–29
  Korean, 76–77
  social, 29, 32, 58, 149
  suppression of, 24–29, 38, 57, 65, 70
  United States, 24–29, 38, 76, 159, 175, 217
  Western, 24–29, 38, 76, 158–59, 175, 217
Mexico
  border with U.S., ix–xi, xii–xiii, 16, 19, 111–13, 136–40, 142–44, 149, 171, 199, 207, 214
  country of, ix–xii, 112, 139, 157, 159, 171, 174, 183, 186, 205, 214

Mexico *(continued)*
  indigenous people of, xiii, 12,
    153–56, 160–61, 214
  invasion of, 170–71, 174,
    177n21, 183
  Sonora, x, 112
Middle East
  Arabs, 27, 101, 118, 120
  Iran, 100, 127
  Jordan, 101, 120
  language, 31
  Lebanon, 101
  Saudi Arabia, 127
  Syria, 101
  United Arab Emirates, 127
  Yemen, 100
  Also see *Israel* and *Palestine*
migration
  Afrikaner, 134–35
  biblical, 140
  European, 11
  from Empire, 140, 148
  Hong Kongese, 62
  U.S., to, 137, 144, 199–203,
    205, 207, 213–14
mine,
  cooper, 155–57
  gold, 3
  land, 76, 85
  minerals, xii, 3, 11, 120,
    153–54, 156, 179
  nickel, 179
  silver, 3
Mitzen, Jennifer, 59
Moltmann, Jürgen, 72
Monroe, James, 168

Mörner, Magnus, 8
Morrison, Toni, 193–94
Motlanthe, Kgalema, 132
Murakami, Haruki, 56–57, 74

Napoleon, Bonaparte, 169
National Security Law,
  China, xiii, 56, 64–66, 68, 72,
  South Korea, 77, 78, 88–89
Norris, Ned, 158

Obama, Barack, 167, 201
Oceana,
  Australia, 28
  Guam, 86, 173, 175
  New Zealand, 113
  Samoa Islands, 175
Olson, Joel, 147
Opium War, 61, 86

Páez, José Antonio, 170
Palestine,
  Bethlehem, ix, xii, 108, 110,
    113–14, 216
  Gaza, xiv, 21–38, 54, 76,
    101–06, 112–15, 128–29, 208
  genocide of, xiv, 21–32, 38, 114,
    128
  Hamas, 24–26, 28–30, 33–34,
    37, 54, 76–77, 114
  as indigenous, 24, 38, 101–3,
    120, 186
  intifada, 31, 103
  land, 21, 32, 39, 101–6, 111,
    113
  Nakba, 22

State of, ix–xiv, 21–38, 54–55,
  76, 100–15, 118, 120–21,
  128–29, 185, 208, 213, 215–16
  West Bank, ix, xii, 108, 110,
  113–14, 216
  See also *Israel-Gaza War*,
  *Israeli-Palestine Apartheid
  Wall* and *Palestine
  Liberation Organization*
Palestine Liberation Organization
  (PLO), 101
Pandor, Naledi, 128
Paredes, Américo, 144–45
Pierce, Franklin, 171
Pinn, Anthony, 188n8
Plato, 186, 189
Polk, James, 170
posttraumatic stress disorder,
  67–68, 145–49, 187
Prasad, Vijay, 94
Puerto Rico, 86, 168, 173–74

Quitman, John A., 171

Rabin, Yitzhak, 101
Ramaphosa, Cyril, 133–34
Reagan, Ronald, 110–11
Rhee, Syngman, 81–82, 84–85
rights,
  human, x, xiii, 2–4, 6–7, 10, 18,
    23–24, 27, 29, 34, 37–38,
    42, 48, 65–66, 90, 103–7,
    120, 122, 128, 162, 187,
    194, 209, 213–14
  property, 2–3, 7, 15, 18–20, 28,
    136, 148, 191

Roosevelt, Franklin D., 81
Roosevelt, Theodore, 176, 209
Rothschild, Walter, 100–1
Rousseau, Jean-Jacques, 2
Rubio, Marco, 165
Runcie, Robert, 124–25
Russia, 78, 93, 100, 127–28,
  see also *Soviet Union*
Russian-Ukraine War, 128

Said, Edward, 141, 148
Saldívar, David, 144
Sau² Zuk¹, 66
Sayles, John, 181–82
Schiller, Nina Glick, 150–51
Schneider, Peter, 49
settler colonialism,
  Canada, 115
  definition of, 102, 104, 113
  European, 4, 22, 38, 100,
    115, 209
  Germany, 115
  Israeli, xiii, 21, 23, 32, 35, 38,
    100–02, 105, 107, 113–15
  of South Africa, 23, 114
  Spain, 157, 169–172
  United Kingdom, 115, 122
  United States, 115, 155,
    173–74, 192, 199
Shalhoub-Kevorkian, Nadera, 32
Shepherd, Benjamin, 74
Sidner, Sar, 26
Smith, Adam, 3–4
Smohalla, 12
Sobukwe, Robert, 119
socialism, 20, 44, 62

Society for Biblical Literature (SBL), 33–38
Soviet Union, 50–51, 78, 81–83, 86–87, 111, 132, 164–65, 180, see also *Russia*
Spanish-American War, 86, 164, 173, 175, 177–78
Spencer, Herbert, 4
Springer, Axel, 28
Stalin, Joseph, 81
Stanley, Henry Morton, 194
Steele, Brent, 59–60
sugar, 169–73, 175, 177–79, 182, 198

Tajfel, Henri, 184
Tambo, Oliver, 124–25, 133
Taylor, Zachary, 171
Thatcher, Margaret, 124
Thomas-Greenfield, Linda, 22
Thompson, Mark, 26
Thurston, John Mellen, 174–75
Tinker, Tink, 11–14
Trump, Donald,
  Administration, 19, 165, 167–68
  campaign, 199–200, 2005
  wall, ix, xii, 19, 111–12, 137, 153, 156, 161
Truth and Reconciliation Commission (TRC), 134
Truth, Sojourner, 198, 201
Tutu, Desmond, 121, 134

Umbrella Movement, 64, 67
United Nations,
  Armistice Agreement, 79, 84
  definitions, 15, 24
  General Assembly, 22, 93, 106, 122, 126
  Human Rights Charter, 23
  military forces, 84–85, 89
  report, 82, 165
  resolutions, 22, 82, 163, 166
  Security Council, 22–24, 122, 126
United States,
  apartheid, xiii–xiv, 15–16, 18, 152, 186–89, 192–94, 197–99, 201–2, 205–8
  Arizona, ix–x, 111–12, 154–60, 214
  California, 111, 159
  Camp David, 94, 103
  Central Intelligence Agency, 164, 177, n21, 209
  Chamber of Commerce, 165
  Civil War, 163, 171
  Colorado, 91, 216
  Democratic Party, 167, 175, 184
  Department of Defense, 84
  Department of Homeland Security, 153
  Department of the Interior, 155
  empire, 78, 81, 83–88, 92–93, 140–41, 144–46, 148–49, 164, 167–81, 210
  Florida, 171
  Hawaii, 86, 175
  Indian Affairs, 154

indigenous people, xiii, 3,
    11–12, 113, 153–56,
    160–61, 185, 192, 214
Louisiana, 171
media, 24–29, 38, 76, 217
military, 21, 23, 81–82, 84–90,
    93–94, 112, 136, 153, 157,
    163–67, 171–79, 209–10
Mississippi, 171
Monroe Doctrine, 170
National Park Service (NPS),
    154, 156, 160–61
New York, 31, 51n27,
    170, 173, 203
passport, xi–xii, 109, 205, 207n2
Republican Party, 31, 136, 167,
    184, 199–200
Senate, 165
settler colonialism, 115, 155,
    173–74, 192, 199
superpower, 22–23, 78–89,
    93–94, 112, 127, 163–67,
    172–81, 186, 203, 205, 209
Texas, ix, 137, 139, 170–71,
    174, 183
See also *Europe: worldview*,
    Puerto Rico, *Spanish-American
    War*, *U.S. Immigration*,
    U.S.-Mexican border wall,
    U.S.-Philippines War, and
    U.S. Revolutionary War
universities
    Arizona, 112, 214
    Brandeis, 30
    Columbia, 30
    Chinese, 216
    Dar al-Kalima, 113, 216
    Denver, ix
    Duke, 33
    George Washington, 30
    Florida, 30
    Harvard, 30–32, 81
    Israeli, 32
    Massachusetts Institute of
        Technology, 30, 32
    Michigan State, 214
    Penn State, 32
    Pretoria, 215
    United States, 29–32, 81, 141
    Vanderbilt, 215
U.S. immigration
    Border Patrol, xii, 144, 153,
        157, 160–62, 200, 208
    Build The Wall (chant), 18–19,
        111, 137, 158, 210
    detention center, 136–40,
        142–44, 149, 160, 200,
        213, 256
    an illegal, 19, 200, 203–8
    Immigration and Customs
        Enforcement (ICE), 112,
        137, 200
    Immigration and
        Nationality Act, 203
    migrants, xi–xii, 17, 19, 139–51,
        162, 193, 199–200, 203–10
U.S.-Mexican border wall, ix–xiii,
    16, 19, 111–13, 136–62, 153,
    156, 161, 171, 199, 207, 214
U.S.-Philippines War, 86

U.S. Revolutionary War, 169

Verwoerd, Hendrik, 116
Vietnam War, 84, 90

Wai⁴ Lou⁴, 57, 66–68, 73–74
White, E. Frances, 194–96
Wind, Maya, 32
Wood, Leonard, 174, 179
World War I, 80, 100
World War II, 22, 79–80, 84, 88
Wounded Knee Massacre, 174

Xi Jinping, 64

yellow economic circle, 57, 66, 70–74
Yoon Suk Yeol, 94
Yuh, Ji-Yeon, 84

Zapata, Emiliano, 8
Zhang, Feng, 60–61
Zuma, Jacob, 132–34